ALONG THE RAMAYANA TRAIL

A cultural journey across India and Sri Lanka

ALONG THE RAMAYANA TRAIL

A cultural journey across India and Sri Lanka

A striking illustration from a mid-19th century *Ramayana* series, capturing the ferocity and drama of the legendary battle scene from the epic.

CONTENTS

An intricate wall carving at the 12th-century Hoysaleswara Temple in Karnataka, India, depicting the fierce battle between Rama and Ravana.

WITH SUPPORT FROM

Dr. Rewant Vikram Singh
Consulting Editor, Sri Lanka

A former diplomat, Dr. Rewant Vikram Singh served as Director of the Indian Cultural Centre in Sri Lanka. An acclaimed academician and author of 10 books, he is currently the Head of the Department of History and Associate Professor at Maharshi Dayanand College, University of Mumbai. His interdisciplinary research spans archaeology, history, and cultural studies.

Dr. Tarinee Awasthi
Consultant, India

An Assistant Professor in the Department of Humanities and Languages at FLAME University, Dr. Tarinee Awasthi received her PhD in Asian Literature, Religion, and Culture from Cornell University in 2022. She is an intellectual historian, and her interests include Sanskrit philosophy and Rama narratives.

PUBLISHER'S NOTE

This book explores the Ramayana *through the lens of culture and belief, reflecting its deep-rooted influence across generations. While the narratives and events are cherished in tradition, they may not necessarily be supported by archaeological evidence. However, the vast array of locations linked to the* Ramayana *highlights its widespread reach, evolving interpretations, and reimaginings across regions. This work aims to present the epic as a living tradition, shaped by history, faith, and storytelling, rather than a purely historical record. Readers are encouraged to appreciate its cultural significance and enduring legacy beyond the confines of empirical validation.*

Created in partnership with the High Commission of Sri Lanka in India to mark the 75th anniversary of the establishment of formal diplomatic relations between India and Sri Lanka.

01

The Story of the Ramayana

◂ Intricate relief carving adorning the exterior of the Gangaramaya Temple in Colombo, Sri Lanka.

THE RAMAYANA RETOLD

A TIMELESS TALE OF DUTY, LOVE, RETRIBUTION, AND REDEMPTION

One of the oldest stories of the Indian subcontinent, the *Ramayana* is a tale of honor and devotion that has traveled across cultures for centuries. The earliest known version of the story comes from a seer, Valmiki, but it may have had more than one composer. This is the story they tell.

The illustrious king Dasharatha ruled Kosala, a powerful, prosperous kingdom along the Sarayu River in the northern plains of the subcontinent of India. He had four sons—Rama, Bharata, and the twins Lakshmana and Shatrughna—from his three chief wives. They were learned, brave, and virtuous, but it was the eldest, Rama, who was regarded truly valorous.

The brothers were yet to turn 16, when the great sage Vishwamitra arrived in Ayodhya, the capital, and asked the king for help. He told of two mighty rakshasas who regularly disrupted his meditation and rituals. Only Rama, the sage told the king, could vanquish them. So a reluctant Dasharatha agreed to let Rama and his brother Lakshmana accompany Vishwamitra to his hermitage.

The wise Vishwamitra taught Rama powerful mantras that would help him kill the rakshasas. He also bestowed upon him the power to summon divine weapons when needed. At the hermitage, the brothers quickly vanquished the rakshasas.

▼ The Tulshibaug Shri Ram temple in Pune, Maharashtra, is adorned with scenes from the epic. This wall painting shows Rama successfully stringing Lord Shiva's bow, making him eligible to marry Sita.

Meeting Sita

The sage then took them to Mithila, where the king, Janaka, was holding a great sacrifice. The keeper of an immensely strong and powerful divine bow, Janaka had vowed to give his daughter, Sita, in marriage to the one who could lift it. None succeeded until Rama lifted the bow, and in one smooth motion, strung it, snapping it in two as he did so. Even as preparations for the wedding began, King Janaka, certain that Rama's brothers could not be any less valorous than he, proposed that Sita's sister Urmila marry Lakshmana.

▶ This 18th-century artwork, titled *Rama on Horseback*, depicts Rama riding a ceremonial horse, flanked by his loyal brothers and Hanuman, who walk alongside him with unwavering devotion.

▲ A Kulu-style gouache painting from the 18th century depicts Rama, Sita, and Lakshmana's departure into exile.

Rama and Sita returned to Ayodhya where they stayed, their kindness and generosity making them popular with the people. Dasharatha, pleased with his eldest son, decided to relinquish the throne in favor of Rama. Preparations for the coronation began, but trouble was brewing. Her envy roused by a handmaiden, the king's second wife Kaikeyi, his favorite, reminded him of two boons he had granted her many years ago. She chose to redeem them now: her son Bharata would be crowned king and Rama exiled to the forests of Dandaka, to live as an ascetic for 14 years.

Rama's exile

A heartbroken Dasharatha begged his queen to reconsider, but she remained unmoved. Distraught, Dasharatha was unable to tell his son what was demanded of him, and so Kaikeyi conveyed his father's orders to Rama herself. The prince received the news with equanimity. He said that it was his duty to ensure his father's vow was fulfilled. Then, he expressed sorrow that his mother Kaikeyi—for he did not differentiate between the three—believed that he would not give up kingship if his brother desired it.

Hearing of the exile, Sita and Lakshmana insisted on joining Rama and the three left Ayodhya.

Heartbroken by what had come to pass, Dasharatha breathed his last. Bharata and Shatrughna who were away at the time, returned to Ayodhya. Bharata, furious with his mother and grieved by the tragedy she had wrought, refused to be crowned—the kingship was not his. Rama was the rightful heir and the most capable of the brothers. Bharata went after the exiles, vowing to bring them all back.

Into the forest

After Rama, Lakshmana, and Sita left Ayodhya, they continued traveling until they crossed the borders of Kosala. Upon reaching the great Ganga River, they dismissed their charioteer and changed into the simple clothes of ascetics. They crossed the wide surging river and continued walking until they reached the forested mountains around Chitrakoot, where they planned to stay for some time.

It is here that Bharata found them. He tried to convince Rama, begging him to return to Ayodhya and take his rightful place as king. But his brother was not to be moved. As far as Rama was concerned, his father had given his word and it was Rama's duty to see that his father's honor was not compromised, even after his passing. After much persuasion, Bharata agreed to return to Ayodhya and rule—but only as regent. He took back a pair of Rama's slippers to place on the throne, so that no one would forget the true king of Ayodhya. Concerned that if Bharata had found them, others would follow, Rama led Sita and Lakshmana further into the wilderness of central India. They were now in Janasthana—the abode of rakshasas, and had many encounters and skirmishes with them. When they finally settled, their hermitage at Panchavati bordered Janasthana.

Surpanakha, the sister of the king of Lanka, Ravana, was also at Janasthana, and one day saw Rama. She was immediately besotted and tried to woo the young prince. Rama wanted nothing to do with her and sent her to the short-tempered Lakshmana, who, exasperated, sent her away, but not before disfiguring her face.

Sita's abduction

When Ravana heard of the insult to his sister, he was furious and, intent on avenging her, arrived at Panchavati with the intention of abducting Rama's wife. He lured Rama and Lakshmana away from the hermitage, disguised himself as an ascetic seeking alms, approached Sita, and carried her away.

Jatayu, the king of vultures, heard Sita's cries for help as Ravana took the princess to his capital in Lanka. He came to her rescue, attacking the king. But Ravana succeeded in mortally wounding the bird and escaping to his kingdom.

Distraught and desperately searching for Sita, the two brothers came upon the injured Jatayu. With his dying breath, the vulture directed them toward Lanka and Ravana. Making their way south across the dense forests of Kishkindha, the brothers forged an alliance with Sugriva, a powerful leader of the vanaras. Sugriva sent rank upon rank of vanaras in all four directions looking for Ravana's Lanka and signs of Sita. It was one of his lieutenants,

▸ A chromolithograph by Raja Ravi Varma depicts Ravana mortally wounding Jatayu by cutting off his wings as the bird tries to rescue Sita.

Hanuman—the son of Vayu, god of the wind—who got news of Ravana's kingdom across the ocean and made the leap to Lanka.

The mighty Hanuman located Sita sitting under a tree in a garden where she was being held captive. He made himself known to her. Then, intending to learn as much as he could about Ravana, Lanka, and its fortifications, Hanuman let himself be captured. Ravana would have preferred to kill the vanara, but was persuaded to let him go as it was dishonorable to execute an emissary. However, to teach the captive a lesson in humility, he ordered that the vanara's tail, his pride, be set on fire before he was freed. Undaunted, the raging Hanuman leapt from rooftop to rooftop, setting alight the capital of Lanka with that flaming tail. Having satisfied himself that Sita was safe, Hanuman then returned to Rama.

Preparing for war

A war was inevitable, but first the mighty ocean had to be crossed. Hanuman could have carried Rama and Lakshmana, but the entire army needed a more practical solution. Their only option was to build a bridge and so Rama, Lakshmana, and the vanaras prayed to the lord of the ocean to appease him. Slowly, the vanaras laid the stones to build the bridge that would help them cross into Lanka. Once it was complete, the army marched across, ready to rescue their queen.

The huge army camped at Ravana's gates and soon a bloody battle began. Mighty warriors from both sides, armed with boons and divine weapons, fought until the earth was drenched in blood and the rivers ran red. One by one, Ravana's powerful sons and relatives fell, until blind with grief and fury, he faced Rama himself. The exiled prince of Ayodhya and the king of Lanka were well matched. They fought blow for blow, arrow for arrow until, on the seventh day, Rama fired Brahma's divine weapon, the Brahmastra, and ended Ravana's life.

Trial by fire

Rama crowned Vibhishana, his ally and Ravana's younger brother, as the king of Lanka. However, he did not immediately rescue Sita. Although she had been abducted, she had lived in the home of another man. Even though Rama did not doubt Sita's purity, she had to prove it to others. Sita bravely walked through fire, and the god of fire himself emerged to testify to her innocence.

▼ This late 18th-century South Indian Kalamkari textile hanging depicts the penultimate battle between Rama and Ravana.

"As long as the mountains and rivers stand on earth, so long shall the story of Ramayana circulate among the people."

Brahma tells Valmiki, Sarga 2, Bala Kanda

Relieved and reassured, Rama welcomed her back. Now that 14 years had come to an end, it was time for Rama, Lakshmana, and Sita to return to Ayodhya. On their return, the overjoyed people of Kosala crowned Rama king.

Under his rule, the kingdom prospered. Then one day, Rama heard whispers of speculation about Sita's fidelity when she was held captive by Ravana, and that there were some who considered him weak for having accepted her back.

Honor-bound to his duty as king, Rama banished his pregnant wife. He asked Lakshmana to abandon her in the forest near the Sage Valmiki's hermitage. Rama's twin sons Lava and Kusha were born there. They grew up under the tutelage of Valmiki, who, having composed the *Ramayana* by then, taught the twins its recitation.

One day, as Rama was performing a sacrificial ritual in the forest, Lava and Kusha appeared before him and started reciting the *Ramayana*. When he learned they were his own sons he sent for Sita. He wanted her to return to Ayodhya as his queen, though only after one last, public test of faith. Sita proved her fidelity again, but then chose to return home to the embrace of her mother, the earth, forever.

The ground broke open and the Goddess Earth emerged, embracing Sita, and taking her back into the earth. She had returned from whence she was born.

A disconsolate Rama took his sons back with him and tried to find peace, but failed. It was time for him to leave the earth.

He first exiled Lakshmana, who then left from his earthly form. Entrusting the kingdom of Kosala to his sons, Rama walked into the waters of the Sarayu River which ran by Ayodhya, and returned to the heavens.

MANY RAMAYANAS

THE MYRIAD FACES OF THE EPIC

The *Ramayana* does not belong to one moment in history. The sheer number of renditions, ranging from academic studies to art and performances that each era has produced, are a testament to the epic's accessibility and popularity.

1

2

3

1. **Valmiki's *Ramayana***
The first version of the epic, it was composed between the 6th century BCE and 3rd century CE; various renditions by other poets were commissioned as recently as the 17th century.

2. ***Dasharatha Jataka***
This Buddhist text, composed between the 3rd and 4th centuries CE, tells the story of Rama as a previous incarnation of Buddha.

3. **The Persian translation**
Commissioned by art patron and commander of Mughal armies, Abd al-Rahim, this 16th-century Persian rendition of the *Ramayana* is one of the finest illustrated copies to exist.

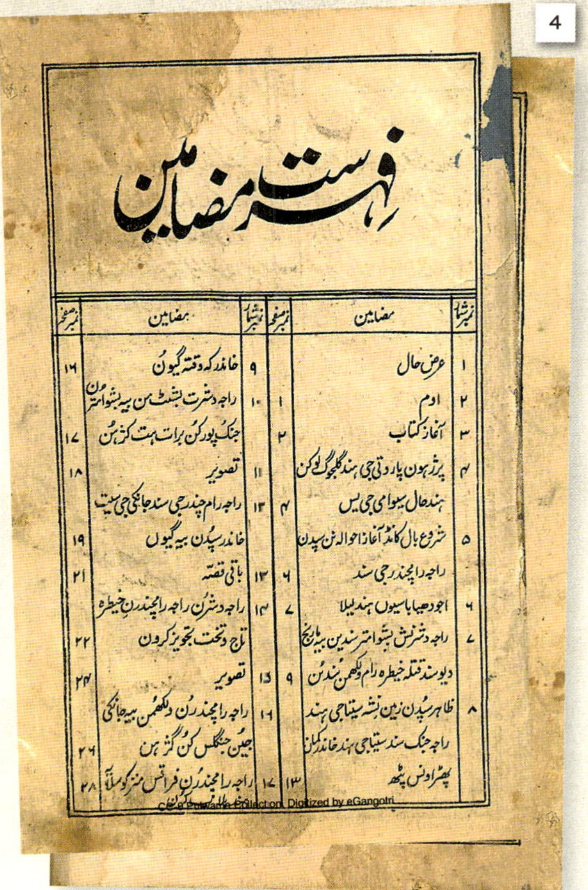

فہرست مضامین

4. ***Ramavatarcharit*** Pandit Prakash Ram Kulgami localized the epic to Kashmir in this retelling from the 19th century. Historically, he was the first to introduce the epic genre in Kashmiri literature.

5. **Urdu retellings** Munshi Jagannatha Khusthar's *Ramayana Khusthar*, Hakim Vicerai Wahmi's *Ramayan Manzum*, Banke Biharilal Bahara's *Ramayana Bahara*, and Ufaq's *Yak-Qafiya Ramayan* gained popularity during the 19th-20th century

6. **Ramlila** These traditional performances with song and recitals, organized annually during the festival of Navratri in fall, depict the story of Rama and his battle against Ravana, highlighting the victory of good over evil. Ramlila was declared an Intangible Cultural Heritage of Humanity by UNESCO in 2008.

▲ This Kangra painting depicts the episode of sage Narada's visit to Valmiki's hermitage to recount Rama's story for the sage.

ESSAY

IN RAMA'S FOOTSTEPS

The story of Rama has been circulating in India for over two millennia. The earliest extant version is the Sanskrit *Ramayana*, which took current form in the early centuries AD. However, the *Ramayana* as we have it is clearly telling a story that's well known—when Rama is introduced in the first chapter, he is already the one whom "people have heard of." The epic is also quite aware of its significance—again, Rama himself says that this story will "effect prosperity even for [him]." It appears that the story was circulating by the middle of the first millennium BC, and some versions of the extant text may date as far back as then, even though the version that we have is later. The Valmiki *Ramayana* enjoys a special status in the religious as well as literary history of India. It is classified as both *kavya*—a literary aesthetic product —and as *itihasa*, or a narrative about the past. In addition, because it is about Rama, an incarnation of Vishnu, it is also used for religious purposes. Even though these uses all seem like they might be mutually exclusive, in practice, they feed into each other.

The many Ramayanas

To think of the Rama narrative in India is just as much to think about the history of its reception. We might start with the reception of the *Ramayana* in the literary and aesthetic traditions of India. Held up as the "first *kavya,*" it shapes the way poetry is thought of. The *Ramayana* is also self-conscious about the poetic process—as Valmiki says, "Grief becomes verse"—something that gets taken up in the later literary tradition.

The Rama story has been retold in various genres of Sanskrit creative literature, including long poems like Kalidasa's celebrated *Raghuvamsha*; the plays of such playwrights as Murari, Bhavabhuti, Ramachandra, or RajaSekhara; and the *Champu Ramayanam* of Bhojaraja. In addition, it was often adapted into various vernaculars as the primary epic in those traditions—the Tamil *Ramavataram* of Kamban, Krttibasa's *Ramayana*, and Tulsi's *Ramacharitamanas* are a few most prominent examples.

Not only are they interesting parts of the Rama tradition, they are also important texts within the literary traditions to which they belong. There were also full-length Sanskrit *Ramayanas*, oriented more toward presenting a theological rather than a literary vision of Rama, like *Adhyatma Ramayana* or *Adbhuta Ramayana*.

In colonial and postcolonial India as well, there has been extensive engagement with the *Ramayana*, both in terms of retellings and commentaries.

The Rama within

As A. K. Ramanujan noted, along with the *Mahabharata*, the Rama narratives provide the "pool of signifiers" through which people negotiate their relationships with one another and with the world. Rama might be held up as the ideal son (because he agrees to be exiled), the ideal brother, or the king who put personal interest aside (as he exiled Sita). Alternatively, he may be held up as the person who mocked a woman (Surpanakha) and then had her mutilated, hid as he shot somebody (Vali), and acted cruelly toward his wife (by exiling Sita). And again, he may just be a lover suffering in separation from his beloved—even if the separation (Sita's exile) is something he caused. In some ways, it doesn't matter which Rama you pick—you have to pick a Rama. Often, if Valmiki's Rama does not fit in with what a poet or devotee needs Rama to be, they can rewrite the story.

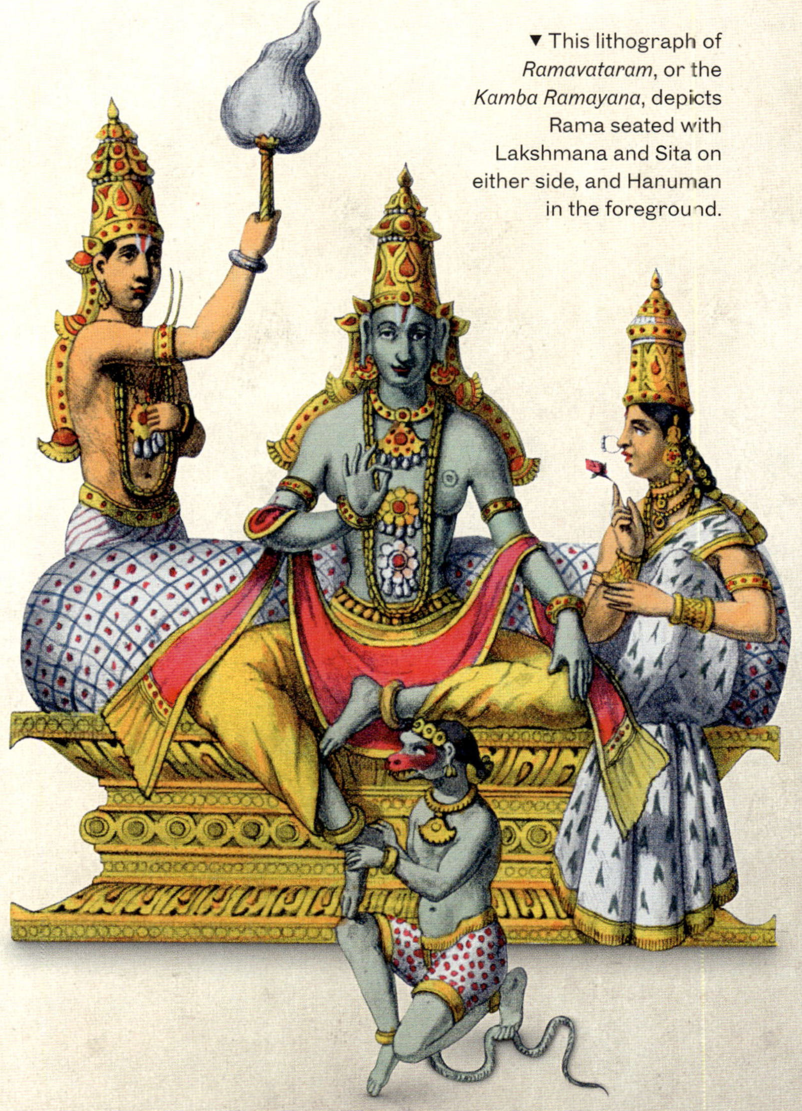

▼ This lithograph of *Ramavataram*, or the *Kamba Ramayana*, depicts Rama seated with Lakshmana and Sita on either side, and Hanuman in the foreground.

A *c.*1775–1800 illustration from Gujarat, depicting pivotal moments from the Aranya Kanda of the *Ramayana* that took place in the Panchavati forest. Starting from the bottom right and moving clockwise, it shows Lakshmana cutting Surpanakha's nose, Rama fighting off the rakshasa army, and Ravana, dressed as a mendicant about to abduct Sita while Rama and Lakshmana chase after the golden deer.

Similarly, people regard Sita as coy and silent, or outspoken and fiery. They may highlight Lakshmana's unconditional devotion or mercurial temper. The point is that these are the characters that have been used for centuries in India to organize the way one relates to the world and to oneself. At the same time, one could regard Rama as the supreme lord, incarnate on earth (to protect the gods from demons, or to extend grace unto his devotees, depending on whom you ask).

Sometimes, even Ravana can become a devotee who is seeking Rama, and because he cannot perform devotional practices for various reasons, he contrives things so that Rama might kill him.

It isn't that figures or events in the *Ramayana* stand for a single set of values. The same event—Sita's exile, for instance—can be read in a variety of ways. At the same time, Rama can be the devotee's son or father or master—even brother-in-law, if the devotee happens to be from Mithila! People celebrate weddings in their own families, in fact, through songs that speak of Sita and Rama's wedding. Different attitudes are grounded in different positions on just what the status of the *Ramayana* is.

▼ A *c.*1800 painting from Kangra, Himachal Pradesh, depicting the siege of Lanka as the city burns and the two armies face each other in a fierce battle.

Sacred spaces

The *Ramayana* can be read as a reflection of societal values over a certain period. Historians can find insights to the processes of state formation during the period of the composition of the *Ramayana*. Literary historians may read the *Ramayana* as a text that not only inspired retellings of its own story, but exerted influence on other narratives like Ashvaghosha's poem about the Buddha. Certain people think of the *Ramayana* as a more or less historical account—they may believe that the events in the *Ramayana* were literally true. Others might read the story symbolically. Yet others might think that Rama and his life constitute an eternally accessible realm which transcends space and time, but is more easily accessed at certain times and places.

How do these different attitudes shape people's approach to places associated with Rama? The Valmiki *Ramayana* itself presents a world that looks very different from our maps—it is organized in concentric circles of land divided up by the sea. While some of the places may sound like those we know, the organization of space is so different from ours that translating them to our maps is futile. For historians, most associations of particular places with Rama don't hold much water. They may identify certain regions as the places where the *Ramayana* may have emerged, but that is really the extent of it. For those who hold Rama to be a historical figure, a lot goes into identifying particular spots, calculating distances, and assessing the plausibility of the claims certain places have to being, for example, Chitrakoot, or Panchavati.

However, for certain kinds of devotees of Rama, these places are not merely about where Rama was, but are about how we can access where Rama is. Thus, the Chitrakoot in present-day Madhya Pradesh, for example, may be the place where Rama spent part of his exile, but the more important thing is that it has the capacity to grant access to that realm where Rama resides now. We find, similarly, the understanding that Sita and Rama ever reside in certain places in Ayodhya, and many devotees seek to serve them there.

Communities from different regions also adopt different attitudes toward various characters in the *Ramayana* – thus, people from Mithila—which is where Sita is from—speak more often of Rama's wedding. Since the wedding is traditionally hosted by the bride's family, they tease Rama as they tease young, shy bridegrooms. In areas where Rama is supposed to be from, his birth is the big event—for people in these areas think of Rama as a child in their family. Some places have been associated with particular moments in Rama's life—Kalidasa, at the beginning of a poem about lovers in separation, tells us that one of them was living in the hermitages on Rama's hill. The water bodies there were purified because Sita would bathe there. The place Kalidasa had in mind is thought to be somewhere in present-day Maharashtra.

Other places may not feature in the Sanskrit *Ramayana* but may still come to be associated with Rama in different ways—the deity at Srirangam (a very important Vishnu shrine in Tamil Nadu), for example, is supposed to have been from Rama's family. The story goes that he gave it to Vibhishana, but the deity decided to stay in Srirangam instead. Other places may be associated just as much with Rama's devotees as they are with Rama—a good example is Bhadrachalam. The temple is associated with the devotee Bhadrachala Ramadasa (Kancharla Gopanna), who is said to have had the temple constructed. Bhadrachala Ramadasa also composed various songs in praise of Rama.

Rama's own path is not singular—different places may claim, for example, to be Chitrakoot, and different stories get added in. Nor is any of these places just a spot on a map. Bhavabhuti, the 8th-century playwright, writes about how vivid Rama's recollection is when he returns to the places where he lived in during exile. For those engaged with the Rama story, these places are all deeply evocative—for those who think of the *Ramayana* as a great work of literature as well as for those who are devoted to Rama, these places remind them of various episodes in the *Ramayana* and allow for aesthetic or religious access to the story. Those who live in these areas are active participants in Rama's story—the young women singing of Rama as their guest and brother-in-law-to-be are not just narrating a story, they are in the story as Sita's companions. To follow Rama's trail, at the very least, is a way of immersing oneself in the experiences of the different communities that are themselves engaged in walking Rama's path or living in places where Rama lived.

▲ A *c.*1830 gouache painting of Ranganatha, a form of Vishnu, reclining on Sheshanaga, the five-hooded serpent, inside the sacred temple of Srirangam in Tamil Nadu, India.

This essay has been contributed by Dr. Tarinee Awasthi.

02

Rama: *An Exiled Prince's Journey*

◂ This *c.*1780 Kangra court painting, from an illustrated folio, depicts Rama, Sita, and Lakshmana at sage Bharadvaja's hermitage.

PROFILE

PRINCE OF KOSALA

Exiled from Ayodhya, Rama ventures through the vast, dark forests of central and southern India. His journey leads him into the wild heart of Kishkindha, then across a treacherous ocean to the island fortress of Lanka, where destiny awaits in the form of a final, epic confrontation.

Rama, the protagonist of the *Ramayana*, means different things to different people—the lord of life and all beings, the ideal man striving for perfection, a flawed husband, or anything in between. Nevertheless, his appeal, and his story, continue to endure among millions of Indians who consider Rama and his reign as the epitome of ideal governance and morality.

▲ This 18th-century illustration shows King Dasharatha with his queens Kaushalya, Kaikeyi, and Sumitra, and their sons Rama, Lakshmana, Bharata, and Shatrughna.

He ... is Rama, the one people have heard of ... He is the protector of all beings, and the preserver of dharma. ... he is grounded in the knowledge of archery.

Narada tells Valmiki, Sarga 1, Bala Kanda

A matter of destiny

Tormented by the powerful king of Lanka, Ravana, the gods appealed to Vishnu, one of the principle deities in Hinduism. Invulnerable, because of a boon, Ravana could only be overcome by a mortal man who—to meet the conditions of the boon—could not be aware of his inherent divinity. Vishnu acceded to the request and took birth in the household of the great king Dasharatha, the ruler of Kosala, as his eldest son Rama.

Rama's story begins in Ayodhya, the capital of Kosala, where he lived and studied with his brothers Lakshmana, Bharata, and Shatrughna—mastering the Vedas and learning the skills of statesmanship and the art of war. Rama's subsequent training under the sage Vishwamitra as he protected the latter's hermitage from rakshasas and then his marriage

▼ This mid-18th century handcrafted playing card from Maharashtra depicts Rama with four warriors.

to Sita, the princess of Mithila, all lead up to the pivotal moment in his story when he begins to fulfill his destiny.

Fated encounters

His exile from Ayodhya sees Rama wander through the forests of India for 14 years, along with Sita and his brother Lakshmana. It is here that his and Lakshmana's ill-fated encounter with Surpanakha, Ravana's sister, leads to Sita's abduction and the ultimate face-off with the feared king of Lanka.

Rama's desperate search for Sita takes him across the lands into Kishkindha, the vanara kingdom, believed to be a part of present-day south India. His alliance with the vanara king Sugriva kicks off the hunt for Sita, followed by Hanuman's journey over the ocean to the kingdom of Lanka.

Subsequently, the vanaras build a bridge over the ocean—perhaps the present-day Adam's Bridge or Ram Setu—so that Rama and his forces can cross over into Lanka.

A series of battles between Rama and Ravana end after the prince of Ayodhya kills the king. After Sita's rescue and trial by fire, the three return to Ayodhya for a peaceful reign. Many versions of the *Ramayana* end here, but Valmiki's tale continues. This final section tells of a pregnant Sita, her exile into the forest and the birth of her twin sons, Rama discovering his children and asking Sita for yet another trial of chastity—in which Sita proves her fidelity and disappears into the earth from where she was born.

The divine vs. the ideal

Most academics agree that Rama was worshipped as a deity at least by the 6th century CE. Over time, however, from being worshipped as an incarnation of Vishnu, he evolved into a deity in his own right—a transformation complete by the 11th–12th centuries, according to written religious records and inscriptions in temples. The continuity between a character depicted as

▼ Depicting a scene from the *Ramayana*, this illustration shows Rama and Lakshmana attacking Surpanakha, Ravana's sister.

an incarnation of a god and praised for his sense of dharma, and a figure worshipped as a god who embodies that dharma is, after all, one that is easily established.

In Valmiki's epic, when Rama returns to Ayodhya after defeating Ravana, his consecration as king marks the beginning of a 10,000-year-long rule. This period is said to be marked by unprecedented peace and virtue among the citizens of his kingdom—the virtue of Rama becomes the virtue of his subjects. The markers of that righteousness, however, are sometimes questioned even by the characters within the *Ramayana*. When Rama chooses to abide by his father's wishes and retire into the forest, Sita challenges him about going alone. She is astonished that Rama did not take into account the commitment he had made as a husband to be together. Rama's decision to test Sita's virtue—not once, but twice —because of idle talk about her fidelity does not go unchallenged by Sita either.

The kingdom of bliss

Order and prosperity—the Kosala of Valmiki's *Ramayana* never breaches the ideal attributes of a kingdom. When the story begins, Kosala is ruled by Dasharatha, who has expanded his empire to ever-rising glory. It is a fertile, bustling, and thriving realm that knows how to protect itself. Thousands of skillful warriors populate Kosala's cities and its people appreciate the finer things in life—parks and groves line its streets, while troupes of actors are always on the move.

Dasharatha is considered to be from the great line of Ikshvaku—descendants of Prajapati, the lord of creatures, under whose rule "the whole world has long been under protection." Ikshvaku was the first king of Ayodhya, the capital of the kingdom of Kosala, which was gifted to him by his father Manu, the first man. The Ikshvaku dynasty followed the law of primogeniture, according to which the firstborn must take over the throne. And so, when Dasharatha chose his eldest, Rama, as the prince regent, he was only following custom.

▲ A gold-plated wooden miniature of the ancient holy city of Ayodhya at the Soni Ji Ki Nasiya Jain Temple, in the city of Ajmer, Rajasthan, India.

As Rama left the kingdom to follow his father's unwilling orders banishing him for 14 years, the learned sages of the realm convened. They considered the ramifications of a land without a king—the rains would stop, no grain would be sown, no garden would be built, no sacred rites performed, and no one would ever sleep peacefully again.

Perhaps another prince of the Ikshvaku line should be named and consecrated as the king, the sages told the great sage Vasishtha. At the time, the prosperity of the land was believed to be inextricably bound to the stewardship of its Ikshvaku kings. Without them, Kosala would cease to be.

Where Rama does not kill Ravana

In the *Paumacariya*, an ancient Jain retelling of the *Ramayana*, Rama does not kill Ravana. A. K. Ramanujan's celebrated essay "Three Hundred Ramayanas" refers to this version as one in which Rama "is an evolved Jain soul who has conquered his passions." He does not need to kill Ravana, leaving the task to his brother Lakshmana, who is condemned to hell while Rama is released from the cycle of birth and death.

So, Rama's brother Bharata reluctantly stands in as a king during Rama's exile, counting down to his brother's return. During the 14-years-long period of Rama's exile, the stage does not return to Kosala—only the news of Dasharatha's death makes its way to Rama. But the spotlight does turn to many friends of Kosala who are fierce protectors of the two princes, Rama and Lakshmana, and Rama's wife Sita. Guha, the forest community chief and an ally of the Kosala court, helps Rama early in his exile. Jatayu, a great friend to Dasharatha, dies trying to stop Ravana from abducting Sita. During the exile, powerful sages all along their route help them because they are friends to the house of Ikshvaku.

The *Ramayana* returns to Kosala when the battle between Rama and Ravana is over. Bharata welcomes his brothers with a magnificent procession. Rama is crowned the king, marking the beginning of a 10,000-year-long glorious period for Kosala, unbesmirched by even the smallest mortal inconvenience. There is no disease, sorrow, the children don't die, and everyone

◄ A painting from *c.*1745 depicting the heroic odyssey of Rama.

Buddhist Kosala

Siddhartha Gautama was born a prince of the Shakya clan in 563 BCE at Lumbini—then a part of the Kosala kingdom. Disillusioned by the transience of the world, he renounced his royal life to go in search of a state beyond the cycle of birth and death. In his wanderings, he is said to have met Bimbisara, the king of Magadha, who invited Gautama to share his kingdom, which Gautama declined. Many of Gautama's discourses were delivered at the monastery of Jetavana in Shravasti, Kosala's capital. King Prasenjit too became a follower, as did many people of Kosala.

believes in the power of truth. But Sita does not get to witness this prosperity—according to Valmiki's *Ramayana*, Rama abandons her to assuage the rumors of infidelity. She bears him two sons—Lava and Kusha—to whom Rama leaves his kingdom when he decides his time on earth is over. The southern regions go to Kusha, as Kosala with its capital at Kushasthali in the Vindhya range, and the northern regions to Lava, as Uttara Kosala whose capital is set up at Shravasti.

Kosala's origins and history

Outside the bounds of the *Ramayana*, Kosala finds mention as one of the biggest and most powerful kingdoms of its time in the other great Indian epic, *Mahabharata*. In it, the kingdom is located east of the Kurus, whose last king Brihadbala—the 115th Ikshvaku ruler—supports Duryodhana in the great war between the Pandavas and the Kauravas. (Brihadbala is defeated.)

Later Vedic texts and Buddhist Pali literature mention Kosala as one of the great kingdoms of Jambudvipa, what is now the Indian subcontinent. Its formation is likely to have been part of the structural evolution of the politics of the Vedic age, when the northern and central parts of the subcontinent began to be ruled by settlements of small, semi-peripatetic units known as *janapadas,* who marked the boundaries between their areas of power by geographical features such as rivers.

Over time, wars, treaties, annexations, and coalitions among the *janapadas* led to the formation of consolidated power centers called *mahajanapadas—maha* or great. Buddhist texts from the 6th century CE mention 16 *mahajanapadas*, among which Kosala is listed as the second (to its southeast lay Kashi, against which Kosala engaged in a constant struggle for supremacy).

At this point, Kosala was ruled by Prasenjit and, after him, his son Vidudabha. The annexation of Kashi brought Kosala into direct conflict with Magadha, the powerful Maurya-ruled *mahajanapada* to the southeast. A resolution was sought through a matrimonial alliance—Bimbisara, the king of Magadha, would marry Prasenjit's sister. But Bimbisara died, and his son and successor Ajatshatru was successful in overpowering Vidudabha. With this, Kosala was absorbed into Magadha.

For a short time after the collapse of the Mauryan empire in 185 BCE, Kosala tried to reassert itself with three dynasties leading the charge. Its glory days, however, were too far in the past and the expansion of the Kushana empire brought with it the end of the Kosala kingdom.

Kosala today

Kosala is identified as the region across both sides of the Sarayu River in present-day south-central Uttar Pradesh. It is believed to have extended from the River Gandak to the Ganges, the Himalayas forming its northern boundary.

This painting on a wooden board portrays Rama and Sita seated on a throne and surrounded by a vibrant assembly of divine figures, including Shiva, Brahma, Ganesha, Hanuman, Jambavan, and Sugriva, and others.

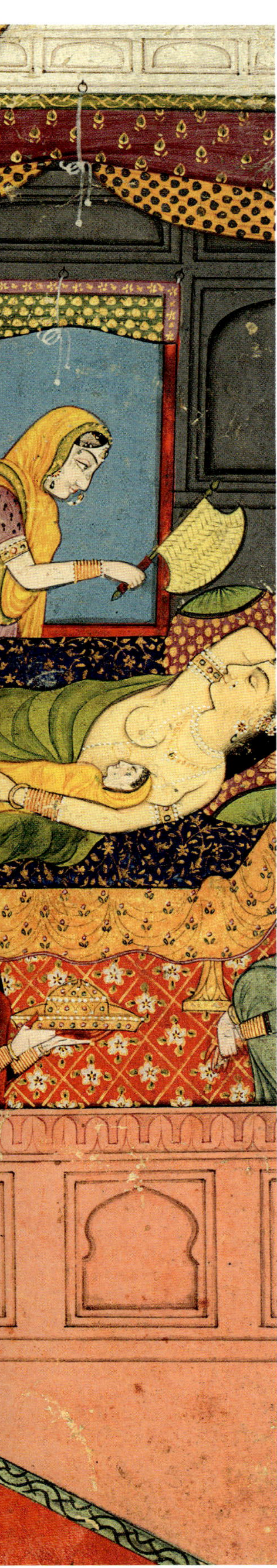

◀ This 18-century painting from the Kangra region of Himachal Pradesh depicts the birth of Rama and his brothers.

RAMA IS BORN

AYODHYA, UTTAR PRADESH (INDIA)

Dasharatha's reign over Kosala, from the capital city of Ayodhya, was one of peace and prosperity, however, the king longed for an heir. Following the advice of a powerful sage, the king held a sacrifice to appease the gods. As he prayed, a divine figure emerged from the holy fire and handed him a bowl of celestial oatmeal meant for his three wives. Dasharatha gave half of the oatmeal to Kaushalya, a quarter to Sumitra, one-eighth to Kaikeyi, and the remainder to Sumitra again. In the days that followed, Kaushalya gave birth to Rama, Kaikeyi to Bharata, and Sumitra, because she received two helpings, to Lakshmana and Shatrughna. All of Ayodhya celebrated for their princes had been born.

In many ways, Ayodhya is a quintessential Indian temple town. Its temples have been the nucleus of both geographical and economic expansion. The narrow by-lanes preserve age-old religious structures, large and small. The town's parallel network of religious organizations, such as the ashrams for ascetics or pilgrims, sustain a pilgrimage-derived economy. Its urban consciousness is sheathed in layers of mythology, often perceived as inseparable from its history.

To many believers of the Hindu faith, Ayodhya is where Rama was born, grew up, and later ascended the throne. This belief is what most of Ayodhya has mapped itself on —with stories that turn the quotidian into the divine, invoking the smallest details of Rama's life story to impart significance to places in and around Ayodhya.

A confluence of cultures

Yet, the town retains traces of its continuing engagement with many faiths and cultures over centuries—as the historical Buddhist center identified as Saketa, as the birthplace of Jain supreme spiritual guides, and the power center for Nawabs of Awadh in the 18th century.

When the British colonial administration undertook the first archaeological survey of Ayodhya in the 1860s, it concluded that the town of Ayodhya could be identified with the ancient town of Saketa—one of the most important centers of Buddhist tradition, where the Buddha spent 16 summers. Scholars have also concluded that the Mauryan emperor Ashoka had built a stupa here. Unfortunately, little of this Buddhist heritage survives in the town today.

▲ The Ram Janmabhoomi Temple, in the city of Ayodhya, Uttar Pradesh, India, is a modern shrine dedicated to the birthplace of Rama.

The legacy of Jainism is easier to trace. Ayodhya is considered to be the birthplace of five Tirthankaras (supreme spiritual guides in Jain tradition), including the first one, Rishabhanatha. Jain shrines line the streets of the town. Many Jain temples are relatively modern—most were built in the 18th century. However, they are believed to be standing on the sites of much older temples. The most prominent of these temples is the Jain Shwetamber Temple, with a 31-ft- (9.4-m-) high marble statue of Rishabhanatha.

For most of modern history however, going back to at least the 19th century, Ayodhya had been the center of legal disputes centered on a mosque, the Babri Masjid, which, a section of Hindus claimed, stood over the place where Rama was born. The disputes were eventually resolved in favor of Hindu claimants in 2019. Now, the temple built on the contested site, the Ram Janmabhoomi Temple, is the town's largest pilgrimage draw.

Rama's home

The Ram Janmabhoomi Temple stands on the city's western edge in a locality known as Ramkot (the citadel of Rama). Consecrated in 2024, it is a relatively new addition to Ayodhya's religious landscape—it is also the most prominent. The 2.7-acre (11,000sq-m) temple is built in the Nagara style with pink sandstone and marble. The Nagara style is typical to temples built in northern India from the 8th century CE, and its distinctive features include a towerlike spire (*shikhara*), inner chamber (*garbhagriha*) for the deity, and pillared hall (*mandapa*) connected to the chamber. In a way, the choice of a centuries-old architectural style for the temple attempts to forge a sense of continuity with a legendary past within which the mythology of the temple is situated.

About 0.7 miles (1.2km) east of the Ram Janmabhoomi Temple lies Dashrath Mahal, with a vibrant, colorful facade. The temple is located on a site identified with Dasharatha's palace from the *Ramayana*. It is where Rama is said to have grown up with his brothers. A 0.1-mile (200-m) walk north of Dashrath Mahal lies the grand Kanak Bhawan, which—as the *Ramayana* mythology goes—stands over the site of a palace Kaikeyi gifted to Sita. The palace is believed to have fallen into disrepair and rebuilt several times over the centuries. The contemporary structure is a sprawling 19th-century temple commissioned by a queen from the royal family of Orchha. *Kanak* means golden in Sanskrit and the temple's golden-yellow hue is a nod to this etymology.

About 0.3 miles (half a kilometer) east of Kanak Bhawan lies another temple complex, Hanuman Garhi. This is believed to be where Hanuman, Rama's loyal

general, stationed himself to guard Ayodhya—Rama had instructed him to do so before he renounced earth. The contemporary structure is located within a four-sided fort with circular bastions in each corner. It is a steep climb to the temple though—up a flight of 76 steps.

The story of Rama concludes at Guptar Ghat by the Sarayu River in the neighboring town of Faizabad, about 6.2 miles (10km) from Hanuman Garhi. Old shrines dedicated to Rama, Sita, and Hanuman line the ghat. It is where Rama is believed to have abandoned his human form and departed for the heavens by walking into the river. It is why many practicing Hindus consider this stretch especially sacred and believe that a dip in these waters will absolve them of their sins.

Legacy of the Nawabs

Ayodhya's time under the Nawab rule—which followed the Mughal period of the 16th and 17th centuries—is preserved in Faizabad, outside the limits of Ayodhya. The Nawabs developed the Awadhi style of architecture. A stunning example of the continuity between Mughal and Awadhi architecture is Gulab Bari. It is the 18th-century tomb of the third Nawab of Awadh, Shuja-ud-Daula, which he built as his final resting place. The tomb is at the center of a garden of roses—*gulab* means rose in Urdu—in the Charbagh layout, a Persian plan in which a garden is split into four through artificial waterways.

About 1.2 miles (2km) from Gulab Bari, in a particularly green part of Faizabad, lies the Bahu Begum ka Maqbara (Bahu Begum's Tomb). It was built in the 19th century for Shuja-ud-Daula's queen, Begum Unmatuzohra Bano, who wielded considerable influence over the Awadh administration. Also called the Taj Mahal of the East, it is an outstanding example of non-Mughal Muslim architecture. The white marble structure has three domes and, with its intricately carved interiors and elaborate wall motifs, represents Awadhi architecture in all its ornate glory.

The "Ayodhya" beyond Ayodhya

As with many Indian places, the name "Ayodhya" is used to refer to a range of geographical or administrative units. There is the present-day town in Uttar Pradesh, on the banks of the Sarayu River, about 93 miles (150km) from the state capital Lucknow and 124 miles (200km) from the pilgrim town of Varanasi. The district within which the town is located is also known as Ayodhya—it was called Faizabad until it was renamed in 2018. There is also an amorphous concept of the ancient city of Ayodhya—expanding beyond the present-day town with the understanding that administrative borders need not interfere with the idea of the legendary or historical city. It is this last idea that explains the geography of places associated with Ayodhya's mythology and history. Most of the important sites are situated in the town, but some are to be found in the neighboring town of Faizabad as well.

▼ The holy ghats along the Sarayu River in Ayodhya witness numerous ceremonies and rituals throughout the year.

◂ Titled *Ahalya*, this 1898 chromolithograph by Indian painter and artist Raja Ravi Varma depicts Ahalya in a garden, leaning against a tree and carrying a basket of flowers.

AHALYA'S REDEMPTION

AHALYA STHAN, BIHAR (INDIA)

The king of gods, Indra, was enamored of sage Gautama's wife, Ahalya. One day, while Gautama was away, Indra took on the form of the sage and approached Ahalya with a proposition to make love. She acquiesced, even though she knew it was really Indra. After they consummated their desire, Ahalya asked Indra to leave and ensure their protection. However, Indra ran into Gautama, who saw the king of gods disguised as himself. Enraged, Gautama cursed Indra with infertility and Ahalya with extreme austerities in an "invisible" state. Thousands of years later, Rama entered the beautiful, but deserted, hermitage on the outskirts of Mithila and liberated Ahalya.

The district of Darbhanga in the northern Indian state of Bihar presented a paradox for its builders—the fertile alluvial plain was an excellent source of clay for sunburned bricks, but these bricks could rarely hold up against the destruction of the recurring floods and earthquakes of the region. This fragility is probably why the temple of Ahalya Sthan in the Ahiyari North village, like a lot of Mithila architecture of the region, retains a pragmatic minimalism—the horizontal tiers of its spire rise from the brick structure underneath, both displaying only the lightest sculpting touches.

The complex has three main temples besides a number of smaller shrines—surrounded by lush greenery, next to a pond called the Ahalya Kund—and a rock with what are worshipped as the footprints of Sita. About 1.9 miles (3km) to the west is another pond, Gautam Kund, believed to be a water body which the creator god Brahma wished into existence so that Gautama would not have to travel too far for a dip in the river.

The Ahiyari North village is about 15 miles (24km) from Darbhanga town. The local belief is that the temple stands on the spot where Rama redeemed Ahalya. In the epic, Rama's encounter with Ahalya takes place as he is on his way to Mithila. Since Ahalya Sthan is less than 37.2 miles (60km) from Nepal's Janakpur Dham—identified as the capital of Mithila as mentioned in the *Ramayana*—believers consider this to be an affirmation of present-day Ahalya Sthan's claim as the site of that meeting.

Since the Darbhanga district and the nearby Madhubani district are part of a cultural and geographical continuum called Mithilanchal (the region of Mithila), Hindu beliefs about mythical episodes converge at many places around Ahalya Sthan. Jagban, 5.6 miles (9km) from Ahalya Sthan, is believed to be the home of Yajnavalkya, a great sage of the Upanishadic age; Kakraul, 15.5 miles (25km) away, is believed to have been Vedic sage Kapila's hermitage; and Bisaul, about 31 miles (50km) away, is considered to be where Rama's mentor, sage Vishwamitra, lived. Beyond legends, the town of Darbhanga—the closest urban center—itself has a rich history. It used to be an influential seat of power in colonial India, home to Bihar's Raj Darbhanga—a royal line that started during the reign of Akbar in the 16th century, and an important center of indigo cultivation. The vestiges of that period of history are found in the red-brick masonry of Darbhanga Fort, once the stately home of the royal family with a 500-year-old Kankali temple, dedicated to their clan goddess Kali.

▲ The ruins of the Rajnagar palace in the city of Darbhanga, Bihar, India, are testament to the rich history of Mithilanchal with unmistakably European pilasters mixed in with Indian elements.

"Invisible to all beings, you will live in this hermitage. And when the unassailable son of Dasharatha, Rama, comes to the forest, you will be purified. Wicked one! By extending hospitality to him, you will be devoid of delusion and lust, and filled with delight, you will take on your own form by my side."

Sage Gautama curses Ahalya, Sarga 47, Bala Kanda

▶ This 18th-century painting depicts Rama, Sita, and Lakshmana in their forest abode, after Rama's banishment from Ayodhya.

A BANISHED PRINCE

CHITRAKOOT, MADHYA PRADESH AND UTTAR PRADESH (INDIA)

Ayodhya prepared to celebrate Rama's consecration as prince regent. However, in the queen's quarters, Manthara, Kaikeyi's maid, had other plans. She goaded the young queen into seeking the throne for her son, Bharata. Kaikeyi called for the king and reminded him of a vow he had once made. She demanded he fulfil his promise by exiling Rama and making Bharata the king. Dasharatha, overwhelmed with grief, could not bear to tell his son to leave. However, Rama, ever obedient, accepted his fate and departed for exile, embracing the life of an ascetic for 14 years. His wife, Sita, and brother Lakshmana followed him into exile. Their first stop was the holy forests of Chitrakoot. This was where Bharata found Rama and begged him, unsuccessfully, to return.

In Hindu mythology, the abundant forests of the riverine Mount Chitrakoot were home to venerated sages and learned ascetics who gave up material pursuits to seek wisdom in peace. The most intensely spiritual spaces are, after all, the ones closest to nature. The natural landscape of present-day Chitrakoot—with its forests, hills, and the river flowing right by—explains the association.

In common usage, Chitrakoot refers to an area spanning the Chitrakoot district of Uttar Pradesh and the Satna district of Madhya Pradesh in India. It is deeply rooted in the *Ramayana* culture, with a number of sites featured in the epic within a 37.3-mile (60-km) radius—at the heart of which lies the sacred Kamadgiri Hill. This lush hill is where Rama is thought to have lived with Sita and Lakshmana for 11½ of his 14 years in exile. Many pilgrims choose to walk barefoot along a 3.1-mile 5-km circumambulatory path around the hill. This path, called the *parikrama*, is lined with temples and shrines. Among the most important of these is the Kamtanath Temple, dedicated to the principal deity of Chitrakoot, which gives the hill its name. Another temple along the path, Bharat Milap Temple, stands over the spot where Bharata pleaded with Rama to return to Ayodhya.

To the south of Kamadgiri, about 2.5 miles (4km) south of the Kamtanath Temple, lies Lakshman Pahari. It is the hill from where Rama's loyal brother Lakshmana is believed to have kept watch

▲ Colorful boats lined up by the steps of Ram Ghat.

during their stay in the forest. About 4.3 miles (7km) east of Lakshman Pahari is Ram Ghat, the splendid Mandakini riverfront. It is where Rama bathed every day while in Chitrakoot. It is also where the 16th-century poet Tulsidas is thought to have composed his retelling of the *Ramayana*, one of the most influential versions of the epic.

The other significant riverside site in Chitrakoot is Sphatik Shila—a flat boulder situated 2.5 miles (4km) upstream from Ram Ghat, and away from the bustle of the central town on the densely forested banks of the Mandakini. The boulder, now enclosed within a pavilion that serves as a temple, is believed to carry the footprint of Rama. It is said that Rama and Sita rested here often as they appreciated the serene natural beauty that surrounded them.

Further out, about 10 miles (16km) from the limits of Chitrakoot town, flows the Gupt Godavari (*gupt* means secret in Hindi) within a two-cave system. The bigger cave has two stone-carved thrones that are said to have belonged to Rama and Lakshmana. The other cave is where, as local lore goes, Lakshmana petrified a voyeur rakshasa who was eyeing Sita as she bathed in a pool. The waters, after flowing through the caves, emerge into a catchment tank before vanishing.

◄ This illustration shows sage Sutikshana reaching sage Agastya's hermitage with Rama, Sita, and Lakshmana.

A LONG EXILE

UTTAR PRADESH AND DANDAKARANYA (INDIA)

Rama, Sita, and Lakshmana spent the initial years of their exile at Chitrakoot, before they continued their journey to the dense and impenetrable forests of Dandaka. They stopped at many hermitages along the way, meeting sages and protecting them from rakshasas. They finally settled down in Dandakaranya, which was to be their home during the final years of the exile. This was where they had their fateful encounter with Surpanakha, which ultimately led to Sita's abduction at the hands of Ravana.

If present-day Ayodhya were home to Rama, Sita, and Lakshmana's home, the exile would follow a route south of the broad sweep of the Gangetic plains, through places scattered across the densely forested Satpura and Vindhya ranges of central India extending to the Western Ghats.

Shringverpur (Uttar Pradesh, India)
The quiet riverside village of Shringverpur in eastern Uttar Pradesh is understood to be the capital of the ancient Nishada community mentioned in the *Ramayana*. In the story, their king, Guha, was Dasharatha's friend. When Rama, Sita, and Lakshmana reached his kingdom, Guha went to see Rama and honored him. A small temple stands where they are believed to have met, a place that has been named Ramchura.

Prayagraj (Uttar Pradesh, India)
The hermitage of sage Bharadvaja was the last stop for Rama, Sita, and Lakshmana before they entered the hilly forests of Chitrakoot. In the story, the hermitage was at Prayaga, the confluence of the Ganga and the Yamuna. Present-day Prayagraj is believed to be the *Ramayana*'s Prayaga, and the Bharadvaja Ashram there marks the place. It is a temple complex lined with shrines dedicated to Hindu gods and sages. About 3.1 miles (5km) east of the temple complex is the Sangam Ghat, one of the most significant sites for the Hindu faith, where the waters of the Ganga meet those of the Yamuna (and, as mythology goes, the invisible Saraswati). Every 12 years, the confluence

is where one of the world's largest religious congregations, the Kumbh Mela, is organized.

Sarbhanga Ashram and Sutikshna Ashram (Madhya Pradesh, India)
The dreaded Dandaka of the epic is identified as the present-day forest tracts of Dandakaranya, which span across the central and western states of India (*aranya* means forest in Sanskrit). Rama's first stop in these woods was at the hermitage of sage Sarabhanga. In the *Ramayana*, Sarabhanga dies just as Rama reaches the place and a gathering of ascetics urge Rama to protect them from the rakshasas living in the forest—a request that Rama accepts.

An ashram and temple memorializing this episode, called Sarbhanga Ashram, lies in the present-day village of Piparawan, which is about 34.2 miles (55km) from Chitrakoot. The ashram welcomes visitors who can join in meditation, spiritual discussions, and workshops. Rama's next stop was the hermitage of sage Sutikshna. The present-day spot believed to be the hermitage, Sutikshna Ashram, is located in the town of Seleha in Madhya Pradesh, about 5 miles (8km) from the Sarbhanga Ashram.

Ramtek (Maharashtra, India)
During their stay at Sutikshna's hermitage, Rama asked him about the great storyteller sage Agastya as he wanted to pay him a visit. Sutikshna gave them directions to sage Agastya's hermitage, which was located in "a beautiful part of the forest, with many trees." Rama, Sita, and Lakshmana stopped at the hermitage for a night. The present-day town of Ramtek is believed to be where Agastya's hermitage once stood. In the northern part of the town, atop the Ramgiri Hill, lies the sprawling Ramtek Gad Mandir (Ramtek Fort Temple)—dedicated to Rama, Sita, and Lakshmana. The temple is likely to have been built in stages, between the 4th and 18th centuries, and preserves traces of the evolution of architectural styles in the region over centuries.

▼ Pilgrims traveling on boats at the Sangam Ghat in Prayagraj, Uttar Pradesh, India, during the Kumbh Mela

▲ The majestic Ramtek Fort Temple in Maharashtra, India, is believed to have been built by Raghuji Bhonsale, the Maratha ruler of Nagpur.

Panchavati (Maharashtra, India)

After a brief stay at the hermitage of Agastya, Rama asked the sage to point him toward a part of the forest where he could set up his own hermitage with Sita and Lakshmana. Agastya directed them to the abundant wilderness of the Panchavati forest by the Godavari River instead. The site, believed to be the forest in the epic, is an area within the city of Nashik in northern Maharashtra, also known as Panchavati. It is from where Ravana, the king of Lanka, is said to have abducted Sita. Situated on the left bank of the Godavari River is Ram Kund, a ghat sacred to Hindu believers—where Rama is said to have bathed while he lived in Panchavati. The ghat was built in the 17th century by the local ruling family, and is a sacred spot for immersing the ashes of those of the Hindu faith.

"The circle of ascetic hermitages was ever the refuge for all beings ... It was inhabited by restrained ancient sages covered in black antelope skin, who appeared like fire or sun, and consumed only fruit and roots. Comparable to the abode of Brahma, it resounded with the sounds of the Veda."

Rama, Sita, and Lakshmana enter Dandakaranya, Sarga 1, Aranya Kanda

One of the holiest cities in the Hindu faith, Prayagraj, which also hosts the Kumbha Mela, is believed to have been one of the places Rama visited while in exile. Seen here are pilgrims gathered to take a holy dip at the confluence of the Rivers Ganga, Yamuna, and mythical Saraswati, on the occasion of the Maha Kumbha.Mela.

GOMIRA MASK DANCE

ENACTING RAMA'S EXILE

The villages of two north Bengal districts in India preserve a centuries-old tradition of a ceremonial masked dance that enacts the exile of Rama.

The blooming of the white, featherlike Kaash flower (*Kans*) in the fields of the Indian state of West Bengal announces the arrival of fall. This is also when the villages of North and South Dinajpur districts prepare for "Raamer Bonobas," the ritual performance of the banishment of Rama. The name means "Rama's exile," and the performance is a form of the Gomira mask dance, staged with elaborately crafted wooden masks, performed year-round, but most often during October and November.

In "Raamer Bonobas," each mask represents a specific character from the *Ramayana*. The performance is entirely improvised and unfolds with no music or chants—only the rhythmic beat of the drum and the cymbal. A performer may go into a trance embodying the traits of the character their mask represents, and at that point, they may represent that character.

The Gomira mask dance itself is performed as an obeisance to local goddesses, derived from the broader Shakti belief system, and to drive away evil forces.

The masks are considered sacred and offered to the local temple – sometimes as pledges for the fulfilment of a wish. They are made of wood that the community believes to be pure—neem qualifies, as do mango, Indian cork, and white teak. After the wood is cut to the required size, it is immersed in water to season and soften it so that sculpting it becomes easier. The basic facial contours are then carved and the openings for the eyes and mouth cut out. Once the front of the mask has been carved, the wood and pulp are carefully scooped out from the inside. The wood is then varnished and hand-painted, traditionally with natural dyes. The makers of these masks are also the performers—and every village has its own troupe.

The performances can be seen in the villages of Kushmandi, Raiganj, and Kunia Danga during the festivals of Dussehra and Durga Puja, around October and November.

▶ **Clockwise from top left:** a Gomira dance troupe; artist carving a mask; distinct garments of the male and female characters; Gomira dancer performing with a burning torch; dancers getting ready for a performance; masks representing different forms of Kali.

◀ The vanara and riksha army build a bridge across the ocean and to Lanka, as Rama and Lakshmana look on, in this *c.*1850 Kangra painting.

RAMA BUILDS A BRIDGE

RAMESWARAM, TAMIL NADU (INDIA)

When Ravana abducted Sita, a brokenhearted Rama scoured the forests and mountains to find her. The vanaras helped him in his search and they finally discovered that Sita was in Lanka. But, Ravana's kingdom was across the vast ocean. Ravana's brother Vibhishana, who chose to be by the prince's side, suggested that Rama petition the ocean for passage. Rama prayed to the god, but the ocean remained unmoved. Angry and distraught, Rama shot an arrow into the deep recesses of the ocean. It was enough for the ocean to relent and it told Rama to seek the help of Nala, son of Vishwakarma, the god of architecture. Nala used his engineering acumen and the help of thousands of vanaras and rikshas to build an immense structure—a bridge across the ocean to Lanka.

While the *tirthasthal* (pilgrimage site) lies at the core of the Hindu belief system, the *dham* (abode) is where gods reside—as an anchor of divinity in this transient, mortal world. Hindu religious thought places four such *dhams* across India—Badrinath in the north, Dwarka in the west, Puri in the east, and Rameswaram in the south. In the *Ramayana* lore, Rameswaram holds immense significance on several accounts.

Rameswaram is believed to be where Rama halted, and strategized his rescue of Sita and the attack on Lanka, after Hanuman brought back word about Sita's whereabouts in Lanka. It is where Ravana's younger brother Vibhishana met Rama, and joined forces with him after Ravana refused to listen to his advice about averting war by releasing Sita from captivity. Rameswaram is also the place where Rama made his victorious return from Lanka after killing Ravana—a sin for which he had to atone by offering prayers to the god of destruction, Shiva. So, there is much to explore in this scenic little town on Pamban Island in the southern Indian state of Tamil Nadu.

Pamban Island reaches out toward Sri Lanka—across the Gulf of Mannar—with a chain of barrier islands, natural limestone shoals, and sand spits. The British called it Adam's Bridge. This chain, or "bridge," is believed to be the remnant of the bridge built by the vanara army for Rama and his forces to cross the ocean into Lanka.

▲ An aerial view of Arichal Munai, the southeastern tip of Pamban Island in Tamil Nadu, India.

Today, Dhanushkodi is a ghost town—lined with the ruins of a temple, a church, a railway station, and houses abandoned after a giant tidal wave hit the bustling town in 1964.

Also linked to the legend of the bridge is the Panchamukhi Hanuman Temple, about 12.4 miles (20km) from Dhanushkodi. The principal deity is a five-faced (*panchamukhi*) form of Hanuman.

A major draw for Hindu pilgrims visiting the temple is a "floating" stone on display. The buoyant stone is a low-density, sedimentary rock that floats on water. This physical property, however, has led to the belief that it is a type of floating stone similar to those used by the vanaras to build the bridge to Lanka.

Rama prepares for battle

About 3.1 miles (5km) east of the Panchamukhi Hanuman Temple lies the Ekantha Ramaswamy Temple. This is one of two temples in Rameswaram associated with the period during which Rama prepared for his battle with Ravana. This 15th-century temple, dedicated to Shiva, lies on the spot where Rama is said to have conferred with the vanaras before the attack on Lanka. The other temple rooted in this part of the story is the Uppoor Veyil Ugantha Vinayagar Temple, 48 miles (77km) from the Ekantha Ramaswamy Temple. The presiding deity is Vinayakar, a form of Shiva's son Ganesha. It is believed that Rama himself installed the deity here to pray for his success before the Lanka

The floating bridge

The former port of Dhanushkodi at the tip of Rameswaram, on the edge of Pamban Island, is the point believed to be where the vanara army started building a floating bridge. The beach in the town is known as Arichal Munai. The word *dhanushkodi* means tip of the bow in the Tamil language—a reference to Rama's bow, a recurring image in Hindu mythological representations. It is where the Bay of Bengal merges with the Indian Ocean, and is the farthest point in India from where one can see Adam's Bridge.

campaign. A pivotal point in Rama's preparation for the face-off with Ravana was his decision to join forces with Vibhishana. The present-day Kothandaramaswamy Temple, 7.5 miles (12km) from Rameswaram, is said to be where Vibhishana sought refuge with Rama. This meeting between the two may have taken place at a different location, Gandamadana Parvatham, according to another version of the local lore. It is a hillock, about 6.8 miles (11km) from the Kothandaramaswamy Temple, and is the highest point in Rameswaram with sweeping views of the ocean toward Sri Lanka.

Rama atones his sin

Rameswaram's most important temple —which lends the town its name—is the Ramanathaswamy Temple, 1.9 miles (3km) from Gandamadana Parvatham. It was built in stages between the 12th and 18th centuries under different rulers, each expanding a part of the temple. Today, the temple's entrance (called *gopuram*) has a 78.7-ft- (24-m-) high tower on one side, and a 125-ft- (38-m-) high tower on the other. These towers lead to three massive, concentric corridors with over 4,000 pillars. The presiding deity is a form of Shiva named Ramanathaswamy. Rameswaram, which means "lord of Rama," refers to Shiva.

One local lore says that when Rama and Sita were on their way back from Lanka, Rama wanted to offer prayers to Shiva to atone for the sin of killing a brahman, Ravana. He asked Hanuman to get him a Shivalinga (a representation of Shiva) from Kashi. Kashi, now called Varanasi, is one of the holiest sites in Hinduism. Rameswaram is popularly known as the Kashi of the south. When Hanuman seemed to take too long, Sita fashioned a Shivalinga out of sand. It is believed that the Shivalinga referred to as Ramalinga worshipped at the temple today is the one that Sita had shaped. The Shivalinga that Hanuman brought back, the Vishwalinga, is also housed in the temple.

Another story goes that as the vanaras built the bridge to Lanka by day, Ravana would destroy their work by night. The king of the rikshas, Jambavan, then told Rama that a way out would be to place a Shivalinga on the bridge—Ravana was an ardent Shiva devotee and would not destroy it. The strategy worked; the bridge to Lanka was completed and the Shivalinga was installed at the site where the magnificent temple stands now.

▼ The magnificent corridors and sculptured pillars of Ramanathaswamy Temple, Rameswaram, Tamil Nadu, India.

CULTURE

BARDS OF RAMKATHA

RAMA GOES TO WAR

From the plains of eastern Uttar Pradesh to the deserts of western Rajasthan and the coastline of northern Kerala, oral traditions among Muslim communities across India celebrate the Hindu epic *Ramayana* as part of their own lore.

This Ramkatha begins with a *qawwali*, the music of Sufism. As the performer recites the story of how Rama waged war in Lanka and defeated Ravana, soft interludes of bhajans or Hindu devotional hymns, accentuate the narrative.

"Lanka ki Chadhai," which means The Invasion of Lanka, is a unique oral retelling of the *Ramayana* by the Jogi community of northern India. The ballad is believed to have been composed more than three centuries ago. The Jogis, the community which preserves the tradition, are part of a Muslim sect that follows the 11th-century Hindu yogi Gorakhnath. While their numbers are dwindling, Jogis reciting the *Ramayana* are still found in villages of eastern Uttar Pradesh and in the Mewat region of Haryana and Rajasthan. In a similar tradition, the Sunni Muslim Manganiar community of western Rajasthan sings the *Ramayana* as bhajans, to the accompaniment of the stringed *khamaicha* and the beats of the *dholak*. While Manganiar performances rely on *dohas*, or couplets, Jogis incorporate longer descriptive verses after each couplet in an oral tradition called *doha dhani*.

Likewise, in northern Kerala, the Malabar Muslim community adapted the *Ramayana* into a localized retelling centuries ago. The *Mappila Ramayanam* is a series of folk songs called Mappilapattu. The lyrics are conversational, and the tunes are structured like *ragas* of Indian classical music but with deep influence of Arabic folk music—reflective of the region's old trading ties with west Asia. The tradition is now a mainstay of performances during Karkidakam, the last month of the Malayalam calendar (from mid-July to mid-August), which is celebrated as the *Ramayana* month when the epic in its many forms is staged across Kerala.

◀ **Clockwise, from top left:** a Langas and Manganiars folk music troupe from Rajasthan; Rajasthani folk dance by an artist from the Bhutte Khan Manganiar Group; sadhus at Magh Mela in Uttar Pradesh; mural depicting a Nath yogi at the Mahamandir Temple, Jodhpur.

A FACE-OFF WITH RAVANA

YUDAGANAWA, NORTH-CENTRAL PROVINCE (SRI LANKA)

The vanara and riksha forces crossed the bridge over the ocean into Lanka and set up camp outside Ravana's fortress to prepare for battle. Under the command of their kings, who pledged fealty to Rama, the armies attacked the citadel and a fierce war broke out. A series of skirmishes and battles followed, and gradually, Rama's forces slew each of Ravana's greatest warriors. Eventually, Ravana rode out to the battleground himself. Rama faced his adversary in a long and fierce combat, and—in the final battle—killed Ravana.

The Wasgamuwa National Park in central Sri Lanka is known for its safaris, especially those to spot wild elephants. In the serene abundance of these forests, a piece of land stands out. In stark contrast to its verdant surroundings, this vast area appears forsaken. This is Yudaganawa, which translates to "battlefield," and local legends and contemporary sources propose that this is the site where Rama and Ravana first engaged in battle. According to these stories, arrows flew across the skies, while maces, bludgeons, and even entire mountaintops and trees were hurled in the fierce confrontation—devastating the land in a way that left lasting scars. However, this connection is not found in traditional versions of the *Ramayana* and appears to be a more recent attribution. Nonetheless, this association with the legendary battle is one of the reasons why the area holds significance as a prominent site on the *Ramayana* circuit in Sri Lanka, which highlights various locations linked to the epic, though the historical accuracy of some sites remains debated.

▼ This intricately carved frieze depicts Rama and Ravana on chariots, unleashing a variety of weapons against each other during the final battle of the *Ramayana*.

The Wasgamuwa National Park lies in the drainage basins of three rivers—Mahaweli, Amban, and Kalu. These rivers are fed by streams originating from Sudu Kanda (White Mountain), the highest point in the national park, which stands 1,540ft (470m) tall. This geography is probably why the region has such rich biodiversity—the dry, evergreen forests of the 37,000-hectare (370sq-km) park are home to nearly 300 species of wildlife and 150 plant species. Besides herds of Asian elephants, which are Wasgamuwa's primary draw, the national park is also known for being home to the leopard, sloth bear, grey slender loris, and southern purple-faced langur.

The park is an idyllic place for camping for those seeking a closer experience of the sweeping nature trails around Yudaganawa. While most of the park is covered with dense forests, there are expansive plains on the southeastern and eastern trails within the park, which are wonderful for hikes.

Yudaganawa also offers an enriching cultural experience. The Buddhist heritage of the place where the park is located is why there are several sites of archaeological significance close by. The most important of these is the ruins of Buduruwayaya, to the southwest of Wasgamuwa (the rock with the statue of Buddha in Sinhalese). Here, a colossal 51-ft (15.5-m) statue of a recumbent Buddha is carved into a limestone rock face, which explains the name.

In Sri Lankan history, the period from the 5th century BCE to the 11th century CE is considered its prime. It is known as the

▼ Almost entirely encompassed by rivers, the Wasgamuwa National Park in Sri Lanka is a sanctuary for wildlife enthusiasts as well as nature lovers.

Anuradhapura period—a time of Buddhist expansion—named after the sacred city of Anuradhapura, its capital (a UNESCO World Heritage Site now). Buduruwayaya dates to the early Anuradhapura period, the 2nd century CE. The statue at Buduruwayaya is one of the three large reclining Buddha statues across Sri Lanka, however, most reclining Buddhas from the period were made of brick, and rock-cut Buddhas were not usually carved on this scale.

Another feature of interest in the park is the Elahera anicut across Amban Ganga, where the Elahera canal branches off. It is only 0.6 miles (1km) south of the Buduruwayaya temple. The 54-miles-(87-km-) long canal carries excess water from the Kala Wewa reservoir in the northern part of the park to the Tissa Wewa reservoir in Anuradhapura (further north) with a remarkably precise, minutely calculated gradient of 3.9–7.8in (10–20cm) every 0.6 miles (kilometer).

What makes it truly fascinating is that this feat of engineering dates back to the late 3rd century CE, when Mahasena—one of the most noteworthy rulers of Sri Lankan history—ruled over these parts.

▶ A fresco of the six-headed deity Murugan at Yudaganawa Temple in Buttala, Sri Lanka.

"Sita! Look, this is the battlefield, a quagmire of flesh and blood, and the site of the great slaughter of the rakshasas and monkeys. Large-eyed one! For your sake, Ravana was killed by me."

Rama to Sita as they return to Ayodhya from Lanka, Sarga 111, Yuddha Kanda

Rama, Lakshmana, and the vanara army confront Ravana and his forces in this lithograph from a 19th-century French publication on Indian religion.

CULTURE

THOLPAVAKOOTHU

A LEGENDARY BATTLE

Intricately crafted leather puppets set against a backdrop illuminated by lamps tell the story of the *Ramayana*—with an elaborate performance of the battle between Rama and Ravana —in this ancient ritual art from Kerala.

No god and no man, the story goes, could counter the might of Darika, the asura made invincible by Brahma's boon. So, the god of destruction, Shiva, created the goddess Bhadrakali, who slayed the asura after a fierce battle. But so preoccupied was she with the battle that she could not watch Rama's victory over Ravana. To placate her, Shiva decreed that all Bhadrakali temples around her battleground would be stages for *Ramayana* performances—with the battle between Rama and Ravana receiving the sharpest focus. This is why, between January and May every year, more than 85 Bhadrakali temples in the Palakkad, Malappuram, and Thrissur districts of Kerala stage Tholpavakoothu plays. *Thol* means leather, *pava* means doll, and *koothu* translates to play. Every temple has a permanent three-walled structure specially constructed for the shadow puppetry performance, which is based on the *Kamba Ramayana*, a 12th-century Tamil retelling of the epic.

Usually staged late in the evening, as many as 160 to 180 flat puppets made of goatskin depict 71 characters in action. A prescribed number of 21 coconut oil lamps cast a soft golden-yellow light on the tightly stretched white backdrop, against which the puppets are held with a thin stick in one hand and manipulated with an even thinner stick in the other. The lead puppeteer, called the Pulavar, must learn over 2,100 verses of the *Kamba Ramayana*, chant the verses relevant to the story, and then explain them to the audience. The accompanying puppeteers respond in chorus while drums, cymbals, pipes, gongs, bells, and conch punctuate the high points of the narrative. Staging the entire play takes 21 days, with seven-hour performances each day.

◀ **Clockwise from top left:** behind the curtain of a shadow puppet performance in Palakkad, Kerala; puppet depicting Ravana; Sita in captivity; shadow puppetry showing a brahman; Ravana and his courtiers as the audience sees them.

▸ This 17th-century painting by Sahib Din, a miniature artist from the Mewar school of Rajasthan, depicts Ravana's funeral.

RAMA'S ATONEMENT

TEMPLES DEDICATED TO SHIVA, ACROSS NORTHERN SRI LANKA AND INDIA

The sin of killing a brahman, Valmiki's *Ramayana* said, was one so great that it would set the killer on course to hell. But it did not refer to the need for Rama to make reparations for killing Ravana, a brahman. Medieval retellings, however, introduced an episode in which Rama realized that killing Ravana was a crime for which he must make amends. The ancient Hindu text *Skanda Purana* described how Rama established a Shivalinga and offered his prayers to atone for his sin. Another version, popular in Sri Lanka, said that as Rama left Lanka aboard Ravana's flying chariot, he was haunted by the crime of killing Ravana. He stopped the chariot and asked Shiva what he must do. Shiva blessed Rama and asked him to install Shivalingas and worship them for atonement.

Along the coast of Sri Lanka lie five Shiva temples that Tamil legend says are the homes of the god of destruction, Shiva. Known as the *Pancha Ishwaram*, which means the five abodes in Tamil, these temples are ancient. Three of them are believed to be where Rama offered prayers to Shiva to seek his grace and absolve himself of the sin of killing Ravana. Two other temples in India, one in the southern state of Tamil Nadu and another in the northern state of Uttarakhand, are also revered sites of Rama's reparations. This intersection (of the worship of Shiva within the universe of the *Ramayana*) is one that happens often over the course of the story of the *Ramayana*. All the primary characters—Rama, Ravana, and Sita—are devotees of Shiva.

Munneswaram Temple and Manavari Temple, Chilaw (Northwestern Province, Sri Lanka)

The magnificent temple at Munneswaram on the western coast of Sri Lanka is considered to be one of the *Pancha Ishwaram*, an ancient temple, which as per local legends predates the events of the *Ramayana*. This is where Rama is thought to have realized that the sin of killing Ravana was following him and is where he prayed to Shiva for a solution.

The recorded history of the temple attributes it to a series of rulers dating back to at least the 15th century—each expanding the temple gradually under their rule. When Portuguese colonists rose in power, they destroyed the temple toward the end of the 16th century.

The temple was renovated by a local ruler in the 18th century. Today, the temple complex has five elaborately sculpted and brightly colored temples dedicated to powerful deities such as Vinayakar (a form of the elephant god Ganesha), Vativampika (a goddess of beautiful form), Aiyanar (a folk deity of fertility), and the principal deity Munnainathar, the lord of antiquity and a form of Shiva. The fifth temple within the complex is a Buddhist shrine. About 7.5 miles (12km) north of the Munneswaram Temple is the equally elaborate Manavari Temple, a shrine where Rama is believed to have installed the first Shivalinga, called Ramalinga, for atonement.

Thiru Koneswaram, Trincomalee (Eastern Province, Sri Lanka)

This is the second site where Rama is said to have installed a Shivalinga to negate his sin. Regarded as the most sacred of the *Pancha Ishwaram*, Thiru Koneswaram is also believed to predate the *Ramayana*. Local lore says that the sage Agastya built the temple following instructions from the god Shiva, who was pleased with Ravana's single-minded devotion to him.

▼ Known for its association with the epic *Ramayana*, Munneswaram Temple in Sri Lanka is an important Hindu pilgrimage site where devotees come to honor Lord Shiva.

The actual structure is likely to have been built in stages since 205 BCE, perhaps even 400 BCE. Significant progress was made during the reign of the southern Indian dynasties of the Cholas and the Pandyas —some of the most powerful empires in the history of the subcontinent. The temple was destroyed by the Portuguese in the early 17th century and a fort was built from its debris. In 1956, eminent science-fiction writer Arthur C. Clarke and underwater photographer Mike Wilson came across its ruins, sculptures, and bronze artifacts, both underwater and on land. They also retrieved a Shivalinga which was then reinstalled at the temple.

The restored shrine opened in 1963, and is now situated within the fort built from its ruins. The temple architecture retains much of its original Tamil influences—detailed sculptures on the spires—with a splash of color at every step. The temple, situated atop a cliff known as Swami Rock, overlooks the ocean.

Near the temple is a notable geological feature called the Ravana Abyss, also known as Ravana Cut or Ravanan Veddu. This deep cleft in the rock face is steeped in local legend. According to local folklore, Ravana created the abyss when he attempted to detach and transport the Koneswaram Temple by cutting through the rock with his sword. This act was intended to appease his mother, who was distressed by her inability to worship at the temple due to her failing health. However, Shiva intervened, causing Ravana to abandon his endeavor, leaving the rock cleft as testament to his attempt. Today, the Ravana Abyss is a point of interest for visitors to the Koneswaram Temple. A statue of Ravana stands near the cliff, symbolizing his association with the site. The location offers a serene environment and panoramic ocean views, making it a memorable spot to visit.

Thiru Ketheeswaram, Mannar (Northern Province, Sri Lanka)
Popularly believed to be one of the oldest Hindu temples in Sri Lanka, this site is where Rama is believed to have installed the third Shivalinga for atonement. Literary and archaeological evidence suggests its existence for at least 2,400 years. As one of the *Pancha Ishwaram* temples, it is believed to have stood here long before the events of the *Ramayana.*

One legend traces its origins to the mythical churning of the ocean in the *Puranas*—an episode in which the gods and asuras together churned the ocean with a mountain to get at the nectar of immortality. The asura Ketu, however, stole the nectar and had to perform penance for the crime. This temple is said to be dedicated to repentance, which gives it the name Thiru-Kethu-Iswaram, meaning the sacred abode of Ketu's Lord. Some legends state that Mayan, Ravana's father-in-law and a renowned architect, built this temple as a mark of reverence.

Thiru Ketheeswaram, too, was destroyed by the Portuguese in the 16th century and rebuilt only in the 1950s. Like the temples of Munneswaram and Koneswaram, this vibrant temple is also based on a Tamil architectural plan.

Ramanathaswamy Temple, Rameswaram (Tamil Nadu, India)
The most important pilgrimage site in the town of Rameswaram, this temple is believed to be another site where Rama installed a Shivalinga and worshipped the god to seek absolution for his crime. The story goes that Sita built a Shivalinga out of sand when Hanuman, whom Rama had sent off to fetch a Shivalinga from the holy city of Kashi (present-day Varanasi), was delayed. Hanuman came back with a Shivalinga anyway, and both were placed within the temple—the one created by Sita was called Ramalinga, and the one brought by Hanuman, Vishwalinga. In Hindu religious thought, the temple is believed to be one of 12 Jyotirlingas—the 12 places on earth where Shiva resides. The present-day temple, built between the 12th and 18th centuries, is a grand structure with 22 holy waterbodies situated within the complex—devotees believe bathing in these waters will absolve them of their sins.

Raghunath Temple, Devprayag (Uttarakhand, India)
While this site is not part of the Sri Lankan traditional tale of Rama's absolution, north Indian narratives place Rama's quest for atonement at this temple in the mountain town of Devprayag. Two rivers sacred to Hindus, Bhagirathi and Alaknanda, meet at Devprayag—riverine confluences are important sites in the Hindu belief—before they flow into the Ganga, the holiest river for Hindus. The main temple in town, Raghunath Temple, is located by the river and is up a steep climb of 100-odd steps. It is believed to be where Rama and Lakshmana both atoned for killing Ravana. The existing temple is likely to have been built in the 9th century. Unlike other sites of Rama's atonement, this temple is not dedicated to Shiva but to Vishnu—whose incarnation is Rama.

▲ This 15th-century bronze statue from Nepal depicts sage Agastya, credited to have built the Thiru Koneswaram temple, meditating on his waterpot.

> **"The Horse Sacrifice is a great ritual,**
> **and purifies of all sin.**
> **May this bull among sacrifices,**
> **the very best—which would be purifying**
> **for you—be pleasing."**
>
> *Lakshmana tells Rama, Sarga 75, Uttara Kanda*

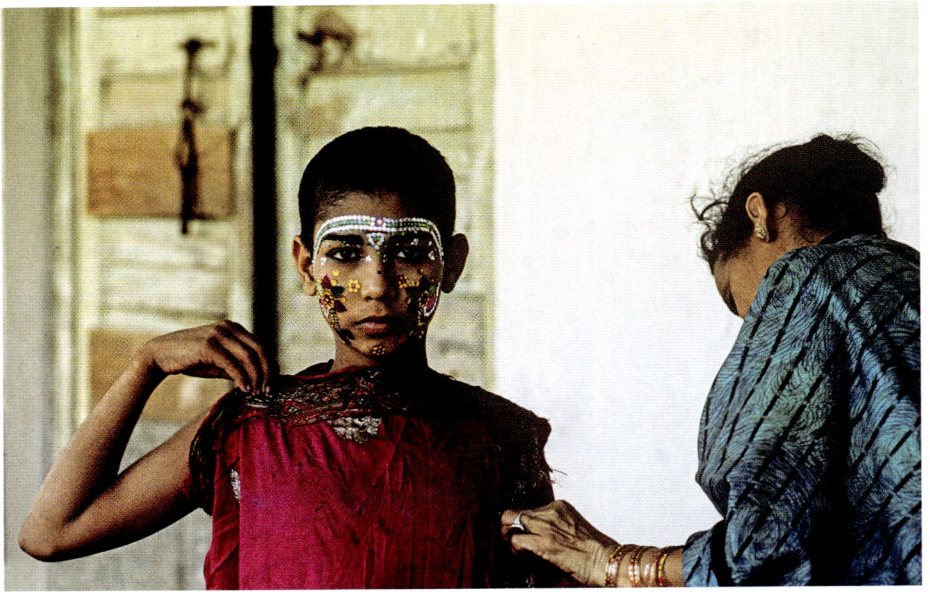

CULTURE

RAMNAGAR RAMLILA

RAMAYANA OVER 31 DAYS

An 18th-century palace serves as the backdrop for one of the oldest performances of the Ramlila, a musical theater enactment of the *Ramayana,* that lasts for a month.

At the Ramnagar Ramlila, everyone is a participant, not a mere spectator. The performance of the musical retelling of the *Ramayana* begins at the 18th-century Ramnagar Fort, on the eastern bank of the Ganga, across the pilgrim town of Varanasi.

As the performance goes on, the lines between the staged and the real seem to blur. The audience travels from one location to another as the drama of Rama's life unfolds. So, when they follow Rama, Sita, and Lakshmana to the banks of the Ganga—represented by a small tank here—they *are* the brokenhearted citizens of Ayodhya, trailing their beloved prince. Shouts of "Jai Siya Ram" follow the boat as it transports Rama, Sita, and Lakshmana across the imaginary river while the crowd crosses the tank on foot to join them on the other side. As Sita sits in captivity in Lanka, women hover around her, sharing her restless wait for Rama.

This performance takes place over 31 days, when all of Ramnagar turns into a stage. Staged under the open sky, natural lighting is preferred—the soft light of traditional lamps illuminating the action when needed. The performers, in traditional makeup and masks, deliver their lines unaided by microphones. The narrators, called Ramayanis, are seated some distance from the action on stage to ensure that their rhythmic recitation of the *Ramcharitmanas* (a 16th-century retelling of the *Ramayana* on which Ramlilas are based) firmly anchors the performance.

The Ramnagar Ramlila begins on Anant Chaturdashi, a fall festival celebrated in September, which is the best time to experience the performance.

◀ **Clockwise from top left:** actor dressed as Rama for a Ramlila performance; fitting for a Ramlila costume; a performer taking on the role of Hanuman; Rama and Lakshmana being carried on the shoulders of Ramlila workers; child actors portraying Rama and Lakshmana at a Ramlila in Varanasi, India.

03

Ravana: *Realm of the Scholar King*

◂ A mural of Ravana at the Thodikkalam Shiva Temple in Kerala in India.

▼ Published in 1782, this illustration by French naturalist and explorer Pierre Sonnerat depicts Ravana, the 10-headed king of Lanka.

PROFILE

KING OF LANKA

Ravana's kingdom, Lanka, was a land of immense wealth and renowned for its prosperity and advancements in arts and sciences. Ravana's intelligence, devotion to Shiva, and strategic prowess strengthened his rule, but his arrogance ultimately led to his downfall. Despite its grandeur, Lanka fell when Ravana's confrontation with Rama ended in his defeat, signaling the end of his reign.

Lanka, in Valmiki's *Ramayana*, is a wondrous place. Seen first through the eyes of Hanuman, the vanara son of the wind god, Vayu, the city, with its golden ramparts, replete with groves and a moat filled with flowers, is vibrant—a symbol of power, almost impenetrable. Much like the city itself, the ruler Ravana, too, is formidable and undefeatable. Such is his power that Hanuman says, on seeing him, "Had adharma not become stronger, this lord of the rakshasas might have become the protector of the world of the gods." Ravana, however, does not listen to Hanuman's advice to follow the path of dharma and return Sita; instead he ends up walking the path to his inevitable destruction.

The might of the lord of Lanka

Ravana was born of a perceived transgression. Kaikasi, the daughter of Sumali, a powerful rakshasa, acting on her father's instructions, asked the sage Visrava to marry her. However, the sage was in the midst of performing a sacred fire ritual, and the hour was inauspicious. So, even though he granted her wish, he told her that the inopportune hour meant her children would be frightful and cruel. Dasagriva, who later came to be known as Ravana, was born, and true to the prophecy, inspired great fear in all the worlds. When his mother Kaikasi told him to aspire to be more like his half-brother Kubera, the god of wealth, Dasagriva, or the one with 10 heads, seethed with envy and resolved to become his equal. For 10,000 years, he performed extreme austerities—going without food, and sacrificing one of his 10 heads every thousand years. Just as he was about to sacrifice his tenth and last head, Brahma appeared, restored his 9 heads, and blessed him with immortality—no god, rakshasa, or divine creature could kill him.

Now invincible, Dasagriva seized Lanka, Kubera's glorious kingdom. In an inevitable face-off, he defeated his half-brother and took control of his flying machine, the Pushpaka Vimana, as a token of victory. It is interesting to note that this machine is referred to as the Dandu-monara in Sri Lanka. This translates to wooden peacock or flying peacock, as its design was reminiscent of the bird and symbolized beauty and majesty. According to Sri Lanka's *Ramayana* folklore, Ravana used the mythical machine for aerial travels and later to abduct Sita.

Dasagriva got the name Ravana after an encounter with Shiva, the god of destruction. While traveling in the flying machine, he discovered he was unable to

▲ A metal statue of the deity Kubera.

pass over a grove as Shiva was there with his wife, Parvati. The angry king uprooted the mountain where the god and his wife sat, and held it up. A calm Shiva pushed it down with his big toe—a playful counter to Dasagriva's arrogance. Dasagriva screamed in pain as his arm was crushed, making the worlds tremble. Realizing he had gone too far, he set about appeasing Shiva. Finally, the god let him go—naming him Ravana, or the one who makes the world scream.

Ravana, as he was now known, became a devotee of Shiva. This incident, called Ravanaugraha or grace to Ravana, is depicted in art and sculpture, as seen in Shiva temples across much of western and southern India, from Maharashtra and Karnataka to Tamil Nadu. Many Shiva temples scattered across south and north India are believed to be places where Ravana worshipped his favored god.

This encounter plays a significant role in Ravana's mythology, emphasizing his complex character, as a fearsome warrior, learned ruler, and a devotee of Shiva. Even though the gods blessed him, Ravana's arrogance, in the end, proved to be his downfall.

A matter of destiny

That much of Ravana's life is predestined becomes apparent in the retelling of his story in the latter half of Valmiki's *Ramayana*, in the Uttara Kanda. It is obvious then that every action of Ravana was a foreshadowing of his inevitable

◀ This 16th-century illustration from the Mughal Dynasty depicts Ravana seizing the Pushpaka Vimana from Kubera.

She saw Ravana, whose energy flashed forth ... The hero was like Death with its jaws open, unvanquishable in battle for the gods, gandharvas, and other beings, and for the great sages.

Surpanakha rushes to Ravana after being mutilated, Sarga 30, Aranya Kanda

end at the hands of Rama, every decision of his keeping him on that path. It is seen in Ravana's encounter with Vedavati, the daughter of a sage. Struck by her beauty and overcome by desire, he approaches her as she performs a severe penance. She rejects him, for she wants to win over Vishnu, the preserver of the universe. Angry, Ravana tries to seize her and Vedavati immolates herself, pledging to be reborn to cause Ravana's destruction. Vedavati is reborn ages later as Sita.

Again, fate sets Ravana's path when he decides to march on Ayodhya, the kingdom of the Ikshvaku. As his armies destroy the city, Ravana attacks the king Anaranya who curses him as he lies dying. Ravana would die at the hands of a king from the Ikshvaku line—as he does 15 generations later at the hands of Rama.

Ravana's inevitable path to destruction begins in the forests of Dandakaranya (believed to be in the present-day Eastern Ghats) with Lakshmana's encounter with his sister Surpanakha. It ends with Sita's subsequent abduction, as Ravana takes her across the sea to his island kingdom. Today, that route to Lanka is believed to be Adam's Bridge in the northern province of Sri Lanka. He then takes Sita to his palace, Lanka's jewel, as Hanuman describes it later—a great citadel believed to be located at what is today the atolls of Great Basses Reef (Maha Ravana) and Little Basses Reef (Kuda Ravana) in Sri Lanka.

The battle of Lanka was a long and bloody one, supposed to have taken place across several regions and key geographical features in Sri Lanka, whether Ravana's caves in the Ella Wildlife Sanctuary, his "airports," such as the one in Horton Plains National Park, or the protected sites of Wasgamuwa, where Ravana is believed to have fought Rama and died.

Leonard Woolf

While the more celebrated literary connection to Sri Lanka might be that of British science-fiction author Arthur C. Clarke, who made it his home in 1956, it was Leonard Woolf, the husband of author Virginia Woolf, who contributed to the popularization of the Ravana geography of southern Sri Lanka. Posted as a civil officer, Woolf put together a list of places identified with parts of what is believed to have been Ravana's kingdom on the southern coast, notes author Justin W. Henry in his book *Ravana's Kingdom*.

Full circle

Researchers studying the *Ramayana* have surmised that Ravana's accumulation of skills and powers may have been necessary to exalt Ravana to the position of a "worthy" antagonist to Rama. As eminent Sanskrit scholars Robert Goldman and J. Masson wrote in an essay about Ravana's position within Valmiki's text, "One would scarcely expect Vishnu to take on human form merely in order to chastise some fairly obscure rakshasa chieftain." This aspect of Ravana's unnerving majesty is narrated in an episode of the *Ananda Ramayana*, a

"Standing in space, I would lift this earth with my arms. I would drink up the ocean. And standing in battle, I would kill Death. I would arrest the sun with my sharp shafts and cleave the earth."

Ravana tells Sita, Sarga 47, Aranya Kanda

retelling often attributed to Valmiki (but which has elements from much later versions of the story and may have been composed by a reader of Valmiki).

After killing Ravana, as Rama rules over Ayodhya in peace, he is struck one day by the sound of laughter. It reminds him of the laughter of Ravana's heads as Rama cut them off one by one. Ravana's heads were laughing because of the thought of dying at Rama's hands, but they frightened Rama. Haunted by this vision, Rama prohibited laughter in Ayodhya. In retellings over centuries, Ravana's end is foretold as a form of divine justice, and elements of excess are brought in throughout the narrative to justify that end.

The Jain retelling of the *Ramayana*, the 3rd or 4th century text *Paumacariya*, presents significant deviations from the traditional Hindu version. In it, Ravana's death takes place at the hands of Lakshmana. In this text, Ravana is an illustrious, learned king who has been wronged in Brahmanical interpretations. He is brought down by his passions—he is desperately in love with Sita, and everything he does is to win her over. In the 12th-century *Kamba Ramayanam* from Tamil Nadu, too, Ravana is a tragic figure brought down by his hubris.

This brings in another aspect of Brahmanical literature that might help frame Ravana's characterization—the idea of moderation. Rama is portrayed as a person who practices

▸ A *c.*1720 painting of Rama, Lakshmana, and Hanuman in a battle with Ravana.

◂ This miniature is from an 1813 volume of the *Ramayana*. It depicts Ravana, enthroned in the center, in his palace guarded by rakshasas.

restraint and patience even at the expense of his happiness and his personal commitment. Ravana is meant to be the opposite—a person who gives in to his passions and cannot stand to deny himself what he wants.

As Goldman notes, Ravana is depicted as the "Other" through his abductions, harem, indulgent lifestyle, and unchecked desire, epitomized by Sita's abduction. The *Ramayana* thus becomes a morality play, illustrating the ideal citizen, with Ravana serving as the necessary foil to Rama's virtuous character.

Setting aside the fatalistic view of Ravana's story, an ethical question still arises: Who was the first aggressor—Ravana, who abducted Sita, or Rama and Lakshmana, who mutilated Surpanakha? This question helps understand how Ravana is interpreted in Sri Lankan culture. While retellings of the *Ramayana* are few in Sri Lanka, its characters and places are widely acknowledged and deeply woven into the country's cultural traditions.

Lanka's mythical legacy and evolution

The Lanka described in Valmiki's *Ramayana* is a city of unparalleled grandeur, one that seems to echo the island's majestic beauty. Perched on the Trikuta mountain, it gleams with wealth and splendor, rivaling the city of gods. Towering palaces, lush forests, and flowing rivers create a vibrant, almost ethereal atmosphere. Ravana's palace, fragrant and magnificent, stands at its heart, while golden ramparts and flower-filled moats reflect the city's perfect blend of beauty and strength. This vivid depiction has long been intertwined with the island of Sri Lanka, strengthening the connection between myth and the living landscape. The idea of linking Lanka in the *Ramayana* to present-day Sri Lanka likely started with 8th-century inscriptions in southern India, when the *Ramayana* was spreading through the region. References to the *Ramayana* appeared in Sri Lankan texts like the *Mahavamsa*, *Dipavamsa*, and *Rajavaliya*, gaining popularity, though classical texts dismissed them as mere folk tales.

By the 9th century, the Chola rulers of southern India seem to have set the seal on the association between the Lanka of the *Ramayana* and Sri Lanka. Tamil communities in Sri Lanka adopted this narrative, stripped of the parts demonizing the inhabitants of Lanka. The other development in this adaptation was the focus on Ravana's devotion to Shiva.

There was no Buddhist adaptation of the epic, however, in the early stages. Later, Sinhala Buddhist authors started putting together chronicles of Sri Lankan history and legend—and Ravana found space as a historical character, a glorious king who stood against the attacks from Indian rulers.

This thread was consolidated further a century ago, when Ravana was understood to be a national hero and not the villain that centuries of religious literature had made him out to be.

Ravana, the healer

Of the innumerable scientific talents Ravana is believed to have possessed, medicinal skill is one which seems to have resonated in Sri Lankan cultural traditions almost as strongly as the legends of his aerial technology. A popular tradition in the island nation attributes several ancient medical texts to Ravana, and grounds the belief that the transmission of Ayurveda, the traditional medicine system in the subcontinent, took place through Ravana.

The Talaimannar Lighthouse on Mannar Island was built in 1915 and served as a beacon for Indian and Sri Lankan ships, guiding them to safety. Talaimannar is the closest point, on the Sri Lankan side, to Adam's Bridge or Ram Setu.

THE FIRST AVIATOR

RAVANA'S "AIRPORTS" ACROSS CENTRAL AND SOUTHERN SRI LANKA

Valmiki's *Ramayana* describes Ravana's legendary Pushpaka as an exquisite, engraved flying palace, encrusted with jewels and gemstones, and covered in silver and gold. The protoaircraft was a gift Kubera, Ravana's half-brother, received from Brahma, the creator and one of the Hindu Trinity. Ravana seized the craft after defeating Kubera. In Sri Lankan lore, Ravana's aircraft was the Dandu-monara or wooden peacock in Sinhalese, which the king used to travel across lands, and was evidence of his advanced technological skills.

If an ancient aircraft had to take off into the skies, an airport high up in the mountains would help. It is perhaps why the terrain of Sri Lanka's central highlands in the south-central part of the country—with its mountains, plateaus, barren patches, and forests—is so closely associated with the story of Ravana's pioneering mastery of aircraft technology and his flying chariots. And while there is no archaeological evidence to support the existence of these fascinating machines, the legends surrounding them continue to endure and captivate.

◂ After Rama defeated Ravana, he left Lanka for Ayodhya along with Sita, Lakshmana, and the rest of his entourage, in Ravana's flying machine, as seen in this painting dated around 1650 from Himachal Pradesh.

Ussangoda (Southern Province, Sri Lanka)

On the southern tip of Hambantota district, an unusual landscape feature interrupts the sandy coastline—a long stretch of red, rustlike soil that is hard like quartz, dotted with dark brownish-red rocks, but barely any vegetation. This is the Ussangoda National Park, a unique ecosystem and one of Sri Lanka's four serpentine sites (areas that have nutrient-poor, heavy metal–rich soil with unusual chemistry).

Local legend says the barren patch was once Ravana's airstrip, which Hanuman set on fire as he escaped after his capture

"With an appearance like fire and the sun, well-built by Vishwakarma, it had golden staircases ... lattice-windows of gold and crystal, and a platform shining with peacock blue and dark blue sapphires."

Hanuman finds Pushpaka in Ravana's palace, Sarga 7, Sundara Kanda

during a reconnaissance mission to Lanka. It is why the soil remains red and the land barren. Local belief also states the possibility that Ussangoda is the site of a meteorite crash millions of years ago. A walk through here ends at a cliff facing the ocean—it is a steep drop. An uneven climb down leads to beaches, where the waves are strong and have been eroding the cliff bit by bit for years. The beaches are important breeding grounds for sea turtles, hordes of which can be seen in shallow waters during the day.

Thotupola Kanda (Central Province, Sri Lanka)

Located within the Horton Plains National Park in the central highlands, in the picturesque Nuwara Eliya district, Thotupola Kanda, with its winding mountain roads and tea plantations, is believed to have been one of Ravana's airstrips. The word *thotupola* means port, dock, or landing place in Sinhalese and *kanda* means mountain. It aligns with the belief that this place could have once been an ancient airport for Ravana's aerial travels. Thotupola Kanda is the country's third highest peak and one of the easiest trails within the Horton Plains National Park. The 1.2-mile- (2-km-) trail begins on a plain and continues—for the most part—with short stretches of tree-lined gradients followed by plains, before a steep trek toward the end that leads to the summit.

The Horton Plains National Park in the central highlands is one of the most popular hiking destinations of Sri Lanka, with dense cloud forests and expansive grasslands on elevations ranging from 3,940ft (1,200m) to 7,546ft (2,300m).

Visitors to Horton Plains can explore this peak, which is accessible via a trail starting near the Pattipola entrance of the park.

Weragantota
(Central Province, Sri Lanka)

The quiet village of Weragantota lies near the town of Mahiyangana, an important Buddhist site in lush and hilly central Sri Lanka. Weragantota is said to have been one of Ravana's primary landing strips and the place where he first landed with Sita. The word *weragantota* means "landing site of aircraft" in Sinhalese. Mahiyangana is dotted with Buddhist temples—a strong local belief is that it was the first place that Gautama Buddha visited when he arrived in Sri Lanka.

Wariyapola
(North Western Province, Sri Lanka)

Like all sites associated with Ravana's aircraft's legend, Wariyapola's name, too, translates into "aircraft landing space" in Sinhalese—*wa* means air, *riya* means vehicle, and *pola* means place. There are two towns with this name; this one is at the Kurunegala in the North Western Province, and the other is at Matale in the Central Province.

Sri Lanka's first satellite

In 2019, Sri Lanka launched its first research satellite into orbit. The satellite was named Raavana 1, after the legendary king of Lanka and a nod to the ancient aerial technology that King Ravana is said to have mastered.

Both are believed to have been Ravana's airstrips. At Kurunegala's Wariyapola, a flat granite plateau is said to be where Ravana would land his aircraft. The town has a rich Buddhist history and is dotted with temples.

Gurulupotha
(Central Province, Sri Lanka)

This remote verdant spot in mountainous central Sri Lanka is where, legends say, Ravana's aircraft service and repair center stood, and where he brought Sita after arriving in Lanka. The name Gurulupotha is understood as "parts of birds" in Sinhalese, believed to be a reference to its role in Ravana's time. Today, Gurulupotha is what remains of an ancient forest monastery. Padhanagaras, as these monasteries are known, were built by the kings in the 8th to 10th centuries for monks belonging to a sect which practiced extreme austerity. These forest monasteries would have a series of twin platforms made of stone, connected by a bridge with a shallow moat surrounding them. Gurulupotha has a similar padhanagara complex, which has been associated with the Ravana legend as a site where Mandodari's palace once stood.

◂ The red-soiled Ussangoda National Park in Ranna, Ambalangoda, Sri Lanka.

SHIVA'S REBUKE

RAVANANUGRAHA SCULPTURES ACROSS SOUTHERN INDIA

As Ravana flew over the golden mountains of Sharavana, his flying chariot came to a halt. He was instructed to turn back as the god of destruction, Shiva, was with his wife on the mountain. Displeased, Ravana displayed his might and uprooted the mountain. But an amused Shiva pressed the mountain with his toe—crushing Ravana's arms and making him roar in pain. Shiva, impressed with Ravana's courage, conferred the name Ravana on him, which translates to "he who makes the worlds scream." This iconic story has been immortalized in sculptures across south India.

Ravana, clearly identifiable by his 10 heads, held up a mountain atop where Shiva and Parvati sat. Shiva was calm, Parvati seeked his reassurance, and Ravana struggled to not be crushed by the weight of the mountain. Called Ravananugraha, where Ravana refers to the Lankan king and *anugraha* means grace or benevolence, this iconography is frequently seen in Shiva temples of the 8th century CE, built under the patronage of powerful dynasties that ruled the Deccan and central India. The sculpture represents Ravana's dual nature—that of a Shiva devotee and of an arrogant king.

Mahakuteswara Temple (Karnataka, India)

Part of the 7th-century Mahakuta group of temples built by the Chalukyas, powerful rulers of south and central India, Mahakuteswara is the most prominent of the many Shiva temples in the complex. It is a captivating example of the confluence of northern and southern Indian architectural styles. Rich engravings cover the walls, many of which depict Ravana's devotion to Shiva—including an intricate Ravananugraha sculpture, which depicts a seated Ravana lifting Mount Kailasha, the strain of keeping it aloft showing on Ravana's face. In a second depiction of Ravana, he is standing on one foot in front of Shiva and Parvati, and in another, he cuts off and offers each one of his 10 heads to Shiva.

▸ Ravana, identified by his many heads and hands, lifts Mount Kailasha in this sculpture on a pillar in Virupaksha Temple, Pattadakal, Karnataka, India.

Virupaksha Temple, Pattadakal (Karnataka, India)
Pattadakal was the capital of the Chalukya dynasty. Its 150-odd temples, like the ones at Mahakuta, blend the northern and southern Indian architectural styles. Of these, nine temples dedicated to Shiva and one Jain temple are major draws. The Virupaksha Temple is the largest of them, and the only temple here that is still used for worship. It was built by a Chalukya queen in the 8th century CE to honor the victory of her husband over the Pallavas of Kanchipuram. The roof of the temple's great hall rests on 16 massive square columns ornamented with finely wrought sculptures. The Ravananugraha here is highly detailed and gives prominence to Ravana, who is depicted with 10 arms and 10 heads, while inhabitants of Kailasha are shown shooting arrows at him in an attempt to make him stop.

Mahabalipuram (Tamil Nadu, India)
This used to be a busy port town between the 4th and 9th centuries, when under the ruling dynasty of the

▲ Shore Temple in Mahabalipuram, Tamil Nadu, India.

formidable Pallavas. The spectacular temples here were sculpted from blocks of granite. Cave temples, carved monoliths, bas-reliefs, and temples at the site are widely considered to be the foundation of temple architecture in India. Known as the Shore Temple complex, it comprises one temple dedicated to Vishnu and two dedicated to Shiva, and is one of the oldest in the country to be built with quarried granite blocks. The Ravananugraha sculpture here is to be found at the Olakkaneshvara Temple, which the British colonial administration had converted into a lighthouse, taking advantage of its location on top of a rock.

Kanchipuram (Tamil Nadu, India)
Known as the city of a thousand temples, Kanchipuram was the capital of the Pallava rulers in the 6th century CE. The built heritage of the town reflects this history, with temples that are outstanding examples of some of the best Dravidian architecture of southern India.

The 8th-century Muktesvara Temple here is a sandstone edifice with beautiful sculptural panels and friezes, including an exquisite Ravananugraha sculpture. The use of sandstone over a hard granite base at Muktesvara and the Kailasanatha Temple, another important temple in the complex, was a move away from the rock-cut temples of the preceding centuries.

Airavatesvara Temple, Thanjavur (Tamil Nadu, India)
This 12th-century temple is one of the three great temples attributed to the powerful Chola rulers of the region. Built in the Dravidian architectural style, the

... Laying his hands on the mountain, he lifted it up along with the animals, serpents, and trees.

Ravana lifts the mountain, Sarga 16, Uttara Kanda

chariotlike temple is adorned with exquisite carvings and sculptures that illustrate stories from ancient Indian texts—one of these is the Ravananugraha frieze. Another frieze, which gives the temple its name, depicts how Airavata, the white elephant of the king of gods, Indra, was cursed and lost his color, regaining it only after bathing in the temple tank and praying to Shiva.

Ellora Caves, Aurangabad (Maharashtra, India)

Carved into the vertical face of the Charanadri Hills is a site with 17 Hindu, 12 Buddhist, and five Jain caves, it is estimated to be from the 6th to 12th centuries CE. One of the finest examples of art can be seen in Cave 29 or Dumar Lena. Six large sculptural panels decorate the halls, arranged in a cruciform around the shrine, all of them narrating stories related to Shiva. Despite the weathering over time, the delicacy of emotion can still be seen in the Ravananugraha here.

Elephanta Caves, Mumbai (Maharashtra, India)

On the island of Elephanta stands a collection of temples cut into the solid basalt rock face. Dated from the 5th to 9th centuries, five of these were Hindu cave temples and two Buddhist. The largest cave is Cave 1, also known as the Great Cave, which is divided into corridors by 24 columns. Dominating its entrance is a 23-ft (7-m) sculpture of Shiva. To the east is the large, but quite badly damaged, panel depicting Ravananugraha.

▼ Intricately carved pillars and a Shivalinga within the main shrine of the Ellora Caves in Aurangabad, Maharashtra, India.

The Airavatesvara Temple in Tamil Nadu was built in the 12th century and is dedicated to Shiva. Its walls and pillars are adorned with intricate miniature carvings and inscriptions.

AN ARDENT DEVOTEE

TEMPLES ACROSS INDIA DEDICATED TO RAVANA'S FAITH IN SHIVA

Valmiki's *Ramayana* told of two separate instances when Ravana engaged with Shiva, the god of destruction. The first was when he tried to uproot the mountain where Shiva was spending time with his wife Parvati, and when he offered prayers to the god in the Vindhya mountains. In the latter, Ravana installed a gold Shivalinga on an altar of sand near the Narmada River and worshipped it. The tradition of Ravana being a Shiva devotee in subsequent literary representations may have originated from this episode. A more explicitly stated narrative about Ravana's faith in Shiva was told in the *Shiva Purana*—in which Ravana cut off nine of his 10 heads to seek Shiva's grace.

A now-obscure tradition, one mentioned in 19th-century colonial records of India, is that the southern part of what is now India was a region where Ravana once ruled. Local legends place the site of Ravana's penance for Shiva's blessings in the mountains of the Himalayas. These stories perhaps help explain how temples dedicated to Shiva came to be known as sites of worship that Ravana himself established.

Mahabaleshwar Temple, Gokarna (Karnataka, India)
The ancient temple in the beach town of Gokarna houses a Shivalinga that Ravana is believed to have placed. The local belief is that Ravana wanted to take Shiva with him to Lanka. He performed

◂ This *c.*1850 painting from Tamil Nadu depicts Shiva sitting atop Mount Kailasha as Ravana attempts to lift the mountain.

arduous penance, and succeeded in obtaining Shiva's blessings and the permission to take a Shivalinga, which held Shiva's essence, to Lanka. He could not, however, set down the Shivalinga anywhere as it would not be possible to pick it up again. The gods, wary of the power Ravana could wield if he saw this quest through, tricked him into putting down the Shivalinga in what is now Gokarna. The temple is said to be built where Ravana put it down—*mahabala* means immense strength in Sanskrit, the origin of the temple's name. The temple is built of granite, in the Dravidian architecture style.

Baijnath Temple, Baijnath (Himachal Pradesh, India)

On the left bank of the Binwa River of the Garur Valley, the 11th-century shrine dedicated to Shiva is located on the foothills of the Dhauladhar ranges in the district of Kangra. The rock-cut temple is built in the Nagara architecture style. Inscriptions say that a temple dedicated to Shiva stood there before the current shrine was built. The local belief is that the Shivalinga here was installed by Ravana—erroneously.

Like at Gokarna, the story goes that Ravana wanted Shiva to move to Lanka from Mount Kailasha. He started meditating to earn Shiva's grace, but that did not work. So, he built a sacrificial fire pit and began to offer his heads, one after the other. When he was about to cut off his last head, Shiva appeared, acknowledged Ravana as his most devoted follower, and restored all his heads.

The name Baijnath is a reference to this part of the story—*baij* is a derivative of *vaid* or healer in Sanskrit, and *nath* means lord. Shiva also granted Ravana's boon, as part of which Ravana would have to carry Shiva in the form of a *linga* to Lanka. There was a caveat—Ravana could not set the Shivalinga down anywhere. There are different versions of what happened next but they all end with Ravana setting the *linga* down at Baijnath, where he eventually set up a temple for Shiva.

Ravana Temple, Kakinada (Andhra Pradesh, India)

On the eastern coast of India, overlooking the Bay of Bengal, stands the Kakinada Temple on a site believed to have been chosen by Ravana. It is said that Ravana created a giant mural of a Shivalinga here as a sign of his faith in the god. The temple gate announces this, framing a huge statue of Ravana against the temple walls. Besides Shiva, Ravana is worshipped here, and like in other places where the king of Lanka is revered, Dussehra, the fall celebration of Rama's victory in Lanka, is marked with quiet prayers and not celebration.

▼ Baijnath Temple in Kangra district, Himachal Pradesh, in India.

CULTURE

RAVANA, THE DEITY

WORSHIPPERS OF THE KING OF LANKA IN INDIA

In pockets of northern, western, and central India, small communities worship Ravana as a learned king, a mighty warrior, and an ancestor to whom they trace their descent.

A village surrounded by urban development clusters in the National Capital Region is the unlikely site for a legend associated with the Lankan king, Ravana. Bisrakh, a village in Uttar Pradesh about 37.3 miles (60km) from Delhi, is believed to be where Ravana was born. Locals say that the name, Bisrakh, is a distortion of Vishrava, the name of Ravana's father, and that Vishrava was their ancestor. The Ravana Temple at the village is dedicated to Shiva, and the Shivalinga at the temple is said to be one that Ravana worshipped.

Some 745 miles (1,200km) south of Bisrakh, Gadchiroli is a town in Maharashtra where a section of the Indigenous Gond community maintains the same belief—that they claim common lineage with Ravana. By this belief, Ravana was an ancient Gond king called Raven, named after a blue-throated bird that was the totem of his clan, and both he and his son Meghanada are worshipped by the Gond community to this day.

Another claimant to Ravana's ancestry is the Kanyakubja Brahmin community of Madhya Pradesh. A village named after him, Ravanagram, is home to a temple with a 10-ft- (3-m-) long reclining statue of Ravana. The local Kanyakubja Brahmin community here offers daily prayers at the temple, and worships him as a deity of prosperity. Also in Madhya Pradesh is a village that considers Ravana its son-in-law because it is said to be his wife Mandodari's birthplace. The same story is narrated in Jodhpur in the neighboring western state of Rajasthan as well, which locals believe was Mandodari's town.

When the rest of the country burns effigies of Ravana during Dussehra, a fall festival marking the triumph of Rama over Ravana, these villages and towns observe a period of mourning—because this was when their protector, their lord, Ravana, was slain.

▶ **Clockwise from top left:** Kathakali performer playing the character of Ravana; mural depicting Ravana in Thodikkalam Shiva Temple, Kerala; a performance of Ramlila at Shriram Center, New Delhi; a 19th-century painting of Ravana; life-size statue of Ravana in Murudeswar, Karnataka; sculpture of Ravana in Meenakshi Temple, Madurai.

▶ A lithograph from the Shekhawati region in Rajasthan illustrating Ravana's palace and the siege of Lanka by Rama's army.

A SPLENDID PALACE

MAHA RAVANA REEF AND KUDA RAVANA REEF, SOUTHERN PROVINCE, SRI LANKA

> Hanuman was enthralled when he first looked at the city where Ravana's palace was. Its golden ramparts made it glow with a radiance as brilliant as that of the sun. The city rang with the sound of jewelry and conch shells. The sweet fragrance of sandalwood wafted through the air. Divided by pathways, there were rows of palaces, seven or eight stories high. It equaled the city of the gods. Upon seeing the palace, Hanuman thought to himself, "Lanka's jewel."

The beach at Kirinda is a portrait of paradoxes. The quiet fishing village has a languid pace with an air of calm—one that even the harshness of the turbulent waters and jagged rocky outcrops cannot offset. Yet, it is considered the gateway to one of the most gripping battle legends of Sri Lanka—the palace of Ravana.

The atolls of Great Basses Reef and the Little Basses Reef—an hour's boat ride from Kirinda—are believed to be what remains of Ravana's citadel. In local parlance, the reefs are called Maha Ravana (Great Basses Reef) and

Kuda Ravana (Little Basses Reef). *Maha* translates to great and *kuda* means little. Even though there are no visible remnants of such a citadel or fort, the stories contribute to the rich tapestry surrounding the reefs. These atolls have now been designated as a marine sanctuary.

Two colonial-era lighthouses stand on the Great Basses Reef and the Little Basses Reef. The 25-mile- (40-km-) long atolls could barely be spotted before a ship got too close—a perilous prospect that was addressed by building the two lighthouses. It was near the Great Basses Reef lighthouse where pioneering science-fiction author Arthur C. Clarke was diving, when he found a shipwreck with thousands of silver coins. The early 18th-century wreck, found in 1961, was identified as a trader ship with a cargo of freshly minted silver coins belonging to the Mughal emperor Aurangzeb. (This was not the only diving discovery Clarke made during his long stay in Sri Lanka.) The Basses continue to be a popular diving site in Sri Lanka, though the diving season is short—from March to April.

▲ The lighthouse at Great Basses Reef.

This coastline is along one of Sri Lanka's most popular nature destinations, the Yala National Park. The southern border of the park stretches over 23 miles (37km) of coastline, offering exciting snorkeling and diving experiences. The 130,000-hectare (1,300sq-km) park is one of Sri Lanka's oldest, and is home to more than 250 species of birds and mammals—its western zone hosts one of the world's largest concentrations of leopards.

Sigiriya Fort

Popular travel literature often points to the ancient 5th-century rock fortress of Sigiriya, in the central Sri Lankan district of Matale, as the storied palace of Ravana. There is academic consensus that the ruins are what remain of a capital built by the 5th-century king Kassapa I, before he was defeated. The association of the Ravana mythology, however, appears to be a later transposition that does not fully resonate with the local lore of the region. The citadel—with elaborate galleries, intricate carvings, and spectacular rock paintings—is, nonetheless, a magnificent site that stands as a testament to Sri Lanka's heritage.

PORTAL TO LANKA

ADAM'S BRIDGE, MANNAR ISLAND, NORTHERN PROVINCE, SRI LANKA

> Under Nala's guidance, the vanara and riksha forces used large boulders and trees to build the long, broad bridge that connected to the northern shore of Lanka. Ravana was surprised to see the bridge and asked his ministers to find out how Rama had achieved such a feat. Popular Sri Lankan lore, however, holds the belief that Ravana built the bridge using floating rocks. These could be brought up whenever required, and would disappear when they were not in use.

A 30-mile (48-km) chain of limestone shoals running through the ocean "connects" southern India and northern Sri Lanka, through centuries of exchange in terms of trade, as well as mythology, beliefs, and legends. Known as the Adam's Bridge, it may have acted as a causeway in the ancient past, an actual physical one, according to several legends across different cultures.

For many Hindus in India, this is the bridge that Rama's vanara and riksha forces built to gain access to Ravana's kingdom. Some, in Sri Lanka, believe it was built by Ravana so that he could travel between Lanka and what is now India. A tradition in Islam, possibly originating from Persian interpretations of the Bible, says that the bridge is where Adam, the biblical first man, landed after his expulsion from Paradise—a story that 19th-century colonial officials,

cartographers, and chroniclers referred to in their records. Geological research, meanwhile, suggests that since the origins of India and Sri Lanka are likely linked, as of an ancient supercontinent that split, it is possible that tectonic changes over hundreds of millions of years in these parts aided the emergence of a bridgelike formation. The theories about the bridge's origin, however, remain contested.

The Dancing Islands

Today, Adam's Bridge appears as a series of sandbanks—parts of which are visible above water level—between present-day Dhanushkodi at Rameswaram, in India, and Talaimannar on Mannar Island in Sri Lanka. As the waters around the sandbanks keep rising and ebbing, the bridge is also known as the Dancing Islands in local parlance—a reference to the seemingly mobile patches of land that form the chain. Adam's Bridge is not a continuous strip of land, and it is not navigable like an actual bridge. The closest point to the formation in Sri Lanka is at Talaimannar. Previously, boats used to take passengers from Talaimannar up to the middle of the waters where the sandbanks were visible up close, but the service was suspended during the Covid-19 pandemic. During low tides, on days with good visibility, parts of the sandbanks can be seen from the beach.

Talaimannar was an important point of transit between Sri Lanka and India under the British colonial administration—through a railway and ferry service that started operating between Talaimannar and Dhanushkodi in 1914. British administrators in the region wanted to build a bridge connecting Talaimannar and Dhanushkodi as well, but the plan was rejected in the British Parliament because of steep costs.

The Talaimannar pier continued to be a key link between India and Sri Lanka until 1964, when a cyclone destroyed

▲ A temple frieze depicting an army of vanaras building a bridge over the ocean.

"I have a great city in the middle of the ocean, called Lanka. It is surrounded by the sea and built on top of a mountain."

Ravana tells Sita, Sarga 45, Aranya Kanda

Dhanushkodi town and damaged the pier. By 1983, ethnic conflict between the Sinhalese majority and Tamils had escalated to a point that Mannar Island—on which Talaimannar lies—became a base for guerrilla operations by the Liberation Tigers of Tamil Eelam (LTTE) insurgents and was considered inaccessible for tourists. When the separatist insurgent group was defeated three decades later, in 2009, Mannar opened up for tourism again.

Today, the pier lies in an isolated part of the Talaimannar beach, next to an abandoned railway line and close to a lighthouse built in 1915—almost a mirror image of the forsaken Dhanushkodi across the ocean.

▼ The remains of the Mannar Fort, Mannar Island.

A pearl haven

The history of Mannar stretches back to the 5th and 6th centuries, with references in the *Mahavamsa*, the revered Pali chronicle of Sri Lanka. This text highlights the region's significance during the reign of Prince Vijaya, one of Sri Lanka's earliest legendary figures. Over the centuries, Mannar's strategic position at the intersection of east-west trade routes made it a crucial port, serving as a primary gateway to the island. Additionally, the region was connected to the ancient Buddhist capital of Anuradhapura via the river, further cementing its role in Sri Lanka's early civilization.

Throughout its history, Mannar has played a pivotal role—as an administrative center for the 14th-century kingdom of Jaffna, a Portuguese outpost in the 16th century, and a British colony by the 19th century.

Mannar's prominence grew during the medieval period, particularly because of its pearl fisheries. The area was renowned for its vast pearl oyster beds,

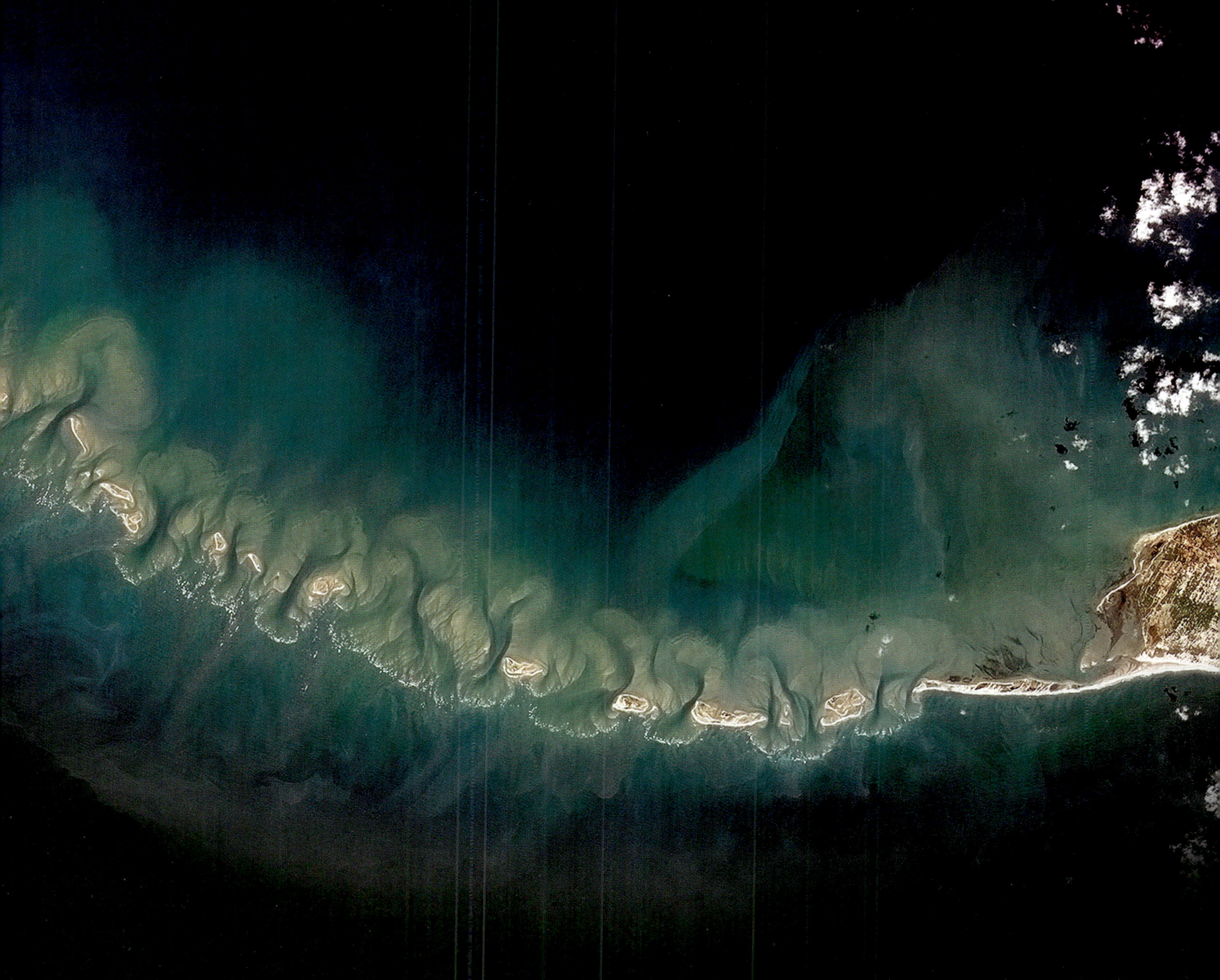

▲ A 2017 satellite image of Adam's Bridge.

known as *paars* or pearl banks, which supplied some of the finest pearls in the world for nearly two millennia.

Traces of the region's eclectic history are scattered across Mannar. The Mannar Fort, built by the Portuguese in 1560, stands near the causeway that connects Mannar to mainland Sri Lanka. It was rebuilt by the Dutch in the 17th century and occupied by the British by the end of the 18th century. The ruins of the limestone, coral, and brick structures are part of a protected site now. A few miles south of Arippu, along the elevated banks of the eroded coastline of Sri Lanka's northwest, lies another notable structure known as The Doric. Sir Frederick North, the first British governor of Ceylon, originally built it in the early 1800s to serve as his residence during visits to the nearby pearl fishery in Kondachchi. The mansion earned the name "The Doric" due to its distinctive architectural style. Over time, it was used by a succession of governors, pearl fishery superintendents, government agents, and other officials. In recent years, the structure has been heavily worn down.

In this 19th-century gouache painting, the vanaras, led by Hanuman, carry boulders to build a bridge across the ocean to Lanka so that Sita can be rescued. Adam's Bridge, or Ram Setu, a chain of natural shoals, is believed to be this mythical bridge.

▸ An artwork showing Ravana entering a cave, from a 16th-century illustrated manuscript of Valmiki's *Ramayana*.

A KING'S SANCTUARY

RAVANA CAVE, UVA PROVINCE (SRI LANKA)

▲ The Ravana Waterfall, a part of the Ravana Ella Wildlife Sactuary in Sri Lanka.

One of the many legends about Ravana deeply rooted in Sri Lanka focuses on his technological genius. Like the mythical airports Ravana is said to have built at a time outside the bounds of recorded history, an intricate network of tunnels is also attributed to him. It is believed that Ravana had these built to connect important parts of his kingdom, and that at the opening of each tunnel lay a cave, which provided Ravana shelter and safe passage during times of conflict.

The topography of Ella is such that grand stories of strategic secrecy are easy to imagine—tall mountains cloaked in dense forests and dotted with cavernous hollows into which anyone could disappear. The nature of this terrain at Ella, a mountain town in the southeastern province of Uva in Sri Lanka, is the foundation on which legends of subterranean escape routes have been built. One of the most popular examples of these is the Ravana Cave.

Located at an elevation of 4,600ft (1,400m) above sea level, the Ravana Cave is a relatively small geological formation and is about 60ft (18.2m) high and 50ft (15.2m) wide. The hike to the cave is steep, up a series of 650-odd uneven steps. The climb, though moderately challenging, offers breathtaking views of the surrounding landscape.

A tunnel connects it to a huge open area with a large, clear lake, as well as openings to several other small caves. Visitors are only allowed up to 0.1 mile (200m) inside the cave, beyond which access is blocked. Excavations done by the archaeological department unearthed evidence that indicates human habitation dating back around 25,000 years.

The cave lies behind an 82-ft- (25-m-) high waterfall known as the Ravana Waterfall, one of the most spectacular in Sri Lanka. The contemporary names of the cave and the waterfall are linked to the local lore about Ravana's network of tunnels and caves, of which the ones at Ella are an important part. Ravana is said to have hidden Sita in this cave, as well as in another at Shtripura, when confronting Rama and his army.

Like many other sites connected to the Ravana story in Sri Lanka, the Ravana Cave is associated with Walagamba, a

king and folk hero from around the 1st century BCE. Also known as Vattagamani, he was the ruler of the ancient capital of Anuradhapura. Walagamba was the son of Saddhatissa, the brother of Duttugemunu. He is believed to have built the Dowa Temple, a rock temple near Ella, as one of the structures in which he sought refuge after an invasion by a southern Indian kingdom.

Today, the temple has a 38-ft- (11.6-m-) high, partially completed statue of the Buddha, carved on the side of a granite boulder. On the top of the boulder lies a small stupa. A little further on lies another stupa inside a cave, which is said to lead to a 6.8-mile- (11-km-) long tunnel that connects Dowa to two other temples. A shorter tunnel, local lore claims, leads to the Ravana Cave. The most iconic imagery at Ella is to be seen at the Demodara Nine Arch Bridge, about 2.8 miles (4.5km) from Ravana Cave. Built in 1919 by colonial planners to get around the region's difficult gradient and terrain, this railway viaduct bridge was made of concrete. Today, the 79-ft- (24-m-) high bridge stands in the midst of bright green tea plantations—and the famous train ride between Kandy and Bandarawela takes a route through this bridge.

The Ravana Cave itself is only about 1.7 miles (2.8km) from the railways station at Ella. However, if time permits, a train from Kandy to Ella offers a spectacular seven-hour ride through lush tea plantations, mountains, valleys, and forests.

The Ravana Falls and the cave nearby are a part of the Ravana Ella Wildlife Sanctuary, and offer an intriguing glimpse into Sri Lanka's folklore and its connection to the *Ramayana*.

A SUBTERRANEAN RETREAT

WORLD'S END, CENTRAL PROVINCE, SRI LANKA

▼ A Sri Lankan postage stamp from 2016 showing the Mini World's End.

A centuries-old Tamil version of Ravana's story introduced a cousin, Peacock Ravana, who ruled over a subterranean Lanka. After Ravana started losing his loved ones and valorous generals, he approached Peacock Ravana for help. Once, during battle, Rama and Lakshmana hid in a fortress made of Hanuman's tail. The way in was through Hanuman's mouth, and the way out was through his ear. However, Peacock Ravana posed as Vibhishana (Ravana's brother who later became Rama's ally) and abducted the two brothers. He hid them in a subterranean cave from where Hanuman rescued them. A 17th-century Sinhala poem, *Ravana Katava*, narrated the same story but turned Ravana into the protagonist of the episode—the ruler with a parallel kingdom underground (Patala Lanka or Pathala Loka). Elements of this story were believed to have inspired the legends of Ravana's network of tunnels and caves.

At a good time on a good day, the sweeping view from World's End encompasses even the southern coast of Sri Lanka, about 62 miles (100km) away. World's End is, after all, an escarpment located at an altitude of 7,021ft (2,140m) on the highest (and windiest) plains of the country—the Horton Plains National Park in the central highlands. This topography also means that visiting it at any time other than on a good day will result in nothing but a wall of mist and clouds. It is a toss-up. Yet, World's End is worth the bet.

Known locally as Pathala Loka, which means the netherworld, it is believed to be where Ravana (or his cousin) hid Rama and Lakshmana after abducting them from the battlefield. It is not hard to see why the story was associated with this landscape—a vertiginous cliff.

The trek to World's End lies on a circular path through grasslands, forests, and streams, and takes about three hours. There are two routes from the base, one of which passes through the plains and another that involves a steep trek through the forest. After walking uphill for 2.5

▲ The Bakers Falls in the Horton Plains National Park, Sri Lanka, plunges down to a gorge covered with rhododendrons and ferns.

miles (4km), the plateau suddenly drops —a plunge of nearly 3,000ft (900m)— into tea plantations in the valley below. The complete circular trek, to World's End and back, is about 5.6 miles (9km).

About 0.6 miles (1km) from World's End is a smaller cliff with a 985-ft- (300-m-) drop called the Little World's End, or Mini World's End. The other major draw of this site is the spectacular Baker's Falls, a 65-ft- (20-m-) high waterfall on a trail known as the Baker's Loop. It is only 0.2 miles (200m) from World's End and lies on the same trekking route.

Besides World's End, two other hiking trails here are quite popular—Thotupola Kanda and Kirigalpoththa, both of which involve trekking up to mountain summits. The 2.5-mile (4-km) trek to Thotupola, Sri Lanka's third highest peak, is considered a fairly easy trek and the 4.3-mile (7-km) trek to Kirigalpoththa, the country's second highest peak, is usually identified as a moderately difficult one.

While these remain the primary draws, the Horton Plains National Park is also an important birding site—with sightings of Ceylon White Eye, Sri Lanka Bush Warbler, Sri Lanka Whistling Thrush, and Dull Blue Flycatcher, among hundreds of others. The forests are home to leopards as well, but they are difficult to spot.

This 1875 painting by French artist Fernand Cormon is titled *The Death of Ravana*.

DEATH OF A KING

MEMORIALIZING THE KING OF LANKA ACROSS CENTRAL SRI LANKA

The battle of Lanka culminated in a direct face-off between Ravana and Rama, but the king of Lanka and the prince of Ayodhya were equally powerful and valorous. Soon, things reached an impasse. Rama, it appeared, needed divine assistance. Help came in the form of Matali, the charioteer to Indra, the king of gods, to aid the prince during the final battle. He advised Rama to use the Brahmastra, a divine weapon belonging to Brahma, the god of creation and one of the Trinity. Rama invoked the weapon, an arrow that never missed its target. It flew through the battlefield and found its mark, immediately killing him. Ravana, the king of Lanka, was dead.

The central highlands of Sri Lanka are home to some of the most deeply rooted Ravana stories in Lankan lore. Nestled between the forests and mountains of two protected nature sites—Wasgamuwa and Knuckles—this stretch commemorates the story of how the king of Lanka fought and died. The surroundings only accentuate the lore surrounding the final battle. It is easy to imagine the plains as the battleground where the two forces faced each other, and the mountains with their high altitude and rocky terrains as the great citadels from where Ravana and his generals strategized their battle plan.

Dunuwila, Matale (Central Province, Sri Lanka)
Beyond the southern limits of the Wasgamuwa National Park, on the Hasalaka-Wasgamuwa road, amid the pristine landscape is a serene lake. The *Ramayana* lore suggests that Rama stood at the shore of this lake to invoke the most powerful divine arrow, Brahmastra, which killed Ravana. The name of the lake, Dunuwila, is said to be a nod to the same—*dunu* means arrow, and *vila* means lake in Sinhalese. Like many sites associated with the *Ramayana* legend in Sri Lanka, there is no archaeological evidence at Dunuwila to tell a visitor about the story. Hills and forests surround the vast grain plains where the lake is situated. If the story of a fierce, long battle culminating in a single moment had to be anchored to a place, it is not too far-fetched to imagine Dunuwila as the place.

Laggala, Matale (Central Province, Sri Lanka)
The Knuckles Range in central Sri Lanka is one of the country's most important biodiversity hot spots. A series of five peaks lends it the appearance of an inverted fist, which is how the name is said to have originated. Toward the tail end of the mountain range at the village of Meemure, about 31 miles (50km) from the Dunuwila Lake, lies the Laggala rock.

The steep, vertical monolithic rock face is at a challenging 4,200ft (1,310m) above sea level. It is one of the most difficult hiking trails in the country and is best done with a local guide.

The *Ramayana* lore suggests that Laggala was quite strategic for Ravana. The word *lag* means target in Sinhala and *gala* means rock. It is believed to be where the watchtower for Ravana's kingdom once stood. Here, Ravana's forces spotted Rama's forces entering Lanka, monitored them, and planned counterattacks. It is believed that this is where Ravana died after the Brahmastra found him.

A local legend speaks of the hill acting like a sundial for the kingdom of Lanka. On a clear day, the view from the top extends from the Thiru Koneswaram temple to the northeast, which supports the tradition that Ravana offered prayers to Shiva from this outcrop.

▲ Dunuwila Lake in Wasgamuwa National Park, Sri Lanka.

▼ View of Yahangala, Sri Lanka.

Yahangala, Kandy (Central Province, Sri Lanka)

The Yahangala mountain in the Knuckles Range is also a bearer of *Ramayana* lore. Ravana was laid to rest here after he was killed in battle—to be guarded by the local deity Gale Bandara for eternity. Yahangala is located in the village of Kalugala, about 18.6 miles (30km) from the village of Meemure. The top of the mountain appears flat, because of which it is also known as Bed Rock Mountain (*Yahangala* translates to bedrock in Sinhalese). Many locals believe that its unique shape gives the impression of a reclining figure, perhaps symbolizing Ravana lying in eternal rest.

The summit offers a breathtaking view of the Mahaweli River, one of the largest rivers of Sri Lanka.

"Impossible to kill for the gods, and so for danavas and rakhshasas, he has been made to sleep on the battlefield by a human on foot ... These [rakhshasas], and we, and you—all have been felled by [you] who didn't listen to your well-wishers who spoke always of your welfare."

Rakshasa women of Lanka lament Ravana's death, Sarga 98, Yuddha Kanda

ARTISANS OF DUSSEHRA

REMEMBERING THE BATTLE OF LANKA

About a month or two before the festival of Dussehra, an obscure urban village in Delhi comes alive in a blaze of color and activity. Here in Titarpur, massive effigies of Ravana and his kin are painstakingly created and later sold in thousands.

In the months leading up to Dussehra—a fall festival celebrating Ravana's defeat—hundreds of Ravanas, Kumbhakarnas (Ravana's brother), and Meghanadas (Ravana's son) line the streets of Titarpur, in the western part of Delhi, India's capital. As the festival nears, they are dispatched to different locations around the country where they will be burnt as part of grand theatrical reenactments of the battle of Lanka in a tradition known as Ramlila.

However, before that, artisans in Titarpur make the effigies with care. Their craft is central to their livelihoods and lends them the local moniker *Ravanwallahs*, which, in Hindi, means the one with Ravana.

The effigies could be anywhere between 2ft (0.6m) and 66ft (20m) high, with up to 10 artisans working on each effigy. It is a long process that may take up to a month to complete. It begins with the creation of a frame made from long stalks of bamboo, which is alternately and repeatedly covered with layers of brown paper and cloth stuck together with a mixture of flour, tapioca starch, and water. The artisans then step in to paint the body of the effigy and embellish it with tinsel.

It is, however, the crafting of the heads that is considered the most important, and the challenge with the Ravana effigy is the creation of 10 heads, each of which portrays an aspect of his character. The arms and legs are fashioned separately.

The entire effigy is put together at the site where Ramlila is enacted. It is here that the actors playing Rama and Lakshmana fire make-believe arrows at the effigies looming over the area, torching them, symbolizing the moment Ravana, Kumbhakarna, and Meghanada were killed.

▸ **Clockwise from top left:** an artisan creating frames for Ravana's 10 heads; Ravana effigy creation in progress; an artist paints the effigy of Ravana; the burning of the Ravana effigy on Dussehra; Ravana, Kumbhakarna, and Meghanada figurines assembled and ready for the final battle; effigies on sale; an artist giving final touches.

विजयश्री रंगमंच

04

Sita:
Trials of a Princess

◂ Hanuman finds Sita in Ashoka Vatika, and pays obeisance to her while telling her of Rama, in this 17th-century painting made in Deccan folk style.

PROFILE

PRINCESS OF MITHILA

Through exile, abduction, and banishment, Sita's journey, as the primary heroine of the epic, is one of courage, devotion, resilience, and piety. This is her story.

The *Ramayana*'s beloved heroine has many names—Vaidehi, Janaki, Maithali—but is popularly revered as Sita, or "furrow" in Sanskrit, referring to the goddess associated with ploughed fields.

Sita is often viewed through multiple lenses. Some see her as the perfect wife, deeply in love with her husband, dutifully following him into exile, remaining true to him when she is abducted, and even later, when exiled. She is admired for her compassion and even choosing to address her situation when there are questions of her fidelity. Some perceive her as a pivotal force, a manifestation of the divine goddess or Shakti. Yet others see her as an equal partner, or a consort who asks thought-provoking questions, challenging Rama on the appropriate conduct of a just king, a good husband, and a true warrior.

In some later renditions of the *Ramayana*, she is also identified as Lakshmi, the consort of Vishnu, one of the Hindu Trinity and the preserver of the universe.

A princess's tale

Her story though begins in Mithila, believed to be either in Nepal or the eastern Indian state of Bihar. It is here that she springs from a furrow when Janaka, the king of Mithila, ritualistically ploughs a field, earning her the sobriquet *ayonija* or not born of a womb. Her wedding to Rama, the crown prince of Kosala, is celebrated by all in the land, and she spends her early years of marriage in Ayodhya, in present-day Uttar Pradesh. Rama's subsequent exile sees Sita follow her husband and his brother Lakshmana into the forests of Chitrakoot and Dandaka across central and southern India.

It is during this time that the brothers encounter Surpanakha, setting off a chain of events that lie at the heart of the *Ramayana*. Sita's request for the exquisite golden deer that she spots in the forest,

◀ Sita, or Seetha Devi, sculpted on a pillar in Ramaswamy Temple in Kumbakonam, in the southern Indian state of Tamil Nadu.

Sita's birth

Indian poet A. K. Ramanujan wrote in his seminal essay "Three Hundred Ramayanas" that in a Kannada folk retelling, Sita is born of Ravana's sneeze after he eats a mango meant to help his wife Mandodari bear a child. In Kannada, the word *sita* means sneeze. Some Jain versions, he wrote, say Sita is Ravana's daughter, but the Lankan king did not know this. A story from Thailand tells of a thieving crow who took sacred rice meant for king Dasharatha to conceive heirs. The bird gave it to Mandodari, Ravana's queen, who ate it and gave birth to Sita.

A mural at the Ramaswamy Temple in Kumbakonam, Tamil Nadu, depicts a boatman ferrying Rama, Sita, and Lakshmana across a river.

Mithila

Kings laid siege to Janaka's kingdom at least twice as they coveted princess Sita. The first was after Janaka announced the test for Sita's hand in marriage—lifting a divine bow. When the assembled kings failed to even grasp the bow, they captured Mithila in anger. Janaka defeated them after the gods gifted him an army. The second time, Sudhanvan, the king of the sacred Sankasya, laid siege to Mithila and demanded Sita and the celestial bow. When his demand was refused, he faced Janaka on the battlefield and was killed. Janaka handed the slain king's empire to his younger brother, Kushadhvaja.

Rama's pursuit of the glorious creature, and Maricha's deception all culminate in her abduction at the hands of Ravana, the king of Lanka.

In some retellings, her abduction is not as straightforward. In the 15th-century *Adhyatma Ramayana*, Rama asks Sita to create Maya Sita, an illusory form of herself for the external world while Sita remains protected by Agni (god of fire). The 16th-century *Ramcharitmanas* by the poet Tulsidas expands on this illusory Sita motif by turning it into a justification for her trial by fire later in the story. Rama used the ordeal as a pretext to retrieve the real Sita who was safe with Agni.

▼ An illustration titled *The God of Fire Rose from the Midst*, depicting Sita's trial by fire, from *Stories of India's Gods and Heroes* by W. D. Monro (*c.*1911).

Sita's trials and divine redemption

Ravana abducts Sita and takes her across the ocean to Lanka, where he first holds her captive in his palace (believed to be in present-day Gurulupotha in Sri Lanka's Dumbara Valley) and later confines her to a secluded grove of ashoka trees. After Ravana's defeat, Sita undergoes a trial by fire in Divurumpola, Sri Lanka, though Indian folklore places it at Sita Kund in India. Upon returning to Ayodhya, whispers about her fidelity lead Rama to banish her. Pregnant, she seeks refuge with sage Valmiki, where she gives birth to twins, Lava and Kusha. Years later, through their recitations of the *Ramayana*, Rama learns the truth about his sons. He calls for Sita to prove her purity, but in a moment of divine grace, the Goddess Earth rises to honor her. As Sita is taken into the earth, gods shower her with praise and flowers rain down. Several sites in both India and Sri Lanka claim the location of this miraculous event.

The sacred heart of Sita's legacy

Several key episodes of Sita's story unfold in Mithila, a region that, though briefly mentioned in Valmiki's *Ramayana*, holds significant importance in the broader *Ramayana* tradition. According to the *Vishnu Purana*, Mithila is named after King Mithi, whose father, Nimi, was cursed by the sage Vasishtha to lose his physical form. The gods churned his body, giving rise to Mithi, and because of this miraculous birth, Mithi and his descendants were called Janaka, or "self-born." Other versions of the *Ramayana* speak about Mithila as Lakshmi's residence.

▲ A painting of Lakshmana returning to Ayodhya while a desolate Sita seeks shelter in Valmiki's hermitage.

Mithila also refers to the ancient Videha Kingdom, established during the Iron Age by Indo-Aryan tribes in the Eastern Gangetic plain. Reflecting this, Sita is often called "Vaidehi," or the "daughter of Videha."

P. S. Sundaram's *Kamba Ramayanam* also vividly portrays Mithila's charm. As Rama visits to meet Sita, he is greeted by bejeweled banners that seem to beckon him to the throne, marking one of the most captivating sections of the Bala Kanda.

The region is known as Tirhut, Tirabhukti, and Mithilanchal, bordered by the Mahananda, Ganga, and Gandaki Rivers, and the Himalayan foothills to the north.

Many interpretations

There are mentions of Sita in texts before Valmiki's *Ramayana*, though she is not very significant, and associated, generally, with abundance and fertility. Further retellings of the *Ramayana*, though, explore the theme of her agency, such as in the *Adbhuta Ramayana*. Here, Sita is a manifestation of Shakti—the embodiment of feminine divine power—and more powerful than Rama. She mocks the tale of Rama slaying the ten-headed Ravana because a thousand-headed Ravana still lives. Rama decides to face him, but it is Sita who eventually defeats the thousand-headed Ravana.

In contemporary times, too, cultural expressions have tried to defy the idea of Sita as a subservient character. One such example is the 2008 film *Sita Sings the Blues*, where Sita's heartbreak is the backdrop against which a deeply personal story of a woman navigating the challenges of her own marriage unfolds. With an even stronger feminist perspective, prominent Dalit activist Du Saraswathi reimagined the *Ramayana* in her Santhimmi plays, in which Sita never dies. She lives on as a symbol of strength for women.

SITA MARRIES RAMA

VIVAH PANCHAMI CELEBRATIONS ACROSS NEPAL AND NORTH BIHAR

When Rama lifted the all-powerful Shiva's bow, strung it, and snapped it with ease, King Janaka of Mithila knew the prince was worthy enough to marry his precious and virtuous daughter, Sita. During the wedding, as the couple circumambulated the holy fire, divine drums played and flowers rained from the sky. The people rejoiced as it was a moment of great celebration in the city of Mithila.

▲ Built in 1874, Janak Mandir is Nepal's largest temple, and features a blend of Mughal and local architecture.

On the fifth day of the waxing phase of the moon in the month of *Agrahayana*, parts of India and Nepal come together to celebrate the union of Sita and Rama. Processions of pilgrims travel to temples dedicated to Sita and Rama, and, in some places, spend up to a week reenacting moments from their wedding. This is Vivah Panchami, a winter festival determined by the lunar Hindu calendar. Interestingly, although this day marks the divine union of Rama and Sita, many people choose not to marry on this day, given the sorrow and challenges Sita faced in her marriage. Nevertheless, Vivah Panchami is celebrated with great enthusiasm and grandeur.

Janakpur (Dhanusha, Nepal)

Often called the City of Ponds, Janakpur in southeast Nepal is believed to be Sita's birthplace. During Vivah Panchami, the city hosts grand ceremonial events, each day reserved for key moments from Rama and Sita's wedding. If their first meeting is reenacted on one day, another day is reserved for the ritual digging of clay to make the wedding platform—a common wedding ritual in the region. At the heart of Janakpur town, the 19th-century Janaki Mandir hosts the more elaborate rituals. The celebrations culminate in a symbolic wedding procession of hundreds of devotees who travel almost 310 miles (500km) from Ayodhya in Uttar Pradesh, India, to Janakpur. The scene then shifts to Rangabhoomi ground, where the entire wedding is reenacted on a grand scale.

Sitamarhi (Bihar, India)

The story of Sita's birth and wedding is entrenched in Sitamarhi and the region around it. Local legends tell of Punaura, west of Sitamarhi, where Janaka rescued Sita, a foundling, from a ploughed furrow. At Panth Pakar, a few miles from the Sitamarhi railway station, stands a tree where Sita rested while traveling to Ayodhya after marrying Rama.

The centerpiece, however, is the Vivah Panchami celebration with the reenactment of the wedding. As part of a tradition that goes back at least a century, symbolic processions from Rama temples head to Sita temples across Sitamarhi. If priests from Sita temples represent her family, those in the processions from Rama temples stand in as Rama's kin. The most splendid wedding ritual festivities are most often seen at the Janki Mandir at Sitamarhi town and the Ma Janaki Janmabhoomi Temple at Punaura.

◂ A frieze depicting the wedding of Rama and Sita.

CULTURE

MADHUBANI ART

A CELEBRATION OF SITA'S WEDDING

Believed to have been commissioned by the king Janaka for his daughter Sita's wedding, Madhubani painting has evolved from a domestic-wall art form into an empowering creative expression for the women of north Bihar and Nepal.

Madhubani art, also known as Mithila painting or Maithil painting, has traditionally been produced by women to commemorate milestones considered important to familial life—births, weddings, religious ceremonies—on the walls of their homes. The *Ramayana* is an important source of subjects, and Sita often appears as a central figure. The wedding of Sita and Rama is a recurring motif, as is *Sita Bidai* (a farewell ceremony for the bride).

Though the historical origin of the art form has not been established, the belief in Mithilanchal, a region spanning Nepal and northern Bihar, is that it came into existence when Sita's father, King Janaka, sought a new art form to celebrate his daughter's wedding. While traditional representations emphasized Sita's role as a wife and mother, in keeping with dominant interpretations, contemporary Madhubani art reimagines her as a figure of agency and resilience. Now, she emerges as a single mother navigating life's challenges, a fearless adversary to Ravana, or a self-sufficient forest dweller—a clear departure from the portrayals of Sita solely as a paragon of loyalty.

The vibrant tradition is still in practice in villages of Mithilanchal. One of the most important of these is Jitwarpur, north of Madhubani town in Bihar, where artists line the lanes across the small village—making intricate paintings on walls, paper, and canvas. Jitwarpur is also home to some of the foremost contemporary Madhubani painters, and now centers its economy on its art—local artists sell paintings made at home. Another significant center of Madhubani art production is Ranti, a village, a few miles south of Madhubani town, where paintings can be bought directly from local artisans.

◀ **Clockwise from top left:** Mithila art on the walls and pillars in a village in Bihar; painting illustrating the *Ram Darbar*—Lord Rama's court; Madhubani paintings depicting nature as well as deities from Hindu epics in Mithila University; Madhubani railway station in Bihar; a Madhubani artist painting a mural; artwork depicting the wedding of Rama and Sita.

Classical Bharatanatyam dancers enact the pivotal event of Rama and Sita's wedding during the performance of a play titled *Sita Swayamvaram*.

THE ABDUCTED

SITA GUFA (MAHARASHTRA, INDIA)

Rama may have rejected Surpanakha's advances, but was wary of retaliation. So, he requested Lakshmana to guard Sita in a mountain cave hidden by overgrowth, in order to keep her safe. Meanwhile, Surpanakha asked Khara, her cousin who ruled over the forests of Janasthana, to fight Rama. A furious Khara challenged Rama, but was defeated. Desperate, Surpanakha then approached her brother Ravana, the king of Lanka, and begged him to avenge her humiliation. Ravana decided to abduct Sita, as revenge. He ordered Maricha to take on the form of a golden deer to distract Rama and Lakshmana. Rama went after the deer to capture it for Sita. When he struck it, Maricha cried out, much like a human. Lakshmana mistook the cry for Rama and rushed to help his brother, leaving Sita behind. Ravana seized this opportunity. He approached Sita while disguised as a mendicant and managed to abduct her.

The northern part of the city of Nashik in India's western state of Maharashtra is key to *Ramayana*'s sacred geography and revered by Hindu devotees. The area, known as Panchavati, lies on the northern bank of the Godavari River and derives its name from five ancient banyan trees (*pancha* means five and *vati* means banyan tree). This is the abundant forest where it is believed Sita, Rama, and Lakshmana lived during their exile.

Within Panchavati, near the banyan trees, lies Sita Gufa. This cave is said to be where Sita was hidden when Rama anticipated retribution after Surpanakha's mutilation, and from where Ravana abducted her. The Sita Gufa, only 9.8ft (3m) high, has a nondescript exterior. It would be hard to miss were it not for the hundreds of people lining up to step inside. (The lines are usually long, especially during religious festivals like Vivah Panchami and Dussehra.) Inside, a low, cramped passage—just wide enough for one person—leads to a narrow, steep staircase that drops into a chamber that has the idols of Rama, Sita, and Lakshmana. Another chamber within the cave holds a Shivalinga, a symbol of the Hindu god of destruction, Shiva. The local lore is that Sita used to worship this Shivalinga. Also within the cave is a meticulously carved stone room, with a stone block fashioned into the likeness of a small bed. While it is not explicitly said to be Sita's bed, it is a nod to the story of Sita's life of plain domesticity spent here.

Down the road from Sita Gufa is the Kalaram Temple. It was built in the 18th century by a Peshwa chief, and is believed to stand over one of the spots where Rama, Sita, and Lakshmana lived during their exile. The temple was also the site of a protest in 1930 led by jurist and Dalit reformer B. R. Ambedkar, demanding the right for oppressed castes to enter the temple.

About 2.5 miles (4km) from the Kalaram Temple lies Tapovan, a green, rocky landscape on the southern bank of the Godavari. It is identified as an important site of meditation for sages in Hindu mythology. The name Tapovan is derived from the Sanskrit words *tapasya*, meaning penance, and *van*, meaning forest.

Within the *Ramayana* universe, it is where Lakshmana deformed Surpanakha by cutting off her nose and ears. This episode is believed to be the source of Nashik's name (*nashika* means nose in Sanskrit).

◄ This 19th-century Kangra painting shows Ravana, in the guise of a brahman mendicant, abducting Sita. Rama and Lakshmana hunt the golden deer in the background.

▲ Sita Gufa in Nashik, India.

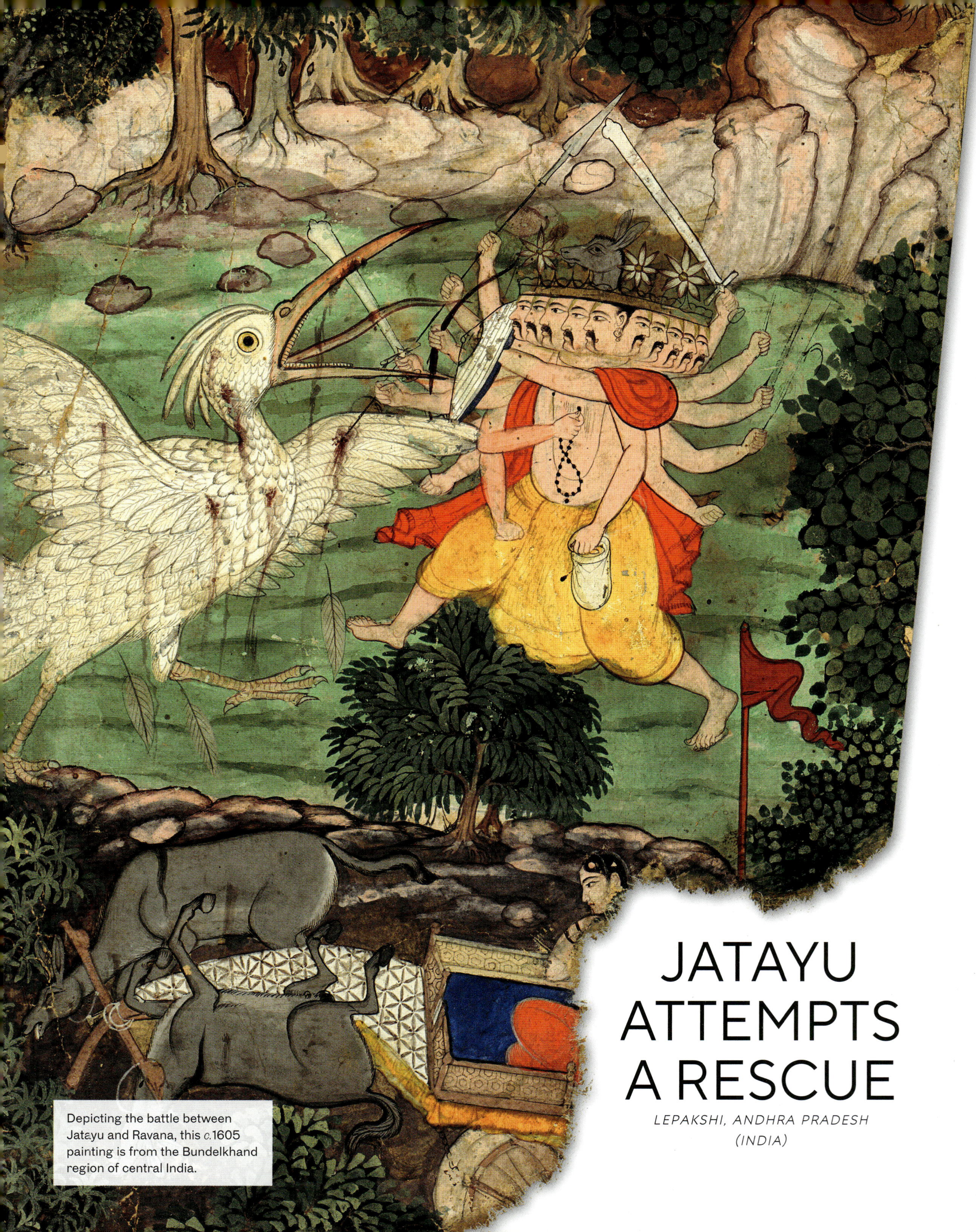

JATAYU ATTEMPTS A RESCUE

LEPAKSHI, ANDHRA PRADESH (INDIA)

Depicting the battle between Jatayu and Ravana, this *c.*1605 painting is from the Bundelkhand region of central India.

The majestic vulture king Jatayu heard Sita's cries for help as Ravana took her away on his flying chariot. A fierce battle broke out between the two mighty warriors. Finally, Ravana swung his sword and cut Jatayu's wings. The mortally wounded bird fell to the ground and Ravana managed to get away. Rama, searching for Sita, came upon the dying bird. In his final moments, Jatayu then told Rama of Sita's abduction.

The village seems to rise out of nowhere. For miles around Lepakshi, a small village in the southern Indian state of Andhra Pradesh, occasional sparsely populated settlements are the only signs of life. Rock-strewn hills line the roads. The drive through the rugged landscape is quiet —and stunning—and does not prepare one for the majestic sprawl that suddenly hits the eyeline as one approaches Lepakshi.

A massive statue of the vulture king Jatayu—perched on top of a boulder with wings spread out—comes into view from afar. The village of Lepakshi is believed to be where Jatayu fell while trying to rescue Sita, and the statue is a monument to that sacrifice. The name is said to be derived from what Rama said when he saw the fallen Jatayu—*"Le pakshi"* (rise, bird in Telugu). The statue lies within the Jatayu Theme Park, which was built in 2015. A flight of metal stairs leads to the top of the boulder on which the statue rests, offering an expansive view of Lepakshi. Another place in India built in a similar manner—a giant Jatayu sculpture resting on a hillock—also claims to be the spot where Jatayu fell. Located at the Jatayu Adventure Center at Chadayamangalam, it is about 31 miles (50km) from Kerala's capital, Thiruvananthapuram.

A temple town

Visible from the top of the boulder at the Jatayu Theme Park and less than 0.6 miles (1 kilometer) away is the Sri Veerabhadra Temple, locally known as Lepakshi Temple. It is dedicated to Veerabhadra, a formidable form of Shiva. Built on a low granite hill called Kurma Saila (tortoise hill in Telugu, a reference to the perceived shape of the hillock), the temple is Lepakshi's primary draw. It was built over three stages from 1,100 CE to 1,800 CE, expanding gradually over centuries. A stunning example of Vijayanagara art, the temple has elaborately carved pillars lining the grand halls around the shrines, and detailed paintings depicting episodes from the *Ramayana* and the *Mahabharata* on its walls and ceilings.

Around 0.3 miles (half a kilometer) from the temple is the Lepakshi Nandi, a gigantic sculpture of the sacred bull Nandi. The 20-ft- (6-m-) high idol has been carved out of a single block of granite and faces west, toward a Naga-linga (a representation of Shiva guarded by a seven-hooded serpent) at the Veerabhadra Temple. It is considered to be a part of the temple architecture because Nandi, Shiva's carrier, is represented in Hindu traditions as Shiva's gatekeeper and is always placed outside Shiva shrines.

◄ Jatayu Theme Park near Lepakshi Temple, Andhra Pradesh, features a majestic statue of Jatayu.

A mortally wounded Jatayu lies on the ground as Lakshmana tries to help the giant bird in this scene from the *Ramayana*, performed in the classical Kathakali dance form of Kerala.

SITA IS BROUGHT TO LANKA

SITA KOTUWA, KANDY (SRI LANKA)

In Lanka, Ravana took Sita to his palace, showed her the palatial rooms, and offered her all manner of comforts. He told the rakshasa women to treat her with respect and kindness. Grief-stricken, she refused his advances. The riches meant nothing to her when she was separated from Rama. Ravana tried to coax her into accepting him as her husband—with kind words and then with threats—but Sita remained unmoved. Furious, he left her in the grove of ashoka trees and ordered the rakshasa women to watch over her.

According to local legends, Ravana's flying machines were assembled and repaired at the ancient site of Gurulupotha. Nestled in the misty Dumbara Valley of south-central Sri Lanka, the journey to this site is as enchanting as the site itself. The A26 mountain road winding up from Kandy to Mahiyangana is a wild ride – with twists and turns and bends and curves so entrenched in local imagination that they are now a shorthand for the route, the 18 Hairpin Bend Road. Toward the end of this spectacular road is Hasalaka, a remote hilly village surrounded by waterfalls. Near Hasalaka lie the ancient ruins of Gurulupotha. A short trek leads to Sita Kotuwa, which translates to Sita's fort in Sinhalese.

The trek to Sita Kotuwa is a descent through layers of forest canopies and rock structures. The last stretch is through a series of narrow stone steps, which lead deeper into the forests. When a clearing emerges, the remnants of two large, ancient platforms become visible—surrounded by moss-covered stone slabs and pillars.

Myth and history

For believers of the *Ramayana* story, the platforms at Gurulupotha are the remains of the inner apartments of Mandodari's fort. The fort, as per local lore, was where Sita was initially held captive after Ravana brought her to Lanka, hence, the name Sita Kotuwa. The belief ties in with another *Ramayana* legend, about Gurulupotha being Ravana's aircraft repair center since he was a skilled aviator.

Archaeological examination has identified the platforms as the remains of a *padhanagara*—a Buddhist monastic structure unique to Sri Lanka—built between the 7th and 10th centuries CE. *Padhanagaras* were meditation centers for monks who chose lives of extreme austerity. The architecture of these meditation centers typically includes two platforms connected to one another with a large stone slab across a shallow moat, like that of Gurulupotha.

The meditative quality of the landscape is evident immediately. Surrounded by forests, the only sound one hears at Sita Kotuwa is that of the waterfall, the Sita Kotuwa Ella, cascading over limestone rocks just 0.1 mile (200m) away.

▲ Ravana offers Sita jewelry in this chromolithograph depicting her captivity in Lanka.

▶ The Sita Kotuwa ruins in Gurulupotha, Sri Lanka.

IN ARDUOUS CAPTIVITY

SEETHA AMMAN TEMPLE, CENTRAL PROVINCE (SRI LANKA)

Torment her so that she will change her mind, Ravana told the rakshasa women who surrounded Sita as she sat in the Ashoka Vatika. It was a grove of abundance and serene beauty, overflowing with flowers and fruits, and every object of desire. In that cornucopian site lay Sita—immersed in grief. Then, one day, Sita heard a voice reciting the story of King Dasharatha and his son Rama. It was Hanuman, the vanara general, dispatched by Rama to find Sita in Lanka. Hanuman told Sita that her husband was preparing to march on Lanka. Sita gave him her hair ornament to take back to Rama. She would not despair. Rama was coming for her.

The Seetha Amman Temple stands as a resplendent splash of colors against the lush greenery of Sri Lanka's most popular hill station, Nuwara Eliya. The temple was built in the early 2000s to honor the belief that the site is part of the *Ramayana's* Ashoka Vatika, the grove in Ravana's palace where Sita spent the longest period of her captivity. It is believed to stand on the site of a much older Sita temple.

The contemporary structure's architecture draws on temples from south India. The entrance has an elaborate arched gateway at the center

▲ This 18th-century painting from Gujarat depicts Hanuman talking to Sita in Lanka's Ashoka Vatika.

of the outer wall. Sculptures of Hanuman stand on either side of the entrance arch as *dwarapalas*—guardian deities.

The main temple tower is in the form of a three-tiered stepped pyramid. Numerous shrines line the circumambulatory path within the temple complex, honoring deities such as Vinayagar, Rama, Sita, Lakshmana, and Hanuman.

The temple is an example of the cultural influence of the Indian Tamil population brought here to work on tea plantations during British colonial rule. The planned town of Nuwara Eliya was established as a retreat for British and Scottish pioneers of Sri Lanka's tea industry in the 19th century. Nuwara Eliya soon became a center of production for the lightest flavors of Ceylon Tea (the proprietary Sri Lankan tea produced in the highlands) and has some of the most beautiful tea estates in the country today. Its cool climate, winding roads through undulating hills, and colonial-era bungalows have lent it the name of Little England.

As one drives southeast, deeper into Nuwara Eliya, the landscape changes—from palm trees to dense forests of eucalyptus trees, with meandering roads leading to mist-shrouded hills. It is here, 3.1 miles (5km) from the hills of Nuwara Eliya, that one finds the area designated as Seetha Eliya where the Seetha Amman Temple stands. The temple is next to a stream, which is said to be where Sita used to bathe. Beside the stream lies a large, flat rock with a giant footprint—believed to be that of Hanuman, who was searching for Sita.

About 1.2 miles (2km) from the temple is the Hakgala Botanical Garden, at an elevation of 5,600ft (1,700m). The experimental garden was developed during the British colonial rule in 1860, but contemporary travel literature refers to it as the site where Ashoka Vatika once stood—as part of a larger landscape that includes the Seetha Amman Temple.

▼ Intricate sculptures depicting deities and mythological scenes adorn the *gopuram*, or entrance gateway, of the Seetha Amman Temple in Nuwara Eliya, Sri Lanka.

A HASTY CONCEALMENT

SHTRIPURA, UVA PROVINCE (SRI LANKA)

When an angry Hanuman started destroying the ashoka grove, the king of Lanka tried to punish Hanuman by setting his tail on fire. However, the vanara managed to escape after setting Lanka ablaze with his tail. Ravana realized that he could not underestimate his enemies. This is also when, local Sri Lankan lore indicates, he decided to move Sita to a secret location. He had built a complex network of tunnels and caves connecting all major parts of Lanka. He hid Sita in one of these caves.

▲ A rock cave at Shtripura in Uva Province, Sri Lanka.

The Shtripura Caves are not the usual bustling tourist hub, but a demanding destination for adventure sports enthusiasts. It is not the kind of cave one simply walks into. One has to climb in, with proper climbing gear, and with local guides. The cave complex comprises a series of three main caves which are interconnected and extend approximately 0.6 miles (1km) in distance. The journey through these caves offers a unique experience as the natural rock formations and the serene environment provide insight into Sri Lanka's rich cultural, historical, and ecological tapestry.

It seems that these interconnected caves were part of Ravana's intricate underground tunnel system, which connected significant areas across his kingdom—such as those now known as Ravana Ella, Sita Kotuwa, and Ramboda. According to local folklore, it is here that Ravana hid Sita after Hanuman set Lanka on fire.

Contemporary travel literature links the name's etymology to the *Ramayana*. *Shtri* means woman and *pura* means town in Sanskrit and Sinhalese, and it must

mean the retinue of rakshasa women Ravana deputed to look after Sita. It is no wonder, then, that this cave complex is also known as the "Women's Town Cave."

The name is important for another reason—Sri Lanka has three caves of the same name. The one associated with the *Ramayana* legend, however, is at Kiriwanagama in the Welimada district of Uva Province—in a remote tea plantation area. It is situated at an elevation of 4,560ft (1,390m) above sea level. The hill on which the cave entrances can be found slopes downward, with a stream at its base. The local *Ramayana* legend says this is where Sita would bathe and a rock near the stream, named Kandu Katta Gala, is where she would sit as she dried her hair.

The Bomburu Ella, a waterfall is just a 9.3-mile (15-km) drive away. The 164-ft- (50-m-) high pristine waterfall is one of Sri Lanka's largest, where waters from several smaller forest waterfalls converge. It is close to the border of Nuwara Eliya, one of the most important sites of the Sita lore in Sri Lanka.

▲ This painting from a 17th-century illustrated manuscript shows a bound Hanuman facing Ravana before his tail is set on fire.

This Paithan painting depicts Ravana's grove, where Hanuman finds Sita, as a toddy palm plantation similar to those found in Andhra Pradesh.

A TRIAL BY FIRE

SOUTHERN SRI LANKA AND NORTHERN BIHAR, INDIA

Ravana was dead, Rama had won, and Sita was rescued, yet what should have been a joyous moment did not feel like one. Sita's virture and purity came into question. Though Rama never doubted her, he asked her to prove her chastity to prevent others from casting doubt upon her. Dejected and angry, Sita agreed to a trial by fire and emerged from the flames unscathed. Her virtue had been proven in the public eye.

The test of Sita's virtue is believed to have taken place at either of two sites located within geographies where the lore of Sita finds deep cultural resonance. The first of these, in Sri Lanka, is near the Nuwara Eliya area, where Sita is said to have been held captive by Ravana. The other lies in Munger, in the north Indian state of Bihar. The region was once controlled by the rulers of Mithila in India, which (as the *Ramayana* story goes) is where Sita was raised by King Janaka. However, the narrative of trial by fire at Sita Kund in Munger is rooted in local folklore tradition rather than canonical texts.

◀ A 17th-century wooden carving depicting Sita undergoing a trial by fire to prove her chastity.

What this highlights is that various *Ramayana* narratives have evolved over time, with regional variations reflecting local traditions and beliefs. Sites, such as Sita Kund, showcase how the *Ramayana* and its events or stories continue to be cherished and reinterpreted in different parts of India and Sri Lanka.

Divurumpola (Sri Lanka)

The bright, white spire stands out against the lush, green fields as one approaches the temple complex. A board identifies it as both Divurumwela, an ancient Buddhist temple, and Seetha Devi Agni Pariksha Place, a site associated with the *Ramayana*. The names "Divurumpola" and "Divurumwela" appear to be used interchangeably in local parlance. "Divurumpola" translates to "place of oath" in Sinhalese, reflecting its historical significance as a venue for solemn vows and sacred ceremonies.

It is where Sita is believed to have faced her trial, entering a fire to prove her purity and emerging unscathed. A spot under a tree within the temple complex is marked as the place where this is supposed to have happened. The complex is only about 2.5 miles (4km) from Welimada town in Sri Lanka's Central Province and about 8.7 miles (14km) from the Seetha Amman Temple at Seetha Eliya, where Sita is believed to have been held captive by Ravana.

Divurumpola is also where a sapling of the sacred Bodhi tree at Sri Lanka's historical city of Anuradhapura—which itself is a sapling of the Bodhi tree under which the Buddha attained enlightenment in Bodh Gaya, India—is believed to have been planted. The temple makes space for both the faiths—magnificent paintings and sculptures depict the story of the life of Buddha as well as the ordeal Sita faced.

▲ Divurumpola/ Seetha Devi Agni Pariksha Place, Central Highlands, Sri Lanka.

Sita Kund (Bihar, India)

This site in the quiet village of Mirzapur Bardah by the Ganga River is another place where, according to local folklore tradition, Sita underwent a trial by fire. She came out of the blaze unharmed, and as she took a dip in these waters, the heat of the fire she had absorbed turned them into a hot spring. Sita Kund is believed to be that hot spring, an important part of northern Bihar's culture of worshipping Sita. The hot spring is enclosed within a gated structure, and small temples dedicated to Hindu deities such as Hanuman are scattered throughout the complex. While Sita Kund is open to visitors all year, the best time to visit is in February during the month-long Magh Purnima Fair, when pilgrims converge on the site to take a dip in the waters of Sita Kund.

In addition to Sita Kund, the site features four other sacred ponds associated with Rama and his brothers. Ramkund lies to the north of Sita Kund, while Lakshman Kund, Bharat Kund, and Shatrughan Kund are situated to its west, each named after one of Rama's brothers.

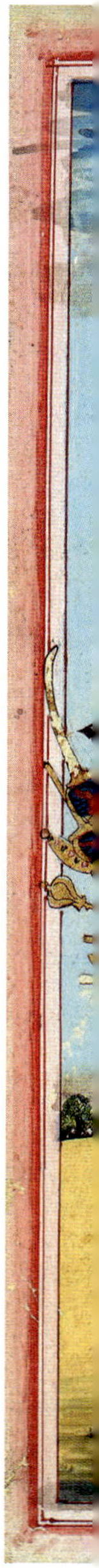

CULTURE

THANJAVUR PAINTINGS

A TESTAMENT TO LOVE

This early 17th-century painting tradition from the southern Indian state of Tamil Nadu elevates the dedication of characters in the Vaishnavite pantheon, such as Rama and Sita, to spectacular glory.

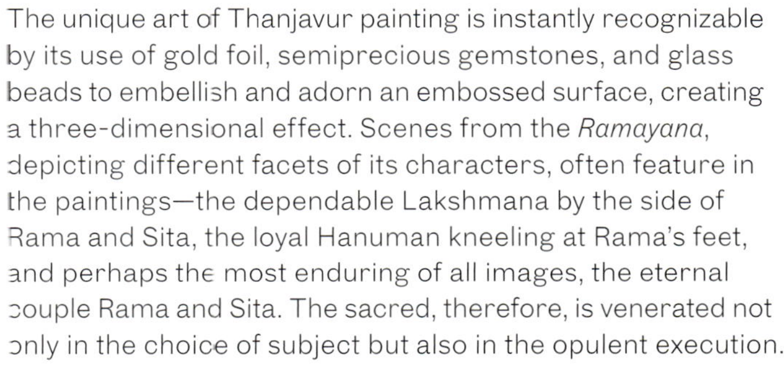

The unique art of Thanjavur painting is instantly recognizable by its use of gold foil, semiprecious gemstones, and glass beads to embellish and adorn an embossed surface, creating a three-dimensional effect. Scenes from the *Ramayana*, depicting different facets of its characters, often feature in the paintings—the dependable Lakshmana by the side of Rama and Sita, the loyal Hanuman kneeling at Rama's feet, and perhaps the most enduring of all images, the eternal couple Rama and Sita. The sacred, therefore, is venerated not only in the choice of subject but also in the opulent execution.

This art form is rooted in the historically remarkable city of Thanjavur. Once the capital of the Chola empire, one of the most powerful dynasties in the Indian subcontinent's history, Thanjavur developed a stunning mural tradition under the patronage of its rulers between the 16th and 18th centuries—most notably, the Thanjavur Nayakas and the Marathas.

Refined over the years, the mural art found expression in a form known locally as Palagai Padam (pictures on wooden planks) and to the world as what we now know as Thanjavur or Tanjore painting. The paintings are made on wooden boards that are covered with cloth. The artist applies gesso (a paste of glue and chalk powder) and starts sketching. Gesso is applied again to introduce contours on which gold or silver foil is then applied. Finally, the artist introduces colors and adds gemstones.

Some of the best examples of Thanjavur painting can be seen at the Government Museum in Chennai and the National Museum in New Delhi.

◄ **Clockwise from top left:** murals depicting Hanuman and Rama's coronation in Thanjavur; a street artist in Thanjavur; painting from c.1820 showing Rama perched on Hanuman's shoulder battling Ravana; traditional rendition of the eternal couple, Rama and Sita.

SITA'S EXILE

SITABINJI, ODISHA (INDIA)

Rama and Sita returned to Ayodhya and spent their time in the capital. However, fate had other plans. Rama learned that the people of the city spoke of Sita's abduction and questioned her time in Lanka, casting doubt on her despite her trial by fire. Distraught, Rama instructed Lakshmana to take the pregnant Sita to the border of his kingdom, across the Ganga River, and leave her there so that she might live with the sage Valmiki. Left with no choice but to accept her fate, the banished Sita withdrew into the forest. The sage Valmiki (a self-referential character, as Valmiki is also the composer of the *Ramayana*) took her into his ashram, where she later gave birth to Rama's sons, Lava and Kusha.

▸ Sitabinji's rock shelters are believed to be where Sita and her twin sons, Lava and Kusha, lived.

Sometimes the natural landscape itself can inspire fascinating storytelling. Imagine massive boulders, standing at slightly inclined angles to each other, with just enough room between them for the spaces to resemble cavelike formations. Could someone have sought refuge here? The answer need not be tied to faith but to the imaginative possibility—whether Sita lived in the rock shelters of Sitabinji after Rama renounced her, as local lore goes, is not necessarily about belief in the *Ramayana*.

Sita's abode

The Sitabinji rock shelters lie between the villages of Danguapasi and Sitabinji, by the Sita River (a tributary of the Baitarani River), about 25 miles (40km) from the hillside town of Keonjhar in northern Odisha. The boulders and rocks strewn across the area have been given names associated with the *Ramayana*. There is a cave where Sita is believed to have given birth to her sons. A boulder is identified as one under which they received their lessons, presumably from Valmiki. A massive rock where Sita is said to have stored her jewelry is called Bhandara Ghara, which means storeroom in Odia.

This last belief, about the Bhandara Ghara, has a counternarrative also associated with the *Ramayana*—it was where a dacoit named Ratnakara hoarded his treasures. Ratnakara later gave up his material possessions and came to be known as Valmiki, the author of the *Ramayana*.

Within the main structure of the rock shelter is a mud-and-brick shrine that houses stone-carved idols of Sita and her sons, Lava and Kusha. Devotees place terracotta horses around the shrine, a way of seeking Sita's blessings. This is where Sita is believed to have taken refuge after Lakshmana left her.

One of the most archaeologically significant formations, however, is a rock shelter shaped like a half-open umbrella—one boulder on top of another—called Ravana Chhaya. The name, meaning the shadow of Ravana, is also associated with a shadow-puppetry tradition in Odisha. The ceiling has tempera paintings, dating back to the 5th century CE, depicting a procession of a royal figure identified as an early king of Odisha's Bhanja dynasty.

Less than 18.6 miles (30km) away lies the Maa Tarini Temple of Ghatgaon, an important site of Shakti worship. It is a vibrantly painted structure built in the traditional Odia style and surrounded by beautiful sal (*Shorea robusta*) forests.

▼ *The Hermitage of Valmiki*, a painting depicting the life of Sita and her sons from c.1820

SITA'S RETURN TO EARTH

KARNATAKA, UTTARAKHAND, UTTAR PRADESH, AND HARYANA (INDIA)

Rama listened to Lava and Kusha narrate Valmiki's *Ramayana* during the course of the horse sacrifice, and realized that the twins were his sons. He requested the sage and Sita to present themselves before him. He asked for forgiveness for abandoning Sita and then requested that she establish her purity once more. Sita agreed. The gods gathered in the heavens, as did Rama and his followers on earth, to witness the moment. Sita joined her hands and prayed to the earth, to give her room if she had never thought of another man. The ground split open and the Goddess Earth emerged. She embraced Sita and seated her by her side. As flowers rained down from the sky, Sita disappeared into the ground.

▲ The Ramalingeshwara Temple in Avani, Karnataka, India.

This is where Sita's story comes full circle. The daughter of the earth, embraced by the goddess, returns to the earth. This conclusion to Sita's story is believed to have unfolded in one of four temples spread across India.

Sita Parvati Temple (Karnataka, India)
The small village of Avani in the southern state of Karnataka in India is about 12.4 miles (20km) from the once-famous gold mines of Kolar. The Sita Parvati Temple at the village can be reached after a fairly steep climb up the rocky terrain of the Avani Hill. According to local legend, the Parvati idol at the temple is one that Sita worshipped. Strewn across the landscape are many structures and idols that refer to the time Sita spent here with her sons Lava and Kusha—such as the Valmiki Hill where the sage Valmiki sheltered Sita, and the Lava Kusha hill where the twins are believed to have been born. At the base of the hill lies the 10th-century Ramalingeshwara Temple complex an architecturally stunning group of temples with shrines dedicated to Rama and his brothers.

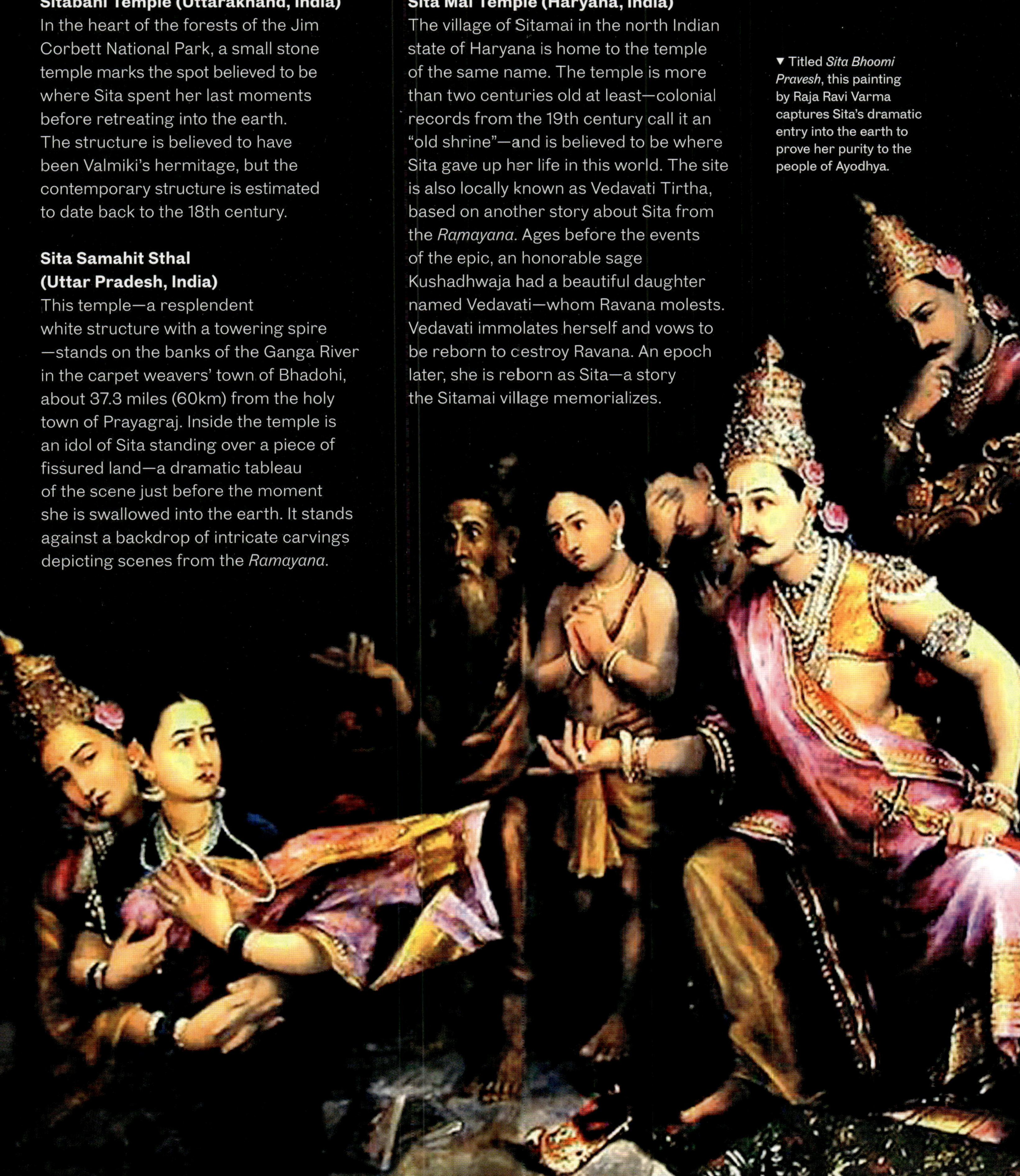

Sitabani Temple (Uttarakhand, India)
In the heart of the forests of the Jim Corbett National Park, a small stone temple marks the spot believed to be where Sita spent her last moments before retreating into the earth. The structure is believed to have been Valmiki's hermitage, but the contemporary structure is estimated to date back to the 18th century.

Sita Samahit Sthal (Uttar Pradesh, India)
This temple—a resplendent white structure with a towering spire—stands on the banks of the Ganga River in the carpet weavers' town of Bhadohi, about 37.3 miles (60km) from the holy town of Prayagraj. Inside the temple is an idol of Sita standing over a piece of fissured land—a dramatic tableau of the scene just before the moment she is swallowed into the earth. It stands against a backdrop of intricate carvings depicting scenes from the *Ramayana*.

Sita Mai Temple (Haryana, India)
The village of Sitamai in the north Indian state of Haryana is home to the temple of the same name. The temple is more than two centuries old at least—colonial records from the 19th century call it an "old shrine"—and is believed to be where Sita gave up her life in this world. The site is also locally known as Vedavati Tirtha, based on another story about Sita from the *Ramayana*. Ages before the events of the epic, an honorable sage Kushadhwaja had a beautiful daughter named Vedavati—whom Ravana molests. Vedavati immolates herself and vows to be reborn to destroy Ravana. An epoch later, she is reborn as Sita—a story the Sitamai village memorializes.

▼ Titled *Sita Bhoomi Pravesh*, this painting by Raja Ravi Varma captures Sita's dramatic entry into the earth to prove her purity to the people of Ayodhya.

05

Following Allies and Rivals

◂ Exiled princes Rama and Lakshmana confer with the vanara king Sugriva and his companions, in this folio created in the Paithan style from Maharashtra, dated 1850.

PROFILE

RAMA'S BROTHERS

Lakshmana remained by Rama's side, Bharata refused to become the king, and dutiful Shatrughna always followed Rama's instructions. Each had a role to play in Rama's destiny and the divine quest for which he was born, and they followed through with intense devotion to him.

▲ A 19th-century statue of Lakshmana from Himachal Pradesh, India.

The gods were distressed. The god of creation and one of the Trinity, Brahma, had granted Ravana, the mighty rakshasa king, unimaginable powers. Everyone and everything was fearful of him. When the gods petitioned Brahma for a solution, he told them of a caveat to his blessing—Ravana could not be killed by a god or semidivine being, but he had failed to ask for protection from death at the hands of a human. The gods turned to Vishnu, the preserver, and asked him to save them.

Vishnu agreed to be born as a man so that he could kill Ravana in battle. For this, he would need allies, so, the gods asked him to divide himself into four parts and be born as four sons to the three wives of the virtuous king of Ayodhya, Dasharatha.

The king, who was performing a sacrifice at that very moment to have sons, saw a divine being emerge from the sacrificial fire to offer him a bowl of celestial rice pudding. If his wives consumed the pudding, the being told him, they would give birth to sons.

Dasharatha divided the pudding, giving half to Kaushalya, the eldest queen, who would give birth to Rama. Sumitra received a quarter and Kaikeyi, his youngest wife, one-eighth. The remaining portion he gave to Sumitra once again, because of which she had twins, Lakshmana and Shatrughana. Bharat was born to Kaikeyi. The children were born on an auspicious day and the gods rejoiced.

Many versions

While this is the narrative in Valmiki's *Ramayana*, other ancient Hindu religious texts, such as the *Puranas,* and some versions of the *Ramayana*, attribute the fraternal ties to another legend.

This story says that Vishnu was born as Rama and massive divine serpent Sheshanaga as Lakshmana. Adaptations of this legend go on to tell that Shatrughna was Vishnu's divine weapon *sudarshan chakra* in a human form, while some believe that Bharata was the manifestation of the *sudarshan chakra* and Shatrughna that of Vishnu's conch.

However, the purpose of these narratives, no matter the variation, remain the same. It was to reinforce the predestined nature of the roles that the brothers were meant to play. Power and glory were not the motivations behind Rama's brothers' descent to earth. They were only there to help Rama fulfil his destiny.

So, even though Kaikeyi asked that Rama be exiled so her son Bharata could be crowned, the youngest brother refused to become king. Instead, he followed Rama and begged him to return and take his rightful place. Rama refused and so Bharata retired to a village from where he managed the kingdom for the duration of Rama's exile. Lakshmana gave up the palace to follow Rama into the forest, to be by his side, as his constant companion.

Rama, the king of Ayodhya, with his brothers Lakshmana, Bharata, and Shatrughna behind him, holds court in this late 18th-century painting from Chamba, Himachal Pradesh.

PROFILE

THE VANARA ARMY

The vanara armies of Kishkinda were key to Rama's victory over Ravana. Their role, too, was a matter of destiny. They were born solely to help the exiled prince fulfil his divine purpose.

Brahma, the god of creation and one of the Trinity, knew Rama's quest was not going to be an easy one. He would need allies. He told the gods to assume any form they wanted to create powerful supporters for Rama. They would be semidivine, borne of apsaras and gandharva women, excellent at warfare, and ceaselessly valiant. So, the gods fathered millions of vanaras, shape-shifters in the form of monkeys who lived in mountains and forests.

A promise of aid

The vanaras answered to the two vanara brothers Vali, son of the god of thunder Indra, and Sugriva, son of the sun god Surya. But the relationship between the brothers soon turned bitter.

Vali was the king of Kishkindha, and Sugriva his aide. One day, Vali's rivalry with the asura Mayavin drew him into a protracted battle within a cave. Sugriva waited for Vali to emerge. Suddenly, a year later, blood poured out of the cave as Vali's cries rang out. Sugriva was convinced that he had lost his brother. He blocked the entrance to the cave, returned to Kishkindha, and became the ruler. But Vali was not dead—he had vanquished his enemy in the cave that night. He returned, seeking vengeance for what he believed was Sugriva's betrayal.

Sugriva fled with his generals to the Rishyamukha mountains, but Vali detained his wife. It was in these mountains that Sugriva met Rama, who was searching for his wife Sita. Rama heard Sugriva's story and immediately felt a sense of kinship with the vanara king. They promised to help each other.

Rama's side of the promise was quickly fulfilled. Sugriva engaged Vali in combat, Rama shot an arrow at Vali and killed him with one strike. Rama reinstated Sugriva to the throne of Kishkindha. Sugriva then asked Hanuman, his powerful minister, to summon vanaras from all corners of the earth—the armies would search for Sita.

The vanaras searched everywhere, but were unable to find any trace. Sita was nowhere to be found. As the vanaras gave up hope, Hanuman, the son of the god of wind, Sugriva's minister Tara, and Vali's son Angada discovered that Sita had been taken across the ocean into Lanka. But, who would leap across the ocean to Lanka? Only Hanuman had the ability to undertake such a difficult task, and so he

"If that hero lives, the army is unvanquished even if it is slain. If Hanuman has given up his life, we are slain even if we live."

Jambavan tells Vibhishana on the battleground, Sarga 61, Yuddha Kanda

◀ A Balinese mask representing Sugriva.

leaped from Mount Mahendra across the ocean into Lanka. He found Sita and gave her Rama's ring, but Ravana's forces captured him. The powerful vanara managed to escape, but not before setting Lanka on fire.

An army of vanaras

On his return, Hanuman told Rama and the vanaras of his discovery. The prince of Ayodhya prepared for war. To invade Lanka, however, they would have to cross the ocean. So, Nala, the architect of the vanaras and son of the god of architecture, Vishwakarma, volunteered his skills to build a bridge through the ocean. The vanaras got to work, flinging boulders, dragging trees, until a gigantic bridge paved their way into Lanka. They stormed Lanka, often with courage, sometimes with trepidation, but pushing forward continuously. Their relentless slaughter wiped out powerful rakshasa generals. Throughout the battle, in moments of despair, vanara generals stepped in to help Rama and Lakshmana. Twice, when the princes were injured, Hanuman brought back lifesaving herbs to revive and heal them.

When Ravana died at Rama's hands, the vanaras roared so fiercely that the rakshasas fled Lanka. Elsewhere, the gods spoke of the king of Lanka's death, Rama's valor, Sugriva's counsel, and the fight put up by the vanaras. Rama's victory was theirs, too.

In this 17th-century painting, vanaras scour the northern, eastern, and western regions for Sita, but are unable to find her. Seated in the middle of the painting are Rama and Lakshmana with Sugriva, surrounded by vanaras paying obeisance to them.

PROFILE

RAVANA'S KIN

The ethical and moral divide is nowhere more evident than among Ravana's family. If one brother walked away because Ravana failed to accept his mistakes, another remained by his side as a trusted warrior. If Ravana's wife wondered how much he was to blame for his fate, his son used his powers to battle the princes of Ayodhya.

The powerful sage Vishravas's curse was irrevocable. Kaikasi, the daughter of the powerful rakshasa Sumali, had disturbed him during a ritual, and the sage had preordained that any children she bore would be cruel and terrifying. Kaikasi pleaded with the sage, and so, he made an allowance—her youngest son would be virtuous. That son was Vibhishana, born free of the curse that set his brothers Ravana and Kumbhakarna on a path of destruction.

An epitome of virtuosity

Vibhishana's predestined path of virtue was consolidated further when he and his brothers performed severe austerities for 10,000 years in the hope of gaining the Brahma's grace. Pleased with the brothers' efforts, the god granted their wishes. Ravana asked the god of creation for immortality, Kumbhakarna for the ability to sleep for many years, and Vibhishana for the ability to adhere to righteous conduct in every circumstance.

▼ This giant statue in Kumbhakarna Gardens, Andhra Pradesh, depicts the scene where the sleeping giant was being woken up by desperate rakshasas.

"Hero! I have been removed from the pleasures of the senses because of your death ... having taken up good acts and bad, you have attained your destiny. I grieve for myself, suffering in separation from you."

Mandodari's lament after Ravana's death, Sarga 99, Yuddha Kanda

So, when Ravana abducted Sita, Vibhishana first urged him to allow her to return to Rama. Even though Ravana was incensed that his brother would not support him, Vibhishana remained true to his beliefs. He left his brother and made his way to Rama and Lakshmana, and sought to help them. Rama's allies wondered why he had abandoned his brother, and whether he wanted the throne of Lanka for himself. The suspicions did not deter Vibhishana, who became a key advisor for Rama's camp.

His advice was pivotal at the most crucial of moments: He advised Rama and his allies to build a bridge when they wondered how they would cross the ocean. He aided them with details of Ravana's citadel, as they entered Lanka. Then, when all hope seemed lost as the vanaras thought Sita had died, Vibhishana reassured them and told them of Meghanada's illusory tricks.

◀ A vessel inspired by the Aranya Kanda of the Ramayana, depicting key scenes from the Dandaka forest.

The redoubtable son

Ravana's son Meghanada emerged as a powerful and formidable warrior during the battle of Lanka. Much like his father, he gained his powers after performing the most severe of austerities while praying to Shiva, one of the all-powerful Trinity. The god of destruction granted him almost complete invincibility. Meghanada unleashed chaos on the battlefield with his illusions, spells, and magical weapons.

His end came at the hands of Lakshmana, who killed him after a prolonged duel, using the divine arrow of Indra, the king of gods. Meghanada had once defeated Indra, earning him the moniker "Indrajit" (*jit* means victory in Sanskrit). Meghanada's death left Ravana shaken. The world, the king of Lanka said, seemed empty.

Great losses

Ravana had already lost too much. He first lost his cousin, the powerful warrior Khara in Dandaka forest, as the latter tried to avenge Surpanakha's humiliation. Then, his mighty and immense younger brother Kumbhakarna died while fighting Rama. On the battlefield, the giant warrior had caused immense havoc, brushing away the trees that were thrown at him, and flinging vanara warriors to the ground. He was finally defeated after Rama cut off his arms and legs before an arrow killed him.

After Ravana's death, his wives lamented his loss. The beautiful Mandodari was beside herself with grief. She had warned him about the fate he was tempting by abducting Sita and challenging Rama. But like the words of Vibhishana, her words too, had fallen on deaf ears.

LAKSHMANA TEMPLES

A PREDESTINED KINSHIP

Ancient temples in central India named after Lakshmana are, in fact, dedicated to Vishnu, the preserver of the universe. The story behind this is one of ceaseless loyalty, predestined ages before the *Ramayana*.

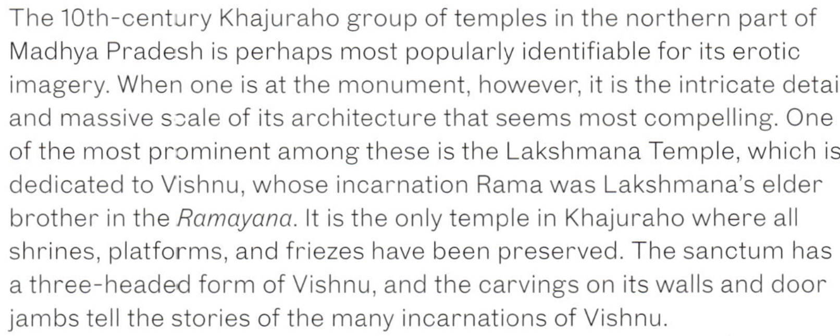

The 10th-century Khajuraho group of temples in the northern part of Madhya Pradesh is perhaps most popularly identifiable for its erotic imagery. When one is at the monument, however, it is the intricate detail and massive scale of its architecture that seems most compelling. One of the most prominent among these is the Lakshmana Temple, which is dedicated to Vishnu, whose incarnation Rama was Lakshmana's elder brother in the *Ramayana*. It is the only temple in Khajuraho where all shrines, platforms, and friezes have been preserved. The sanctum has a three-headed form of Vishnu, and the carvings on its walls and door jambs tell the stories of the many incarnations of Vishnu.

About 373 miles (600km) south of Khajuraho, in the neighboring state of Chhattisgarh, stands another Lakshmana Temple at the archaeological site of Sirpur. It was a seat of power for the rulers of South Kosala between the 6th and 8th centuries. Excavations have unearthed the remains of the township, with several Hindu and Buddhist monuments. Here, too, the Lakshmana Temple is among the best preserved ones. Built in the 7th century, this temple is also dedicated to Vishnu, with carvings that depict his many incarnations.

The tradition at the root of this seeming contradiction lies in Hindu texts that identify Lakshmana as the massive divine serpent Sheshanaga on whom Vishnu rests. The 12th-century Tamil retelling of the *Ramayana* by Kamban refers to the logic of the incarnations in the story—Rama is Vishnu, Sita is Vishnu's consort Lakshmi, and Lakshmana is Sheshanaga. This part of the story is used to explain why Lakshmana had to die before Rama—so that Vishnu's repose, Sheshanaga, would be ready for him when he went back to heaven after abandoning Rama's physical form.

◄ **Clockwise from top left:** sanctum of the Lakshmana Temple in Khajuraho with a shrine for Vishnu; intricate sculptures adorning the porch wall; sculpture of the Varaha avatar of Vishnu; a relief carving of Vishnu on the temple walls; facade of the Lakshmana Temple in Khajuraho, India.

WAITING FOR RAMA

NANDIGRAM, UTTAR PRADESH (INDIA)

Bharata failed to convince Rama to give up the idea of an exile and return to Ayodhya to be crowned king. Distraught, he retired to the small village of Nandigram near Ayodhya. He ruled over Kosala as a devoted steward, consecrating Rama's slippers, and shedding all royal accoutrements to lead an austere life, much like an ascetic. After 14 years, Rama, on his way back to Ayodhya from Lanka, stopped at Nandigram to meet Bharata. On seeing him, Bharata was overwhelmed with joy. He welcomed him, and then, gently placed Rama's feet in his slippers and said, "I return your kingdom to you."

▼ Bharatkund in Nandigram, Uttar Pradesh.

If the period of Bharata's secluded rule was marked by a sense of deep humility, the mythical seat of his power retains that modesty. A quiet, unostentatious stop on the way to Ayodhya, the village of Nandigram is about 12.4 miles (20km) south of the temple town on the Sultanpur highway in eastern Uttar Pradesh. It is not a bustling tourist destination nor is it a busy pilgrim town, but it is where two important events of the *Ramayana* are believed to have played out: Bharata's reluctant rule over Kosala in Rama's absence and Rama's meeting with Bharata after returning from Lanka.

Excavations that began in the 1970s as part of a project to determine the archaeology of *Ramayana* sites had concluded that the origins of the settlement at Nandigram was at least as old as that of Ayodhya. (However, the evidence—as pointed out by scholars such as historian Hemant Dave—came from a mound called Rahet on the southern bank of the river, while Nandigram lies on the northern bank of the river.)

At the heart of this *Ramayana* lore in present-day Nandigram lies Bharatkund, a large lotus-covered pond considered sacred by Hindu pilgrims—the *Skand Purana* says that a dip in its waters washes away all sins.

On the northern bank of Bharatkund, overlooking the waters, is a temple complex dedicated to Bharata's long wait. A small temple—locally called a cave—is the place into which Bharata is believed to have retreated while holding fort for Rama. A little further away, another temple marks the spot where Hanuman is believed to have met Bharata, telling him the story of Rama's victory and Sita's rescue just as the royal couple are on their way back from Lanka. In addition to the shrines to Rama, Bharata, and Hanuman, the temple also has on display what are believed to be Rama's slippers—the ones Bharata worshipped and consecrated when Rama was away.

On the opposite bank of Bharatkund is a cremation ghat of great significance to Hindus. Bharatkund is believed to be one of the most important places for offering prayers to ancestors, in a ritual called *pind daan*, before they proceed to Gaya in Bihar. The busiest time at Bharatkund i s during *Pitru Paksha*, a fortnight in fall during which Hindus pay homage to their ancestors.

▸ Titled *The Return of Rama*, this illustration by K. Venkatappa is part of Sister Nivedita and Ananda K. Coomaraswamy's book *Myths of the Hindus and Buddhists.*

عمل قاسم

◄ A folio from a *Ramayana* manuscript during the Mughal rule. The artwork, created with ink, opaque watercolor, and gold on paper, depicts Rama striking down Khara with an arrow.

KHARA'S KINGDOM

NASHIK, MAHARASHTRA (INDIA)

Khara ruled over the forests of Janasthana with an army of thousands of rakshasas. His cousin, the Lanka king Ravana, had given him the kingdom and the army, and sent his sister Surpanakha to stay with him. This is where Surpanakha approached Rama and Lakshmana, and faced rejection. When she flew into fury and tried to attack Sita, Lakshmana stepped in and cut off her nose and ears. A furious Khara sought to take revenge and sent his best warriors to fight Rama. However, the exiled prince of Ayodhya fought them all and then killed Khara himself.

The Godavari River is known as the "Ganga of the south"—an epithet that bears deep resonance for the devout. Like the Ganga, the Godavari River is believed to have purifying powers that wash away all sins. The ancient city of Nashik in northern Maharashtra is by the banks of this river—rendered significant by the holy river and by the religious mythology that surrounds it.

Nashik is believed to be where Khara's kingdom Janasthana, as mentioned in the *Ramayana*, once stood and where Surpanakha's encounter with Rama and Lakshmana took place. The name, Nashik, is assumed in some local legends to have been derived from Surpanakha's story—her nose was cut off, and "*nashika*" means nose in Sanskrit. In the *Ramayana* universe, Nashik was home to the ashrams of many sages—whose austerities and day-to-day lives Khara disrupted.

Nashik is part of the Shakti mythology as well. Sati, wife of the destroyer god Shiva, was incensed when Shiva was not invited to a rite (every other god had been invited). She killed herself, and Shiva was unable to bear the grief. He carried her body across the skies, and parts of it fell in places across what is now India. Nashik is believed to be where her chin fell.

The city is also one of four places in India where the Kumbh Mela is held. One of the most important Hindu religious congregations, the Kumbh Mela is held over weeks—four times in four specified places in a span of 12 years. It is believed that the gods and the asuras worked together to extract the nectar of immortality from the depths of the ocean. As the gods took the nectar up to heaven, four drops fell on earth. These were at Prayag, Haridwar, Ujjain, and Nashik.

▲ Ramkund in Panchavati at night, illuminated during the Kumbh Mela.

Sacred spaces

The ghat of Ramkund, built in the 17th century, is of great significance to the city's *Ramayana* lore. Its waters are believed to bestow *moksha* (eternal liberation) on anyone who bathes in it. This is where, it is believed, Rama used to bathe when he lived in these forests with Sita and Lakshmana. Ramkund is also where the ritual Simhastha bathing festival is organized every 12 years. Around it is Lakshman Kund and Sita Kund, with similar associations—that Lakshmana and Sita used to bathe in those waters. These water bodies all lie within an area known as Panchavati, much like, it is believed, the beautiful and abundant Panchavati forest Rama lived in. A cave temple dedicated to Sita stands here as well. It is said that Ravana abducted her from here. Close to it, the striking 18th-century Kalaram Temple is a revered pilgrimage site with a distinctive black statue of Rama, Sita, and Lakshmana —not a common representation of the Hindu god. The main structure stands within a fortified enclosure supported by 96 pillars, with its east-facing entrance marked by an arched portal.

A few miles from Kalaram Temple lies the verdant retreat of Tapovan. The waters of the Godavari River flow through

"Go and be by the side of your brother Khara, who has abiding power. Your brother will be the lord of fourteen thousand extremely mighty rakhshasas in battle and in the granting of gifts ... Let that hero go quickly to protect the Dandakas."

Ravana tells Surpanakha, Sarga 24, Uttara Kanda

weather-beaten rocks in this tranquil space, believed to be where Lakshmana cut Surpanakha's nose.

About 9.3 miles (15km) south of Nashik, a pleasant drive up to the picturesque hilltop of the Deolali Cantonment Area leads to the 500-year-old Khandoba Temple. While the temple is dedicated to Shiva, its deity, Khandoba, is said to have come into being when two rakshasa brothers, Malla and Mani, received a boon from Shiva which made them invincible. Intoxicated by their newfound power, they terrorized the people. Shiva then took on the form of the warrior Khandoba, and vanquished them. Shiva is believed to have rested atop this hill after defeating them.

To the west of Nashik, about 18.6 miles (30km) away from the city, on the base of the Brahmagiri Hill, lies the celebrated Trimbakeshwar Temple. The temple is dedicated to a three-eyed Shiva, Trimbaka, and the contemporary structure was built in the 18th century. It is believed to be one of the 12 Jyotirlingas, divine manifestations of Shiva's luminous power, across India. This is where the Godavari originates.

Buddhist traditions

Just outside Nashik, on the Nashik-Mumbai road, stunning caves carved into the rock face of the Trirashmi Hill are a testament to the region's rich Buddhist legacy as well.

The caves, Pandav Leni, have been dated back to a period between 250 BCE and 600 CE. Accessible after a 200-step climb up the hill, the caves are structured in the form of *viharas* (monasteries) with one *chaitya* (prayer hall). They house magnificent idols of Buddha and Jain Tirthankaras. Despite the seeming association of the name with the Pandavas from the other great Indian epic, *Mahabharata*, the caves were originally known as Pundru Caves in Pali (*pundru* means yellow in Pali). Over time, the name evolved to Pandu and eventually Pandav.

◄ Pandav Leni in Nashik, Maharashtra, are a group of 24 ancient caves dating back to the 2nd century, carved during the reign of the Satavahana dynasty

"Wind replied to Anjana '... I am not harming you. Fortunate one! Let there not be any fear in you ... Your son will be heroic and intelligent.'"

Vayu tells Anjana, Sarga 65, Kishkindha Kanda

► A late 19th-century handcrafted shadow puppet on leather from Andhra Pradesh, possibly depicting the vanara general Hanuman.

BIRTH OF HANUMAN

HILLS OF SOUTHERN INDIA

A curse turned Anjana, a celestial nymph and wife of the vanara general Kesari, into a vanara. She could, however, change her form at will. One day, the god of wind, Maruta or Vayu, caught sight of her as she assumed a human form, clad in yellow silk, adorned with garlands and ornaments, and was captivated by her beauty. Overcome with desire and love, he embraced her. An agitated Anjana demanded to know who wanted her to break her vow as a faithful wife. Vayu told her that he would not harm her—his embrace alone would bear a child. That child was the mighty Hanuman, who became one of Rama's most loyal followers.

The birth of Hanuman follows an encounter on the top of a mountain. So, several hilly places—from the plateaus of central India to the hills of southern India—have adopted the legend as their own. Believed to be where Hanuman was born, these places draw their names from Hanuman's mother, Anjana.

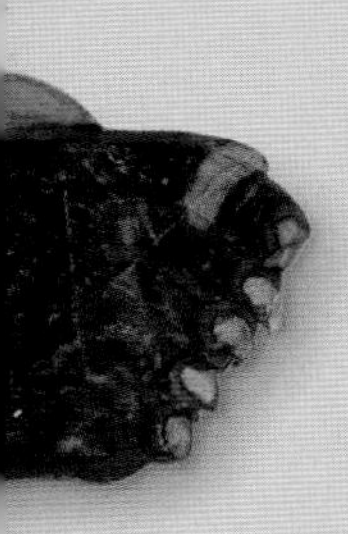

Anjaneri (Maharashtra, India)

The Anjaneri village in northern Maharashtra is surrounded by the green craggy terrain of the Anjaneri Hill, believed to be where Anjana gave birth to Hanuman. A challenging trek up the Anjaneri Hill leads to the Anjaneri Fort. Many rock-cut Jain caves from the 12th century line the path, which offers stunning views of the landscape. A temple dedicated to Anjana lies closer to the top and near the fort. A cave here is believed to be the place where an anguished Vayu cradled the child Hanuman, as he lay injured. He had leaped into the sky to grab the sun, angering the god of thunder, Indra, who in turn had hurled his thunderbolt at him. Hanuman was later revived and granted many boons.

Anjan Kund (Gujarat, India)

Tucked away in the Sahyadri Hills, Anjan Kund is a village 21.8 miles (35km) from Ahwa in Gujarat and 74.5 miles (120km) from the holy city of Nashik in Maharashtra. There are three places in the village believed to be associated with Hanuman's birth and childhood—Anjani Hill where Anjana is supposed to have performed a penance, Anjani Cave where local lore says Anjana gave birth to Hanuman, and Anjani Kund, a small body of water near the cave. This is where, devotees believe, Anjana would bathe Hanuman when he was a child.

Anjan (Jharkhand, India)

This village in Jharkhand's Gumla district, too, associates itself with Hanuman's birth. About 2.5 miles (4km) from the village is a hill, named Anjani, which also has a cave. This is where the nymph is supposed to have lived. A temple nearby is dedicated to her with an idol of Anjana cradling the child Hanuman in her lap. The village is linked to another Hindu legend. An ancient king is believed to have built a hyperbolic 300 temples and 300 tanks to worship Shiva, the destroyer, at what is now Anjan.

Anjanadri Hill (Karnataka, India)

Across the Tungabhadra River, opposite Hampi, the Anjanadri Hill is a craggy elevation with a breathtaking view of the boulder-strewn landscape. Local legends say this hill is where Hanuman was born. The river can be crossed in a traditional coracle ferry—available at multiple points near popular landmarks such as Virupapur Gadde, Kodandarama Temple, or Vittala Temple—to reach the

▼ A temple dedicated to Hanuman atop the Anjanadri Hill in Karnataka, India.

base of the hill. Then, a zigzag 575-step climb leads to a temple on top of the hill, dedicated to Hanuman (who is known in southern Indian traditions as Anjaneya). Besides a rock-carved idol of the god, the temple also has shrines honoring Rama and Sita. The climb to the top of the hill is worth it, with stunning views of expansive coconut plantations, paddy fields, and the Tungabhadra River. The ruins of Hampi are across the river and is where, it is believed, the kingdom of Kishkindha once stood.

Anjanadri Hill
(Andhra Pradesh, India)

The seven sacred hills of Tirumala are believed to represent the hood of Sheshanaga, the serpent god with five hoods. One of those hills is Anjanadri, a pilgrimage for those who believe that Hanuman was born there. A spring here, Swami Pushkarini, is believed by devotees to cleanse all sins with a single dip.

About 2 miles (3km) away is the Akasha Ganga waterfalls. This is where, it is believed, Anjana performed severe austerities. Lost in penance, she went without food for days. Worried about her, the god of wind dropped a fruit into her hand every day—which was all she ate. She became pregnant after eating the fruit and gave birth to Hanuman.

The beautiful waterfall is also the source for all the water used for the rituals at the temple. Tirumala is widely known for its Ventakeswara Temple, one of India's richest and most visited Hindu temples.

▼ Tirumala Hills in Andhra Pradesh, India.

MICKEY MOUSE

Artists and devotees dressed as Hanuman often attend processions on Hindu festivals such as Hanuman Jayanti (commemorating Hanuman's birth) and Diwali (festival of lights).

SUGRIVA'S SANCTUM

HAMPI, KARNATAKA (INDIA)

Help came from the most unexpected of quarters. As Rama and Lakshmana searched for Sita, they encountered the terrifying Kabandha. A giant with neither a head nor a neck, a single eye on his chest, and the face on his stomach, Kabandha attacked the brothers. Rama managed to cut off his right arm and Lakshmana his left. As Kabandha lay dying, he thanked the two princes—this was his salvation. He then told them to find the vanara king Sugriva, who lived in a cave on the Rishyamukha mountain, east of the Pampa Lake, in Kishkindha. It would be a daunting quest, Kabandha warned Rama, but worth his while, for the vanara had a vast army that could help him find Sita. So, the two princes set off to find Sugriva, who would go on to become their staunch ally.

The rugged landscape in and around Hampi in southern India's eastern Karnataka—the last capital of the 14th-century Vijayanagara empire—stands over what is believed to have been a part of the Kishkindha kingdom. It is no surprise then that key locations in and around the ancient town are linked to the epic—from the lake where Rama took a dip, the cave where Sugriva sought shelter, to the place where the two princes met Hanuman. Besides this, the vast ruins of temples and palaces at Hampi display stunning bas-relief sculptures that also draw on stories from the *Ramayana*.

Waiting for Rama

In a secluded valley, surrounded by boulder-strewn hills on three sides, lies a lake. It is here that Shabari, it is said, met Rama. The woman, an elderly ascetic, had waited years to meet the

◂ Rama, Lakshmana, and the vanara king Sugriva talk about the search for Sita in this painting from Punjab Hills, dated the early 1700s.

prince and, on seeing him, offered fruits she had collected from the forest on the banks of the Pampa River.

He accepted her hospitality, after which she asked for liberation—it was her time to die. Rama gave her leave to do so, and she departed for heaven. In later versions, Shabari tastes each berry before offering them to Rama. (This is perceived as a breach of the norm because of the idea that half-eaten food is unfit for consumption, as well as an indication that Shabari belonged to a community considered to be on a lower rung of the social hierarchy. Rama chose to overlook this.)

The lake, a few miles from the historic village of Anegundi on the northern banks of the Tungabhadra River, is also said to be where Parvati performed penance for Shiva. A shrine to Shiva and Parvati marks this event.

Meeting a friend

After liberating Shabari, Rama and Lakshmana made their way to the Rishyamukha mountain and Sugriva's home. This is where they met Hanuman for the first time. It is believed that Rishimukh Hill, a couple of miles from Pampa Sarovar on the northern bank of the Tungabhadra, is that very mountain. Today, it provides a sweeping vantage point for the stunning ruins of Hampi across the river.

Sugriva's Cave

Hanuman took the brothers to meet Sugriva who, fearing his brother Vali, had retreated to a cave on the Rishyamukha mountain. Vali had been cursed by a sage, which prevented him from entering the mountain. When the princes met Sugriva, he gave them the shawl and ornaments Sita had dropped while being carried to Lanka. It is believed this meeting took place at a cave in Hampi, which is located on the opposite side of the Tungabhadra from Rishimukh Hill, and is a natural formation close to the Kodandarama Temple. Locals believe that this temple is the location where Rama killed Vali and crowned Sugriva as the king of Kishkindha.

▲ Sugriva's Cave *(top)*; Virupaksha Temple *(below)*, in Hampi.

Cursed and banned

The Matanga Hill, just over half a mile from Sugriva's Cave at Hampi, is located at the center of the ruins, and is the highest point in the area. This is supposed to be where the sage Matanga's hermitage once stood. The sage cursed Vali and prohibited him from entering the Rishyamukha mountain, after the vanara killed an asura. A short trek up the stepway brings one to the exquisite Veerabhadra Temple on top of the hill. One path leads to the Achyuta Raya Temple, a magnificent example of Vijayanagara architecture.

A LEAP ACROSS THE OCEAN

MAHENDRAGIRI, ODISHA (INDIA)

Sugriva's search parties looked for Sita everywhere, until Vali's son Angada met the vulture king Sampati, who told them that Sita had been taken across the ocean to the island of Lanka. But, how would they cross the ocean? The vanaras realized that there was only one among them powerful enough to leap across the ocean: their general, Hanuman. The vanara, who was also the son of the wind god, was delighted. He took on an immense form, roared, leaped from the great mountain Mahendra with such force that he nearly crushed it, and flew toward Lanka.

There is often an element of arduousness to pilgrim trails that seek to be an end in itself—if you have made it, you were worthy; if you do not, you were never meant to. Mahendragiri in India's eastern state of Odisha may not be among the toughest religious treks in India, but completing it does require more than a whim. It is a little out of the way, remote even, and the trek does require a certain amount of hardiness. When one reaches the destination, however, it is easy to see why nature evokes spirituality. For as far as the eye can see, the tranquil land is cloaked in forests and hills.

Mahendragiri is part of an unbroken chain of hills from the Mahanadi to the Godavari in the Eastern Ghats and, at an elevation of 4,920ft (1,500m), is a fairly high formation. It is perhaps the reason why local legends suggest that the site called Hanuman Kuda is the place from where Hanuman leaped across the ocean.

Epic connection

The forest-covered hill is believed to be a Kula Parvata, or the mountain of a clan, mentioned in the ancient Hindu religious texts of the *Puranas*. It is associated with two other legends besides that of Hanuman. One is of the Pandavas—the five brothers at the center of the story of the *Mahabharata* who sought refuge here with their mother, Kunti, during their 12-year

◀ Mahendragiri, the second-highest point in Odisha.

exile. The other is of Parashurama, the sixth incarnation of Vishnu who did his penance here and never died.

Markers of these stories line the trek route. At the foothills on the eastern side lies the Kunti Temple. A short walk up leads to a temple dedicated to Yudhisthira, the eldest of the Pandavas, and then the second brother, Bhima. Each of these is a stone temple—sparse, unembellished. The formation named after Arjuna, the third brother, is a cave temple dedicated to Shiva.

From the top of the hill, originates the Mahendra Tanaya River, which merges with the Vamsadhara in the neighboring state of Andhra Pradesh. This is also where the smaller fiefdoms of the 2nd-century BCE Kalinga (roughly corresponding to the state of Odisha) organized themselves.

▲ A Liebig collectors' card dating 1931 depicts Hanuman as he leaps across the ocean to Lanka.

WHERE IS SITA?

RAMBODA, CENTRAL PROVINCE (SRI LANKA)

▼ The unique Puna Ella Falls, Ramboda.

Hanuman crossed the ocean and upon reaching Lanka started scouring the glorious city for signs of Sita. He was enthralled by its magnificence. He saw the palaces of great rakshasa warriors and wandered through them in hopes of finding Sita. He chanced upon Ravana's palace and entered the inner apartments, but was flummoxed. There was no trace of Sita. As he leaped from one part of the palace to another, he spotted a beautiful grove with silver and gold trees. He entered, climbed to the very top of a tree, and looked around. Suddenly, he saw her. Sita, crestfallen, despairing, sitting under a tree, and waiting for Rama.

In the central highlands of Sri Lanka, past the lush tea plantations of the hill station of Nuwara Eliya as one drives north, lies Ramboda. At an elevation of nearly 3,300ft (1,000m), this small village is a cool refuge in a warm country, and offers spectacular views of the green landscape. Perched on a hill is a temple dedicated to Hanuman, the Ramboda Bhaktha Hanuman Temple. This is where Hanuman is believed to have rested as he looked for Sita. Built in 1999 by an organization founded by Indian spiritual thinker Chinmayananda, the temple has a massive 16ft (4.8m) Hanuman statue carved out of granite. Every *poya* (full moon), thousands of devotees arrive to participate in the special prayers that are held here. Hanuman Jayanti, or Hanuman's birthday, is celebrated in spring and is another good time to visit the area. The festivities take place for 10 days, culminating in grand prayers and spectacular parades.

The anchors of the *Ramayana* associations of this area possibly lie in the history of the tea gardens around it. Here, 19th-century colonial administrations brought in Tamil people to work on the plantations, who brought with them their cultures and belief systems. Evidence of the gradual development of these *Ramayana*-centered narratives lies in the local lore built around the landscape.

At Ramboda, a stretch of barren land near the temple, called Chariot Path, is believed to mark the route along which Ravana took Sita to the ashoka grove

▶ Sita looks at Rama's ring as Hanuman looks on from his hiding place in the tree, in this painting from the late 1800s, created under the patronage of Abd al-Rahim, an important minister in Mughal emperor Akbar's court.

where Hanuman eventually found her. A pond nearby has been named Sita Tear Pond, said to have been formed out of Sita's tears as she waited for Rama. In fact, the name of the village, Ramboda, is tied to the *Ramayana* story as well. The Tamil word for Ramboda, *Rampadai*, means Rama's force. So, it is also said to be where Rama set up one of his army camps for the vanara and riksha forces during the battle of Lanka. Across the temple lies a mountain range known as Ravanaboda, where Ravana's army is said to have been stationed during the battle. The local lore is that the silhouette of the mountain line resembles a reclining Hanuman—and so, the colloquial name for the range is Sleeping Hanuman.

Ramboda is best known for its breathtaking waterfall. The Ramboda Falls (also known as the Puna Falls) drops from a height of 360ft (110m) on one of the highest plains of the central highlands. It cascades down two tiers of rock, with stark white water dropping into a rocky pool. Nature enthusiasts can make the 1.2-mile- (2-km-) uphill trek to reach the stunning site.

MANDODARI'S WEDDING

MADHYA PRADESH AND RAJASTHAN (INDIA)

As Hanuman searched for Sita, he wandered through the inner apartments of Ravana's palace in Lanka, and saw a beautiful queen. This must be Sita, he thought. But it wasn't. This was Mandodari, Ravana's chief queen and a comfort to Sita during her captivity. The princess was born to the apsara Hema and the master architect of the danavas, Maya. It was Maya who chanced upon Ravana when he was out on a hunt, and offered him Mandodari's hand in marriage. Ravana did not waste a moment—he lit a sacred fire and married her. Pleased, Maya presented him with a javelin that would never miss its mark. Ravana later used this weapon to strike down Lakshmana on the battlefield of Lanka.

The *Ramayana* does not identify any terrestrial location for Mandodari's birth and the early years of her youth. Later Hindu traditions in India have adopted Lanka's pious queen into the canon of "ideal" wives to be revered. As an extension of this interpretation, it is believed that two ancient towns in western and central India, both with rich archaeological histories, are where Mandodari grew up and married Ravana.

Mandore (Rajasthan, India)

It is believed that Mandodari was born in the ancient town of Mandore, about 12.4 miles (20km) from Jodhpur. A red stone temple with rock carvings, known as Ravana ki Chhanwari, is said to be the pavilion where Mandodari married Ravana. Contemporary belief holds that Ravana is the local community's kin.

Less than a mile from the temple is Mandore Garden, once the cremation grounds for the powerful rulers of Marwar. Now it hosts an annual festival, the Veerpuri Fair, in the month of Shravana in the Hindu calendar (which falls in the rainy season between July and August) to commemorate the heroes of what is now the state of Rajasthan. This garden also has a Hall of Heroes with images of legendary local heroes carved out of a massive rock. The festival is said to have originated in the 17th century when the ruler of Mandore

▼ The temples in Mandore Garden, Rajasthan.

survived a challenging battle and built a memorial to those who showed courage in testing times. Behind the gardens are the ruins of the 6th-century Mandore Fort, the ruling clan's capital until the 15th century, after which it moved to Jodhpur.

Mandsaur (Madhya Pradesh, India)
About 93.2 miles (150km) from the Hindu pilgrimage site Ujjain, is Mandsaur, a town in northern Madhya Pradesh, also believed to be Mandodari's birthplace. Here, Ravana is worshipped on Dussehra, his effigies are not burned, and the king of Lanka is considered to be part of the town's ancient familial history. In the town's Khanpur neighborhood, a towering 35ft (10.6m) statue of Ravana stands as a symbol of this reverence.

Like Rajasthan's Mandore, Mandsaur, too, is an ancient town—its archaeological heritage dates back to at least the 5th century CE. The revered Pashupatinath Temple, dedicated to the god of destruction, Shiva, is on the banks of the Shivna River. Just a few miles from the temple is the Mandsaur Fort, a massive 15th-century fortification with 12 gates.

▶ Mandodari admonishes her husband Ravana as guards patrol the palace grounds, in this painting, dated around 1605, possibly from what was once the kingdom of Datia in present-day Madhya Pradesh.

VIBHISHANA MEETS RAMA

KOTHANDARAMASWAMY TEMPLE, TAMIL NADU (INDIA)

▼ In this *c.*1790 painting, Hanuman, accompanied by Vibhishana, is depicted approaching the brothers with a handful of herbs to revive them.

Like Ravana's wife Mandodari, Vibhishana too is portrayed in a virtuous light in Valmiki's *Ramayana*. One of Ravana's younger brothers, he was shocked when Ravana abducted Sita and tried to reason with him to return her. He reasoned that there was no point in provoking a powerful man, such as Rama. Ravana paid no heed and castigated his younger brother. Vibhishana decided to leave Ravana and sought refuge with Rama and Lakshmana and offered his help to defeat Ravana. While some vanaras cautioned Rama as Vibhishana could have been a spy, Hanuman chose to trust him. Rama agreed and accepted Vibhishana as his friend and ally.

▲ Kothandaramaswamy Temple, Dhanushkodi, Tamil Nadu, India.

Detached from the Indian mainland, Pamban Island lies off the southeastern coast of Tamil Nadu—connected via a spectacular bridge halfway to Dhanushkodi, the last point on the Indian side leading to Adam's Bridge in Sri Lanka. The island has a temple dedicated to a bow-wielding Rama, the Kothandaramaswamy Temple, where Vibhishana is believed to have sought refuge with the prince after leaving Ravana. It is also said to be where Rama consecrated Vibhishana as the king of Lanka after Ravana's defeat. The temple lies at the core of the Vibhishana lore in this region.

The temple might feel a little out of the way and is only accessible through a narrow street that leads to it without much fanfare. There is an unusual minimalism to its design—sparse arches, unembellished roof, and unadorned corridors. It displays modern influences with some elements of traditional temple architecture, such as the ornate dome that crowns its roof. The temple is surrounded by the ocean and the view, along with the unassuming construction, makes it a beautiful point for quiet reflection.

Inside, the sanctum are idols of Rama, Lakshmana, Sita, Hanuman, and Vibhishana. The walls are adorned with beautiful paintings depicting stories from the *Ramayana*. Among the few structures to survive the 1964 cyclone, the temple was restored in the late 1970s.

According to another local legend, a small temple atop a hillock, near the Kothandaramaswamy Temple, is where Vibhishana met Rama. Called the Gandamadana Parvatham, it is the highest point of Rameswaram, with an enchanting view of the island and the wide expanse of the ocean all around.

"All welfare to you; I will leave—may you be happy without me. Nightstalker! The words spoken by me as I ... tried to restrain you, did not please. Men who are overtaken by death ... don't accept beneficial speech uttered by well-wishers."

Vibhishana tells Ravana before leaving Lanka, Sarga 10, Yuddha Kanda

▶ This illustration from a 16th-century manuscript depicts Rama, Lakshmana, and the vanara and riksha forces laying siege to Ravana's citadel.

SUGRIVA DECLARES WAR

DEWUNDARA OR DONDRA, SOUTHERN PROVINCE (SRI LANKA)

To reach Ravana's citadel in Lanka, the vanara army crossed a bridge that they built across the ocean and camped near Mount Suvela. Vibhishana told Rama, Lakshmana, and Sugriva all he knew about Ravana's fortifications and military strength. With a plan in place, they climbed Mount Suvela to survey Lanka. They observed Ravana's citadel and stationed their forces at strategic points. Sugriva positioned himself at the central encampment with millions of vanara soldiers, west of Rama's post. Rama sent Vali's son Angada to Ravana with a message of threat and doom. Ravana ordered his soldiers to kill the messenger, but Angada escaped. The vanara army laid siege to the citadel. When Ravana saw his city being surrounded by the vanara and riksha forces, he ordered his troops to go into the battlefield with full force. The battle of Lanka had begun.

The ancient port town of Dondra is at the southernmost point of Sri Lanka, about 3.7 miles (6km) from the city of Matara in the Southern Province. In local *Ramayana* lore, Dondra is believed to be the place where Sugriva set up an encampment for his army and launched the attack on Ravana's forces.

One of the most important religious sites in town is the Upulvan Devalaya, also known as Sri Vishnu Maha Devalaya or simply Vishnu Devalaya.

The striking blue temple is constructed on vaulted arches as a three-story building. It is flanked by a 60ft (18m) Buddha statue. According to local legend, Dondra was once the seat of a lotus-blue guardian-deity, Upulvan. In early Buddhist chronicles, Upulvan is described as Sri Lanka's guardian deity. As Hindu influences gradually blended with Sri Lankan Buddhist traditions, Upulvan became increasingly identified with Vishnu, and the temple gradually became known as Sri Vishnu Maha Devalaya.

The Upulvan Devalaya is said to have been built by the 7th-century king Dapulla I, with subsequent kings expanding the temple complex. It is thought to have once spanned an extensive area as a Buddhist monastic complex, with gilded roofs that were visible from afar. In the 16th century, the Portuguese destroyed the temple, which King Rajasinghe II of Kandy rebuilt in the 17th century. Some regional folklore also draws an association with the *Ramayana*, with the belief that the temple was built to commemorate the divine intervention of Vishnu in the battle between Rama and Ravana.

Another popular site toward the north of the town is the Weherahena Buddhist Temple. It is widely regarded as one of the most spectacular temples in the region, with a colossal seated Buddha statue. The temple features thousands of wall paintings depicting stories from the *Jataka Tales* and intricate carvings.

One of the most charming spots in Dondra is a 19th-century lighthouse. While it is not open to the public, the location warrants a visit for the spectacular views of the Indian Ocean and adjoining lagoons.

▲ The unique, blue-colored Upulvan Devalaya Temple combines elements of traditional temple and Buddhist architecture.

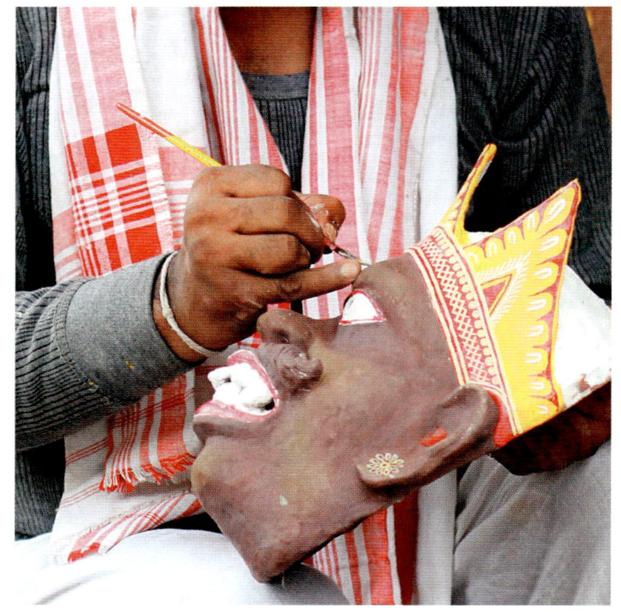

CULTURE

BHAONA MASK DANCE

REPRESENTING RAVANA'S ACOLYTES

A riverine island in northeastern India preserves a mask-making and performance tradition based on Hindu texts. Its most spectacular manifestations are representations of supernatural beings, such as the rakshasas of the *Ramayana*.

Every year Majuli loses a little bit of itself. The changing environment has not been kind to this riverine island in the Brahmaputra, and it has been eroding inch by inch. Rooted in this shrinking island is a spiritual tradition that moved away from rituals and wove cultural expression into its religious practices. In the 16th century, a neo-Vaishnavite culture emerged in Majuli, centered on the institution of the Satra—monasteries where communities gathered to engage with religious texts and, later, cultural forms. Bhaona, a folk drama, belongs to this tradition. It is based on one-act plays composed by the poet Sankaradeva, who led the neo-Vaishnavite movement. Called Ankiya Nat, the plays narrate episodes from Hindu mythology featuring Vishnu and his many forms, such as Rama, and have been traditionally performed in the prayer halls of satras.

Performers of Ankiya Nat don elaborate Bhaona masks, meant to reflect the essence of the play's characters. The most striking are those representing the rakshasas from the *Ramayana*. The masks vary in size—massive ones cover the head and torso (*bor mukha*), large face masks that are flexible (*lotokari mukha*), and small masks for the face (*mukh mukha*). The size corresponds to the power of the mythical characters. For instance, *bor mukhas* are used for larger-than-life characters, such as Ravana or Kumbhakarna, *lotokari mukhas* for those like the rakshasa Trishira, and *mukh mukhas* for those like Surpanakha and Maricha. One can experience this tradition at the Notun Samaguri Satra, about 8 miles (13km) from the Kamalabari Ghat, where the ferry from Nimati Ghat in Jorhat lands. The ideal time to visit is during the annual Raas Mahotsav, organized in October and November.

◀ **Clockwise from top left:** artist applies color to a mask; a *bor mukha* mask; artist creates frame of a mask using bamboo; Bhaona performers rehearse before a show; some examples of Bhaona performances; artist gives final touches to a mask.

MEGHANADA'S PENANCE

PATALKOT, MADHYA PRADESH (INDIA)

The battle of Lanka began and it soon became clear that the most terrifying and formidable adversary would be Ravana's son Meghanada. The Lankan prince had performed seven elaborate sacrificial rituals to earn favor from Shiva, the god of destruction and one of the Trinity. Pleased, Shiva granted Meghanada formidable powers: from an indestructible flying chariot and a quiver of arrows that would never run out, to a weapon to crush his opponents. He was also given the power of illusion, which made it impossible for gods and asuras to track his movements during battle. The powers made him unassailable on the battlefield.

▲ The Satpura ranges surround Patalkot and are home to the Bharia tribe.

So dramatic is the sweep of Patalkot's terrain that the only way to truly appreciate it is from a distance. Looking down from the hilltop of Tamia, about 15.5 miles (25km) away, one begins to see why Patalkot inspires stories of the grand mythical. This horseshoe-shaped valley, spread across 8,000 hectares (80 sq km) in southern Madhya Pradesh, is 1,300ft (400m) deep, lined by a steep gorge and covered in dense forests. Its depth is often assumed to be the reason the valley got its name—in Sanskrit *patal* means the netherworld and *kot* means fort.

The legend around this etymology has also lent itself to stories—built on myths—that reimagine Patalkot as a portal to subterranean routes and distant worlds. Therefore, to the believers of the *Ramayana* tradition, Patalkot is the point from where Meghanada made his way back to Lanka through an underground route after gaining Shiva's grace.

Patalkot has been home to the Gond and Bharia—Indigenous communities that practice subsistence agriculture. The Meghananda myth became associated with these communities due to an Indigenous festival, the Meghanada Festival, celebrated annually by the Gond around the time of Holi. While some scholars think that

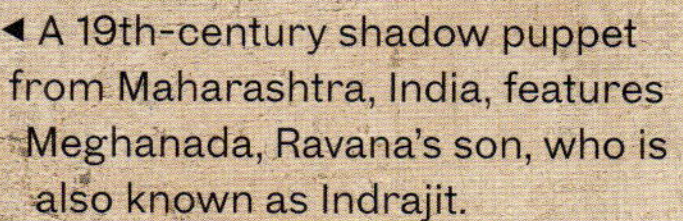

◄ A 19th-century shadow puppet from Maharashtra, India, features Meghanada, Ravana's son, who is also known as Indrajit.

this festival has nothing to do with the Meghanada of the *Ramayana,* and the name allowed dominant Hindu communities to associate the Indigenous celebration with Hindu rituals, others believe the festival is part of the Ravana-worship culture prevalent among the Gond, and observed in other parts of India. During the festival, the community erects a pole of wood symbolizing Meghanada, called Khandera, and all gather around it in celebration.

Besides the religious and the mythical, the valley's secular celebrations are also spectacular occasions. Indigenous dance forms—such as the Bhadam, Saitam, Saila, and Ahirai—are performed during weddings, to the accompaniment of traditional musical instruments like the *dhol* (a two-sided drum) and cymbals.

The Bharia community comprises skilled artisans, making objects out of the leaves of wild dates—locally called *chhind.* This is a probable source of the name of Chhindwara, a town 50 miles (80km) from Patalkot and the district within which it lies.

QUEST FOR REVIVING HERBS

NORTHERN AND SOUTHERN INDIA, AND SRI LANKA

Twice Hanuman leaped into the sky and flew to the Himalayas to retrieve life-saving herbs, and twice, he brought an entire mountain back with him. Both the instances are iconic moments in the *Ramayana*. The first was when Meghanada's arrows struck Rama and Lakshmana. As they lay injured on the battlefield, Hanuman flew between Kailasa and Rishabha to search for medicinal herbs. But the herbs made themselves invisible, so an exasperated Hanuman uprooted the entire mountain of medicinal herbs and took it back with him. After the princes of Ayodhya were revived, he returned the mountain to the Himalayas. With the death of Meghanada, a furious Ravana took the battlefield and injured Lakshmana. As a distraught Rama mourned his brother who lay unconscious, Hanuman returned to the Himalayas. Once more, unable to find the herbs and worried that he would be too late, he lifted the entire mountain and took it back with him. At the battlefield, the physician Sushena gave Lakshmana the medicines and the prince opened his eyes.

Jagged mountains laden with dense forests across an axis from northern India to southern Sri Lanka are believed to mark the trail of Hanuman's flight to seek the medicinal herbs that would revive Rama and Lakshmana on the battlefield. Many of these sites have expansive medicinal plant covers, which might explain their association with these legends.

Jakhu Temple (Himachal Pradesh, India)

As per local legend, the first stop on Hanuman's quest was the Jakhu Hill in present-day Shimla, where the vanara general stopped to ask the sage Yaku for directions to the mountain of healing herbs. A temple on the hill marks the spot where this encounter took place. It is about 1.2 miles (2km) from Shimla's

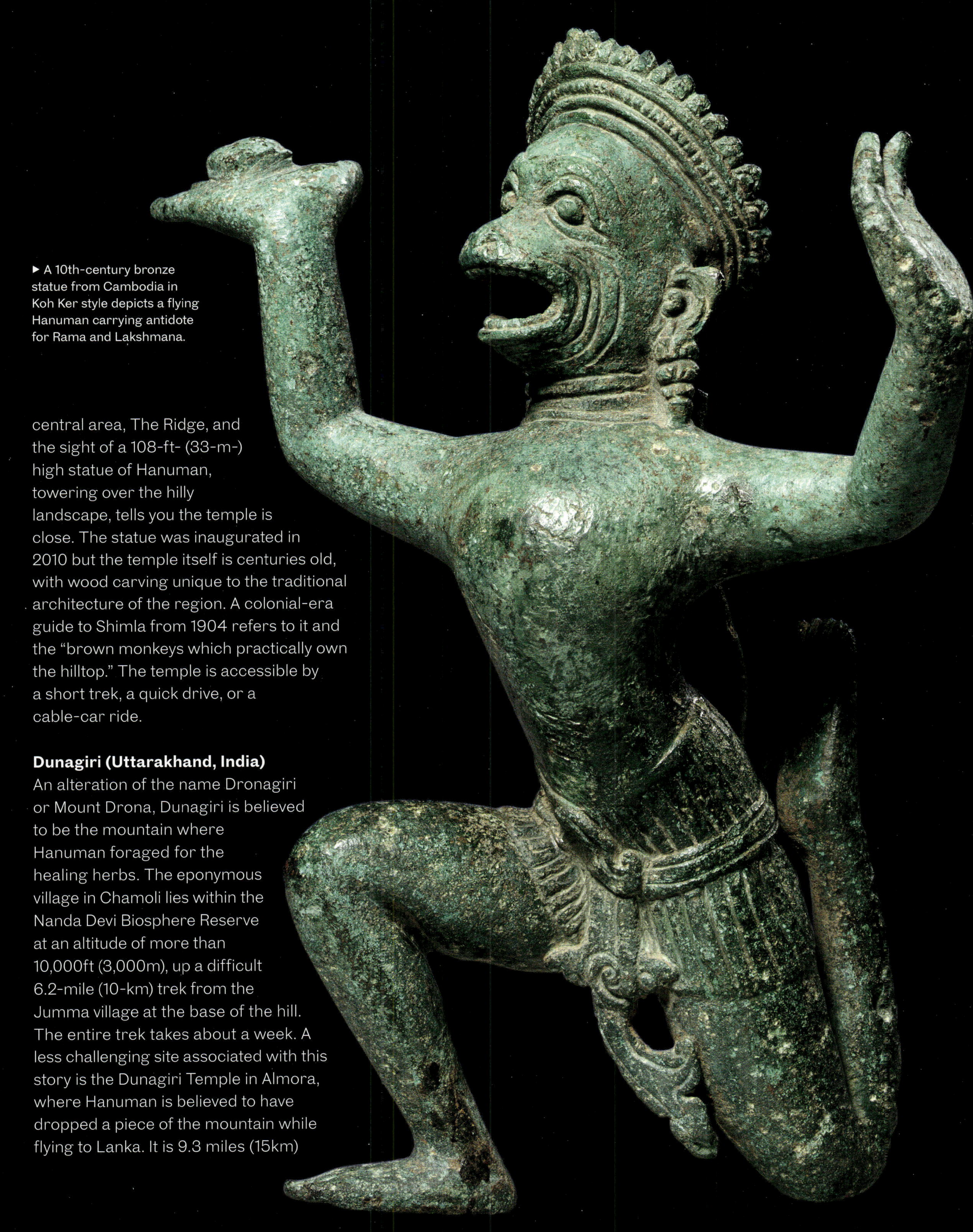

▶ A 10th-century bronze statue from Cambodia in Koh Ker style depicts a flying Hanuman carrying antidote for Rama and Lakshmana.

central area, The Ridge, and the sight of a 108-ft- (33-m-) high statue of Hanuman, towering over the hilly landscape, tells you the temple is close. The statue was inaugurated in 2010 but the temple itself is centuries old, with wood carving unique to the traditional architecture of the region. A colonial-era guide to Shimla from 1904 refers to it and the "brown monkeys which practically own the hilltop." The temple is accessible by a short trek, a quick drive, or a cable-car ride.

Dunagiri (Uttarakhand, India)
An alteration of the name Dronagiri or Mount Drona, Dunagiri is believed to be the mountain where Hanuman foraged for the healing herbs. The eponymous village in Chamoli lies within the Nanda Devi Biosphere Reserve at an altitude of more than 10,000ft (3,000m), up a difficult 6.2-mile (10-km) trek from the Jumma village at the base of the hill. The entire trek takes about a week. A less challenging site associated with this story is the Dunagiri Temple in Almora, where Hanuman is believed to have dropped a piece of the mountain while flying to Lanka. It is 9.3 miles (15km)

Having gone to the herb mountain, the glorious Hanuman became concerned, not recognizing the great herbs. Then, a thought rose in the immeasurably powerful son of wind: "I shall leave with the mountain peak itself."

After Lakshmana is struck a second time, Sarga 89, Yuddha Kanda

away from the town of Dwarahat, which itself is about 124 miles (200km) from Jumma village. The path leading up to the temple is a steep climb, comprising 365 steps.

Sanjeevi Hills (Tamil Nadu, India)
About 62 miles (100km) from the culturally significant pilgrim town of Madurai, a group of hillocks in the textile town of Rajapalayam is believed to be the fragments of the mountain of healing herbs that Hanuman carried to Lanka. It is a popular hiking trail, ending at a temple dedicated to the Hindu god of war Murugan, or Kartikeya, on top of the hill.

Ritigala Mountain (North Central Province, Sri Lanka)
According to local Sri Lankan folklore, as Hanuman flew back carrying the mountain of healing herbs, fragments of it broke off and scattered across various locations in Sri Lanka. One such site is Ritigala, renowned for its rare medicinal plants and herbs, many of which are not found elsewhere on the island. This has reinforced the legend that a portion of the mountain, bearing the Sanjeevani herb, fell here. The presence of non-native plant species is often cited as compelling evidence linking Ritigala to the *Ramayana*.

▼ Sanjeevi Hills form the southernmost tip of the Western Ghats range in Tamil Nadu.

Designated as a "strict nature reserve" because of its rich but sensitive biodiversity, all of Ritigala is not open to the public. Parts that are open lead to the stunning ruins of a massive monastery complex in the Ritigala forest. The monastery was built in the 9th century for an order of Buddhist monks who practiced extreme austerities, and was abandoned around the 12th century. Ritigala is about 31 miles (50km) from Anuradhapura, an ancient seat of power for nearly 1,300 years. A UNESCO World Heritage Site, Anuradhapura is one of the most sacred Buddhist pilgrimage destinations in the world, known for its massive stupas, ancient monasteries, and advanced irrigation systems, making it a major tourist and historical site in Sri Lanka.

Dolukanda Mountain (North-Western Province, Sri Lanka)

Like Ritigala, Dolukanda Mountain is also the site of an ancient forest monastery belonging to the Pamsukulika sect—an order of Theravada Buddhists who practiced absolute asceticism. The monastery, Arankele, lies at the foot of the mountain. Dolukanda Mountain is believed to have been the herbarium of Buddhadasa, a king of Anuradhapura in the 4th century CE.

About 12.4 miles (20km) from the city of Kurunegala, Dolukanda Mountain, like Ritigala, is home to rare medicinal plants, many of which are similar to those found in the Himalayan region. This has reinforced the legend that Dolukanda Mountain is one of the sites where a fragment of the healing mountain fell as Hanuman, carrying the life-saving Sanjeevani herb, rushed to save Lakshmana.

Rumassala Mountain (Southern Province, Sri Lanka)

Some 3.1 miles (5km) from the port city of Galle, Rumassala has long been known for the diversity of its rare medicinal plants, many of which are not native to Sri Lanka. As in the case of Ritigala and Dolukanda, this lends itself to the story of Hanuman's quest to bring healing herbs from the Himalayas to the battlefield at Lanka—Rumassala is also considered to be one of the spots where a piece of the mountain fell.

▲ The Japanese Peace Pagoda at Rumassala Mountain, Sri Lanka.

A steep climb from the western end of the Unawatuna beach to the top of the mountains leads to the Japanese Peace Pagoda, which offers a breathtaking view of the seascape. It is also famous for coral reefs, making it a popular spot for snorkeling and diving.

When British science-fiction writer Arthur C. Clarke made Sri Lanka his home, the Unawatuna beach was where he lived for more than a decade.

The beautiful Jungle beach in Galle, Sri Lanka, located at the foot of the Rumasalla Mountain, is known for its calm, clear waters.

A PRAYER FOR VICTORY

GAYATHRI PEEDAM, CENTRAL PROVINCE (SRI LANKA)

As the battle of Lanka raged on, Meghanada used an illusion to make the vanaras believe that he had killed Sita. As Rama, Lakshmana, and the vanaras grieved, Meghanada withdrew to a shrine to perform a ritual that would make him invincible. Vibhishana learned of his nephew's plans and informed Rama. He told the exiled prince to send Lakshmana to disrupt the sacrificial ritual. This was the only way to kill Meghanada, Vibhishana told them. Lakshmana rushed to a banyan tree inside a huge grove—the site of the sacrifice— while Hanuman drew Meghanada out. Meghanada emerged and Lakshmana challenged him to a direct combat. Vibhishana acted as Lakshmana's second and the duel began. After a prolonged fight, Lakshmana used a divine arrow that belonged to god Indra to strike Meghanada. It was enough to kill him. Meghanada had finally been vanquished.

Nestled in the northern part of Nuwara Eliya, a charming hill town in the Central Province known for its cool climate, colonial architecture, and picturesque landscapes, is Gayathri Peedam, a temple dedicated to Veda Mata (the mother of the *Vedas*) or Gayathri. Surrounded by lush greenery and sprawling tea plantations, the temple offers a serene and peaceful atmosphere. It is believed to stand at the site where Meghanada was performing the ritual for his success in the battle in Lanka.

Local lore adds that it is also where earlier the three principal deities—creator god Brahma, preserver god Vishnu, and destroyer god Shiva—appeared to acknowledge Meghanada's power because of his arduous prayers.

Swami Murugesu Maharishi, a popular spiritual leader of the region and also known as Gayathri Siddhar, founded the temple in the 1970s to spread the teachings of the Gayathri Mantra. Gayathri Peedam has a fairly simple architecture—the exterior is plain and modern, while the sanctum follows a traditional design.

Depictions of Shiva and his wife Parvati, Vinayagar (a manifestation of Ganesha, the Hindu god of wisdom, and the son of Shiva and Parvati), and Subramanyam (a manifestation of Kartikeya, the Hindu god of war and another of Shiva's sons) adorn the entrance. A five-headed idol of Gayathri in a meditative posture lies at the center of the sanctum and is surrounded by different forms of the goddess—such as Rama Gayathri, Vishnu Gayathri, and Krishna Gayathri. The tower above the

◄ The hilly plains of Nuwara Eliya, behind Lake Gregory.

sanctum showcases influences of north Indian architectural styles, and a stucco Shivalinga sits on the roof.

Other connections

The landscape of Nuwara Eliya is dotted with places associated with the Ravana mythology. The Hakgala Botanical Garden, for instance, is believed to be part of the larger Ashoka Vatika within which Sita was held captive. The Seetha Amman Temple is where Sita is thought to have been detained during her captivity in Lanka. One possible explanation for this could be the history of the town, developed out of a virtually uninhabited piece of land by colonial British administrators who set up tea plantations in the hills. Tamil workers were brought in to work on the plantations, and the stories from the *Ramayana* traveled with them.

For a panoramic view of the Nuwara Eliya town, head to the Lover's Leap Waterfall, about 4.3 miles (7km) from the town's center, or to the Moon Plains, a wide valley with circular plains and breathtaking views, about 1.2 miles (2km) away.

▼ This *c.*1820 painting depicts Meghanada attacking Rama and Lakshmana with arrows that turn into snakes, while the vanara and riksha forces try to repel the attack.

◂ This carving of Vibhishana with his consort Sarama is from the temple at Kelaniya. It depicts Lakshmana crowning Vibhishana by placing a garland around his neck.

VIBHISHANA IS KING

KELANIYA (SRI LANKA)

The battle of Lanka ended. Ravana was dead. The throne of Lanka lay empty. Rama turned to Lakshmana and instructed him to crown the wise Vibhishana as the new king. Lakshmana followed his brother's instructions and the people of Lanka were delighted to witness the consecration of Vibhishana, who had always remained devoted to Rama.

The story of the Kelaniya Raja Maha Viharaya Temple is intertwined with the ebb and flow of Sri Lanka's history. In popular imagination, its fate is linked to that of the nation. It is believed to have been constructed before the country's recorded history. Over centuries, it is said to have fallen into ruins and rebuilt more than once.

Overlapping histories

The temple at Kelaniya is located about 6.2 miles (10km) from Colombo. Last rebuilt in the 18th century, it is said to have been modeled on the temple destroyed by the Portuguese in the 16th century. However, it is known for another enduring history. The temple is supposed to have lodged a shrine to Vibhishana for at least six centuries and is said to be the spot where Vibhishana was consecrated as the king of Lanka. The western wall of the temple has an image of Vibhishana being crowned by Lakshmana, while the northern wall has one of Rama.

It is, however, a Buddhist temple and one of the many sites of the confluence of Buddhist and Hindu religious cultures. Intricate friezes portraying elephants (signifying fortitude in Buddhist thought), dwarfs (representing wealth), and geese (symbolizing the transmission of the Buddha's teachings) adorn the main building. Within the central hall lies a reclining Buddha, surrounded by 19th-century murals depicting Kandyan art and scenes from *Jataka Tales*, an ancient collection of Buddhist morality stories. Vibrant paintings portray Vibhishana—depicted as a rakshasa with distinctive features—alongside Saman, one of the island's guardian deities, in a celestial assembly.

Next to the temple lies the Kelaniya Stupa, believed to house a jeweled throne on which the Buddha sat during his third visit to the island (if and when the Buddha visited Sri Lanka has been a subject of debate among scholars for a while now). It has an imposing 18-ft- (5.5-m-) tall statue of the Bodhisattva Avalokitesvara, an enlightened embodiment of compassion.

▾ Sri Lankan tradition holds that Vibhishana's palace was situated on the banks of the Kelani River, near the present-day town of Kelaniya, which is named after the river.

CULTURE

SHATRUGHNA TEMPLES

VANQUISHING LAVANA

Rama's youngest brother, Shatrughna, plays an understated role through most of the epic, but communities across India revere the adventures of this impetuous prince and his many facets.

Considered the birthplace of Krishna, an incarnation of the creator god Vishnu, the city of Mathura in western Uttar Pradesh is steeped in Hindu culture and religion. One of its founding legends can be traced to the *Ramayana*.

When Rama was asked to confront the rakshasa Lavana, a nephew of Ravana, he sent Shatrughna to face him. Shatrughna waited until Lavana went foraging for food, leaving behind his magic lance that made him invincible. He killed the rakshasa with a divine arrow Rama had given him. Lavana's kingdom went to Shatrughna, and its capital is said to have been what is present-day Mathura. The Lavanasura Cave in the southern part of the city is believed to have been Lavana's abode, and a small temple of Shatrughna lies on the bank of a pond, Krishna Kund, at Maholi.

Another legend associated with Rama's youngest brother is commemorated in the lush landscape of Thrissur, in central Kerala, where a rare sanctuary devoted to Shatrughna is located. The Payammal Shatrughna Temple is an integral part of the revered Nalambalam set of four temples dedicated to the four princes of Ayodhya. Here, Shatrughna is believed to have been an incarnation of the creator god Vishnu's *sudarshan chakra* (a divine discus-shaped weapon). The architecture of these temples reflects a distinct Kerala style, characterized by the generous use of wood owing to the area's rich forest cover.

The hilly pilgrimage town of Rishikesh in Uttarakhand also has a temple dedicated to Shatrughna, next to the iconic Ram Jhula bridge. Its deity, Badrinarayana, is considered an incarnation of Vishnu.

▸ **Clockwise from top left:** Shatrughna slaying Lavana, from a 16th-century illustrated manuscript; a 19th-century depiction of Shatrughna as a young prince; a 13th-century copper sculpture from Tamil Nadu depicting Vishnu holding the sudarshan chakra in his right hand; entrance to the Payammal Shatrughna Temple in Kerala, India.

RAMA RELINQUISHES POWER

SHRAVASTI, UTTAR PRADESH (INDIA)

Yama, the god of death, arrived in Ayodhya and requested a private audience with Rama. Honoring his request, Rama instructed Lakshmana to stand guard at the door, warning him that anyone who dared enter would face death at his hands. As fate would have it, at that very moment, sage Durvasa arrived, demanding to see Rama immediately. When Lakshmana asked Durvasa to wait for Rama, the sage was furious and threatened to curse Ayodhya and its kings for all time to come. Lakshmana offered his life so that Durvasa would spare everyone else. So, Rama was forced to banish Lakshmana in order to honor his commitment. He was consumed with grief. He decided it was time to leave the world and bequeathed the kingdom to his brother Bharata. Bharata rejected the throne and asked Rama to anoint his sons, Kusha and Lava, instead. Rama then handed southern Kosala to Kusha and the northern regions to Lava, and prepared to leave the living world. Kusha set up as his capital, the city of Kushavati in the Vindhya mountains, and Lava established the city of Shravasti.

▲ Monks offering prayers at the ruins of the Jetavana Monastery in Shravasti, Uttar Pradesh, India.

The ancient town of Shravasti in northern Uttar Pradesh is an undeniable example of the confluence of Buddhist lore and Hindu mythology. Located by the Rapti River, it was the capital of the Kosalan kingdom from the 6th century BCE to the 6th century CE. Long known as one of the eight important centers associated with Buddhism, Shravasti is where the Buddha is said to have performed "the Great Miracle." When challenged by a nonbeliever, he levitated his body as fire leaped from his shoulders and water flowed from his feet.

The Ikshvaku lineage

In the *Ramayana* lore, Shravasti is believed to be where Rama's son Lava set up his capital and ruled over southern Kosala. Historians of the colonial period found no contradiction here—the lineage of

▶ This folio from a late 16th-century illustrated manuscript of Valmiki's *Ramayana* depicts Lava and Kusha chanting a poem before Rama.

Lava and the Buddha was the same, from the house of the Ikshvaku of Kosala, and the continuity in mythology and history of their capital was only to be expected.

Therefore, even though there is no site in Shravasti that commemorates any event of the *Ramayana* specifically, the city is said to have been passed down to generations of Ikshvaku rulers all the way from Lava to the Buddha.

The Jetavana Monastery is Shravasti's most prominent site. A wealthy merchant Sudatta, also known as Anathapindika, is believed to have donated the monastery to the Buddha, who spent much of his time here. There are ruins of temples and stupas dating back to 1st–2nd centuries CE at the site, among which stands the Gandhakuti (fragrant chamber, where the Buddha lived) as well as the Kosambakuti (meditation chamber). The grounds, once covered with a mango grove, has a Bodhi tree that Anathapindika planted from a sapling of the Mahabodhi tree—the sacred fig tree under which the Buddha attained enlightenment.

A little over half a mile away stand the ruins of the Angulimala Stupa. The story goes that Angulimala was a dreaded dacoit, whose name was derived from a necklace of the little fingers of his victims that he would wear (*anguli* means finger, and *mala* means necklace in Sanskrit). An encounter with the Buddha transformed him, and he gave up the life of cruelty and ruthlessness. The stupa is said to have been built by Angulimala for the Buddha. What remains of it now is a terraced structure on a rectangular platform—one can discern walls, a plinth, and a raised platform with stairs.

CULTURE

KALAMKARI

THE GRAND NARRATIVE

The temple town of Srikalahasti in the southern state of Andhra Pradesh in India preserves a centuries-old technique of painting to narrate stories, myths, and legends from the *Ramayana* on cloth.

Impossibly fine line drawings and a palette of softened colors make Kalamkari paintings immediately recognizable. The most starkly distinguishing aspect of the art form, however, might be the characters it portrays. They have distinct elongated eyes, animated hands, they are intricately ornamented, and when a character is a god—or a king—they don elaborate headgear. The key characters of the *Ramayana* are often both, royalty with a touch of the divine. In fact, Kalamkari has been immortalizing them in a tradition that goes back to the 15th century.

Kalamkari art is hand-drawn and then painted, and is likely to have originated from religious narrative traditions. The oldest surviving paintings have stylistic similarities to the temple murals of the Vijayanagara period, when Kalamkari paintings appear to have been used as hangings behind idols of gods, as canopies, as screens, and as visual references for reciters of episodes from epics such as the *Ramayana* or the *Mahabharata*. Since the primary association of the art was with the temple, it is only natural to find Kalamkari production centers emerging around temple towns.

The most important of these is Srikalahasti, a riverside town 24.8 miles (40km) from the pilgrimage center of Tirupati. Srikalahasti was the nodal point of Kalamkari production and trade between the 15th and early 20th centuries, largely due to its religious importance (tied to its Shaivite culture), its position by the river (an abundant supply of water is essential to the process), and the patronage of feudal landlords (the production process was expensive). A brief period of decline followed but by the 1950s, Srikalahasti's artisans organized themselves into workshops and started training others—the practice continues to this day in its traditional form, with its arduous 20-odd stages of production.

◂ **Clockwise from top left:** artist painting a Kalamkari design; outline of the design drawn on a fabric; painted fabric being washed in a tank of water; a *kalam* (pen) made of bamboo and natural vegetable dyes used for painting; Kalamkari depicting the story of the *Ramayana*.

06

The Ramayana's Trail

◂ This appliqué textile from *c.*1870–85, created by Burmese artist U. Paw Hnyun, depicts scenes from the *Thiri Rama*, the Burmese version of the *Ramayana*.

WHY RAMAYANA ENDURES

2,500 YEARS OF REINVENTION

The lives and adventures of Rama, Ravana, and Sita have been recounted and retold by saints, poets, scholars, and performers for centuries. Its abiding relevance is rooted in the powerful metaphor at the heart of the story—the triumph of righteousness.

Beyond its narrative allure, the *Ramayana* has played a crucial role in shaping collective identities and values of cultures across geographies and over centuries. It has provided a shared framework for moral and ethical conduct, influencing societal norms and individual behavior. Its characters, particularly Rama, Sita, Hanuman, and Ravana, embody virtues and vices that continue to serve as moral exemplars and cautionary figures.

Ramayana across cultures

The primary reason for widespread acceptance is that the *Ramayana*, wherever introduced, has become thoroughly infused with elements that are familiar and comfortable to the local people. Such adaptations ensure that the story—whether seen in visual art, experienced in performance, or read—resonates with and appeals to the local audience, making it relatable across different cultures and societies.

So, when the epic traveled to a non-Hindu culture, religious elements of the receiving society ended up finding a place in the retellings. Myanmar, Laos, Cambodia, and Thailand, for instance—nations where Theravada Buddhism is the dominant faith—have come to have preeminent *Ramayana* traditions with Buddhist inflections, reinterpretations, interpolations, and adaptations. These versions draw from the *Dasharatha Jataka*, which came into circulation around the 2nd century CE, and explicitly describe Rama as the Great Being, or Mahasatto, representing the Buddha in a previous life. He exemplifies Buddhist virtues, remaining calm upon hearing of his father's death and teaching others about the impermanence of life.

In Malaysia and parts of Indonesia, where the majority of the population had converted to Islam by the 16th century, Muslim retellings emerged with several adaptations. In the popular *Hikayat Seri Rama*, the main characters are reimagined and localized, such as Rama, no longer a god but still a figure to be emulate.

Through the localization process, people found it easy to relate to many characters in the *Ramayana*. Rama, depicted as the ideal ruler, is often likened to the reigning monarch, embodying deep moral integrity, a strong sense of duty, and the ability to bring peace, prosperity, and protection to the realm. Sita represents the faithful and devoted wife, willing to sacrifice and endure for her love and commitment to her husband. Hanuman, the loyal soldier, demonstrates unwavering duty to the ruler and realm. These characters mirror deeply held beliefs in social hierarchy, including familiar roles and positions within society that resonate with the local population. Ravana, the embodiment of evil in Valmiki's *Ramayana*, provides an antagonist to root against. Yet, in most versions, he possesses redeeming qualities, making him a deeper,

more multidimensional character who expresses a wide range of emotions and feelings.

Global themes

The universality of the *Ramayana*'s story can also be understood from the perspective of Russian folklorist Vladimir Propp, who identified common structural elements in folktales—such as the hero's quest, the villain, the helper, and the magical agent—that recur in narratives across cultures. When analyzed through Propp's narrative functions, the *Ramayana* also follows the timeless structure of folktales.

For instance, Propp's first function, in which a family member "absents himself from home," is fulfilled when Rama, Lakshmana, and Sita are exiled to the forest. Propp's fifth function, in which "the villain receives information about his victim," is evident when Ravana learns about Sita's beauty from his sister Surpanakha, who is humiliated by Rama and Lakshmana. Function eight, in which "the villain causes harm or injury to a member of the family," is a pivotal moment in the *Ramayana* when Ravana abducts Sita. Rama's journey to rescue Sita follows several of Propp's subsequent functions, including the hero being tested (function 12), receiving a magical agent or helper (function 14), and the hero and villain engaging in direct combat (function 16).

At its heart, then, the *Ramayana* is a familiar story of the human condition. Originating as a distinctly Hindu epic with sacred and religious undertones, the *Ramayana* has been seamlessly integrated into various spiritual and religious contexts, adapting to the diverse cultures and societies it encountered. As a result, the *Ramayana*'s characters could easily be perceived as Hindu, Jain, Buddhist, or Islamic.

◄ A 19th-century Burmese wood carving from Myanmar depicting Rama and Hanuman.

RAMAYANA OUTSIDE SOUTH ASIA

HOW THE EPIC TRAVELED ACROSS ASIA

The *Ramayana's* influence extends significantly beyond the Indian subcontinent, having permeated into cultures across Asia through networks of trade, migration, religious missions, and cultural exchanges.

During the early centuries of the last millennium, historian Santosh N. Desai explains, the *Ramayana* traveled out of India through three primary trade routes. The northern land route carried the epic from Punjab and Kashmir into China, Tibet, and East Turkestan. The southern sea route transported it from Gujarat and southern India to Java, Sumatra, and Malaya. The eastern land route brought the story from Bengal into Burma, Thailand, and Laos. Vietnam and Cambodia received the narrative partly from Java and partly from the eastern land route.

Religion, trade, and politics

The essence and values of the *Ramayana* story made their way into China through the Buddhist *Jataka Tales*, forming part of the *Tripitaka* canon. These stories reached Japan through the Silk Route.

The story traveled to southeast Asia as Indian traders were often accompanied by priests, scholars, and monks, and played a crucial role in disseminating Indian culture and religion as they traveled for trade in spices and gold. Hinduism is believed to have arrived in southeast Asia around 200 BCE, initially influencing regions like Java and Sumatra. During the same period, the Khmer rulers of Cambodia began adopting Hindu practices, and by the 8th century CE, had fully embraced it, incorporating the *Ramayana* into their culture and constructing Hindu temples.

Diplomatic relations and the establishment of Indianized kingdoms in southeast Asia facilitated the *Ramayana*'s transmission. Kingdoms such as Funan (1st to 6th centuries CE), Champa (2nd to 17th centuries CE), Srivijaya (7th to 13th centuries CE), and Majapahit (13th to 16th centuries CE), which embraced Hindu and Buddhist practices, incorporated the *Ramayana* into their courtly traditions and literary works, underscoring their political and cultural connections with India.

Meanwhile, Buddhist monks and Hindu priests established religious centers and taught local populations throughout the Indonesian archipelago. This led to the creation of local adaptations of the *Ramayana*, such as the *Kakawin Ramayana* and the *Ramayana* Ballet of Yogyakarta and Bali.

In Thailand, Indian missionaries, along with traders, introduced the *Ramayana*, which evolved into the *Ramakien*, with influences from the Khmer title *Reamker*.

▸ A mural depicting the story of the *Ramakien* on the walls of Wat Phra Kaew—the Temple of the Emerald Buddha in Bangkok, Thailand.

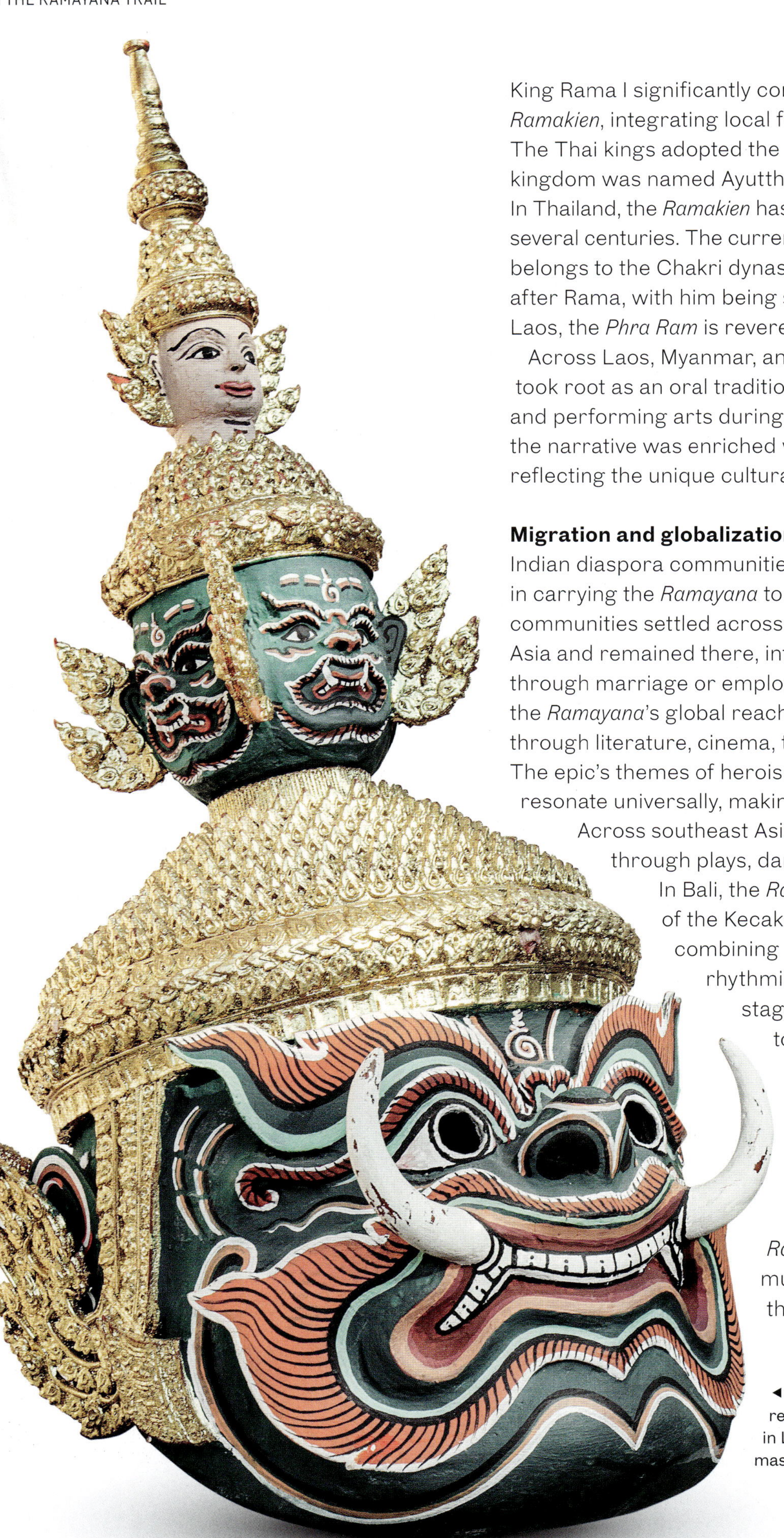

King Rama I significantly consolidated and adapted the *Ramakien*, integrating local folklore and royal symbolism. The Thai kings adopted the title Rama, and their old kingdom was named Ayutthya, after Rama's city, Ayodhya. In Thailand, the *Ramakien* has stood as the national epic for several centuries. The current monarch, King Vajiralongkorn, belongs to the Chakri dynasty, where each ruler is named after Rama, with him being styled as Rama X. Similarly, in Laos, the *Phra Ram* is revered as the national epic.

Across Laos, Myanmar, and Malaysia, the story initially took root as an oral tradition before evolving into festivals and performing arts during the medieval era. As it spread, the narrative was enriched with local values and beliefs, reflecting the unique cultural perspectives of each region.

Migration and globalization

Indian diaspora communities played a significant role in carrying the *Ramayana* to new regions. Many trading communities settled across various regions of southeast Asia and remained there, integrating with local communities through marriage or employment. In contemporary times, the *Ramayana*'s global reach has expanded significantly through literature, cinema, television, and the Internet. The epic's themes of heroism, devotion, and moral integrity resonate universally, making it relevant in modern contexts. Across southeast Asia, the story has been kept alive through plays, dance dramas, and puppet shows. In Bali, the *Ramayana* is performed as part of the Kecak dance, a captivating spectacle combining intricate choreography and rhythmic chanting. This dance, often staged for both local audiences and tourists, highlights the cultural and religious significance of the *Ramayana* in Balinese Hinduism. Similarly, the Javanese Wayang Kulit shadow puppetry tradition frequently features episodes from the *Ramayana*, blending storytelling, music, and visual artistry to keep the epic alive. Malaysia also has

◄ A traditional mask representing Ravana used in Lakhon Khol, a Cambodian masked theater performance.

▲ A traditional puppet show in Myanmar, representing the legends of *Zatdaw* (Buddhist Jataka) and *Yamazat*—tales inspired by the Indian *Ramayana*.

its version of the Wayang Kulit puppet theater, adapted to reflect local cultural and religious contexts.

Thailand and Myanmar share a rich tradition of classical dance and theater rooted in the *Ramayana*. The Thai *Ramakien* is a crucial element of traditional dance-drama known as Khon, characterized by elaborate costumes, intricate masks, and stylized movements. Myanmar's *Rama Zatdaw* performances are notable for their vibrant costumes, intricate puppetry, and the use of music to enhance the storytelling experience.

The Cambodian *Reamker* is performed during significant festivals and royal events. Cambodian classical dance, with its graceful and symbolic movements, brings the *Reamker* to life, emphasizing the epic's moral and spiritual themes. In Laos, the epic survives as *Phra Lak Phra Ram*, performed in temple ceremonies and cultural festivals.

The epic has also manifested on screen. The Indian television series *Ramayan*, directed by Ramanand Sagar, aired from 1987 to 1988 on the television broadcaster Doordarshan and had a profound impact on global television. It was telecast in over 55 countries, earning a viewership of 650 million and becoming a cultural milestone. A unique Indo-Japanese collaboration, *Ramayana: The Legend of Prince Rama*, is an animated film by Yugo Sako. This adaptation is remarkable for its fusion of Indian and Japanese animation styles, bringing the story of Rama to a younger audience through vibrant animation and engaging storytelling. *Sita Sings the Blues*, directed by Nina Paley, is an American animated film that blends the *Ramayana*'s narrative with autobiographical elements and 1920s jazz music. This highly stylized and personal interpretation contrasts the epic's events with the director's own life experiences, providing a contemporary and feminist perspective on Sita's story.

Tourists watching the Kecak Dance at Uluwatu Temple in Bali, Indonesia, as rhythmic chants and powerful movements bring the *Ramayana* to life against a stunning cliffside backdrop.

BIR PILSENER

THE EPIC ACROSS BORDERS

HOW THE EPIC TRAVELED OUTSIDE INDIA

2

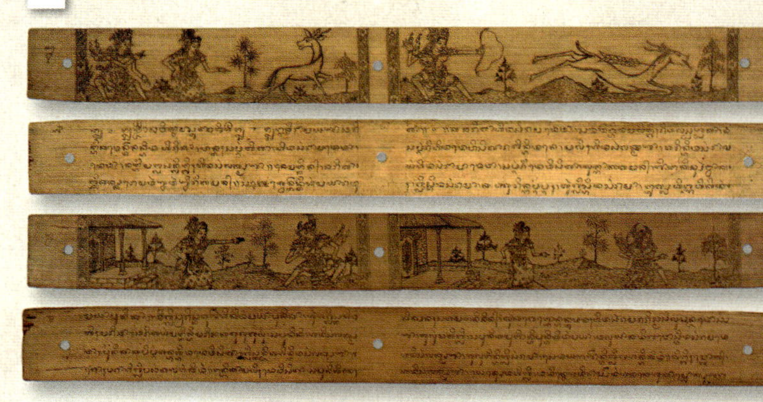

The *Ramayana* has been translated in various languages and different cultures. As a direct result of either trade relations or the spread of religion, it traveled as far as Russia and Mongolia, to Cambodia and Indonesia, and more. The *Ramayana* has influenced the shaping of historical and cultural bonds across India and other countries, and continues to do so.

1

3

1. **Prambanan Temple** These stunning 9th-century bas-reliefs depict stories from the *Ramayana* in Indonesia. It was declared a UNESCO World Heritage Site in 1991 and is one of the largest Hindu temples in Southeast Asia.

2. ***Kakawin Ramayana*** This manuscript is of a 10th-century Javanese retelling of the *Ramayana* from Indonesia. The poem is a rich amalgamation of ancient Sanskritic cultural components, adapted to a Javanese setting.

3. **Angkor Wat** These famous 12th-century bas-reliefs depict episodes from the *Ramayana* and are carved into the walls. The vast complex of Angkor Wat in Cambodia comprises over a thousand buildings.

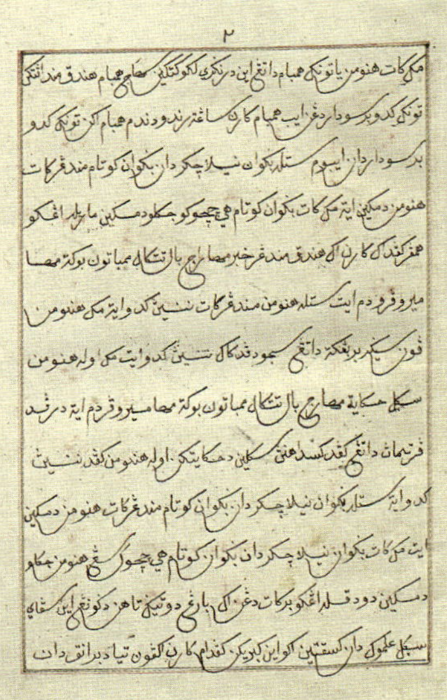

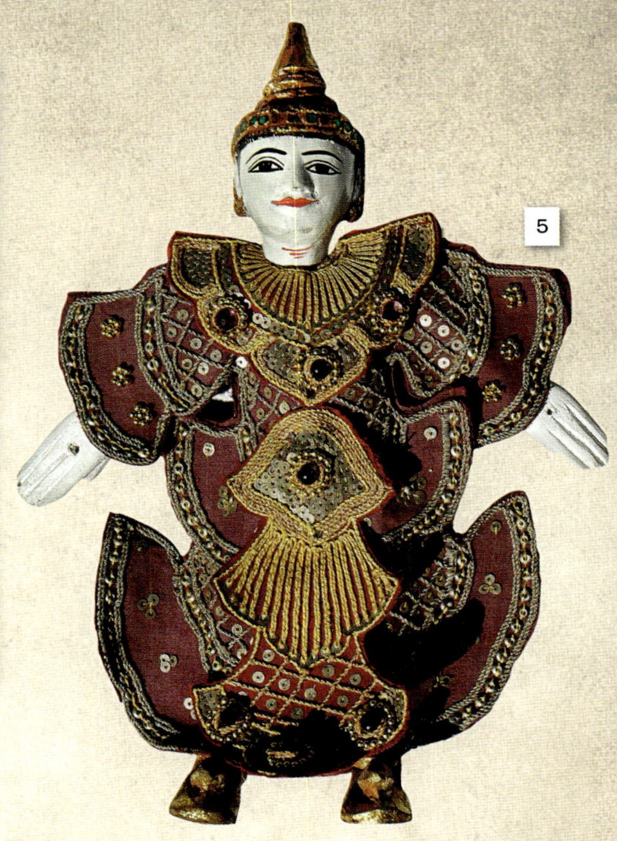

4. **Hikayat Seri Rama** Compiled and written down in what is now Malaysia between the 13th–15th century, it is not a translation of Valmiki's *Ramayana* but a combination of Javanese, Cambodian, and Malay retellings of the epic.

5. **Yama Zatdaw** A Burmese puppet, used in theater performances of the *Ramayana*. *Yama Zatdaw* is the Burmese version of the *Ramayana* and *Dasaratha Jataka*.

6. **Phra Lak Phra Ram** This cultural touchstone in the history of Laos has both the brothers Lakshmana and Rama in its title. Here we see it being performed at the Royal Ballet Theater of Luang Prabang.

CHINA AND JAPAN

TALES OF BUDDHIST VIRTUE

The oldest record of the *Ramayana* outside India appears in China, where a Jataka form of the story was translated in the 3rd century CE. Japan later adapted the tale from the Chinese Buddhist canon, transmitted along the Silk Route.

When Buddhism arrived in China in the 1st century CE, it introduced a body of stories and themes that had a deep impact on Chinese culture. Among these were the *Jataka Tales*, which includes versions of the story of the *Ramayana*. Over centuries, these narratives were gradually integrated into the Chinese Buddhist canon of sacred literature, known as *Tripitaka*.

One story from this canon features Rama as a Bodhisattva whose enemy is not Ravana but a maternal uncle who seizes the throne. Rama withdraws into the forest and does not fight. In the forest, his wife is abducted by a serpent who poses as a sage—and then Rama goes on a quest to rescue her. Another story draws from Valmiki's *Ramayana*, but does not mention Sita's abduction or the battle in Lanka. The focus, instead, is on filial duty. Rama is sent into exile because of his stepmother's wishes. Bharata pleads with him to return to the capital and rule over the kingdom, but Rama refuses. Bharata rules as a regent, with Rama's sandals placed on the throne. When Rama returns, he urges Bharata to continue ruling but Bharata persuades Rama to take the throne Rama was destined for.

Tibet

While some Buddhist versions of the *Ramayana* did travel to Tibet from China, Tibetan literature developed its own *Ramayana*-inspired stories around the 8th–9th century CE. These stories mention Sita's abduction and her banishment. They also say that Sita was Ravana's daughter, but since it was foretold that she would be the reason for Ravana's destruction, she was thrown into the sea. She was saved by Indian farmers who gave her to Janaka.

Japanese adaptations

As the first global trade route, the Silk Road connected China to far-flung civilizations, and the transmission of stories and cultures was made easier. Around the 8th century CE, the story of the *Ramayana* is thought to have reached Japan because of the exchange that took place with the movement of Buddhist monks and traders between the two countries on this route. Although rooted in Valmiki's story, the adaptations are likely to have been based on the Chinese versions of the story or on oral traditions that reached Japan through travelers from India.

One of these Japanese texts, *Sambo-ekotoba*, was composed in the

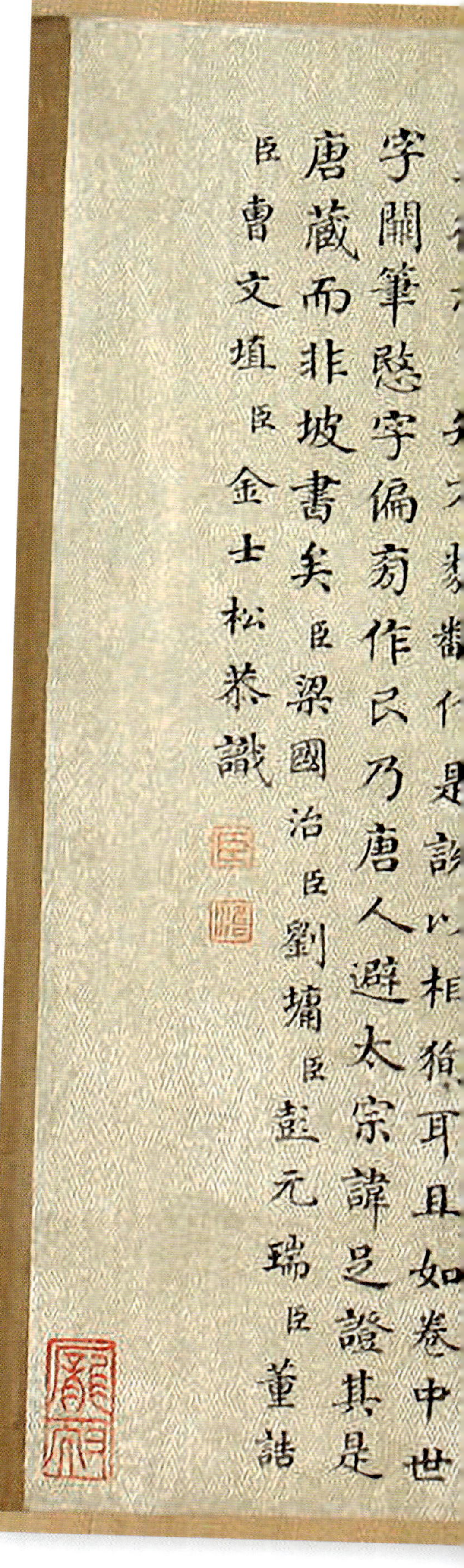

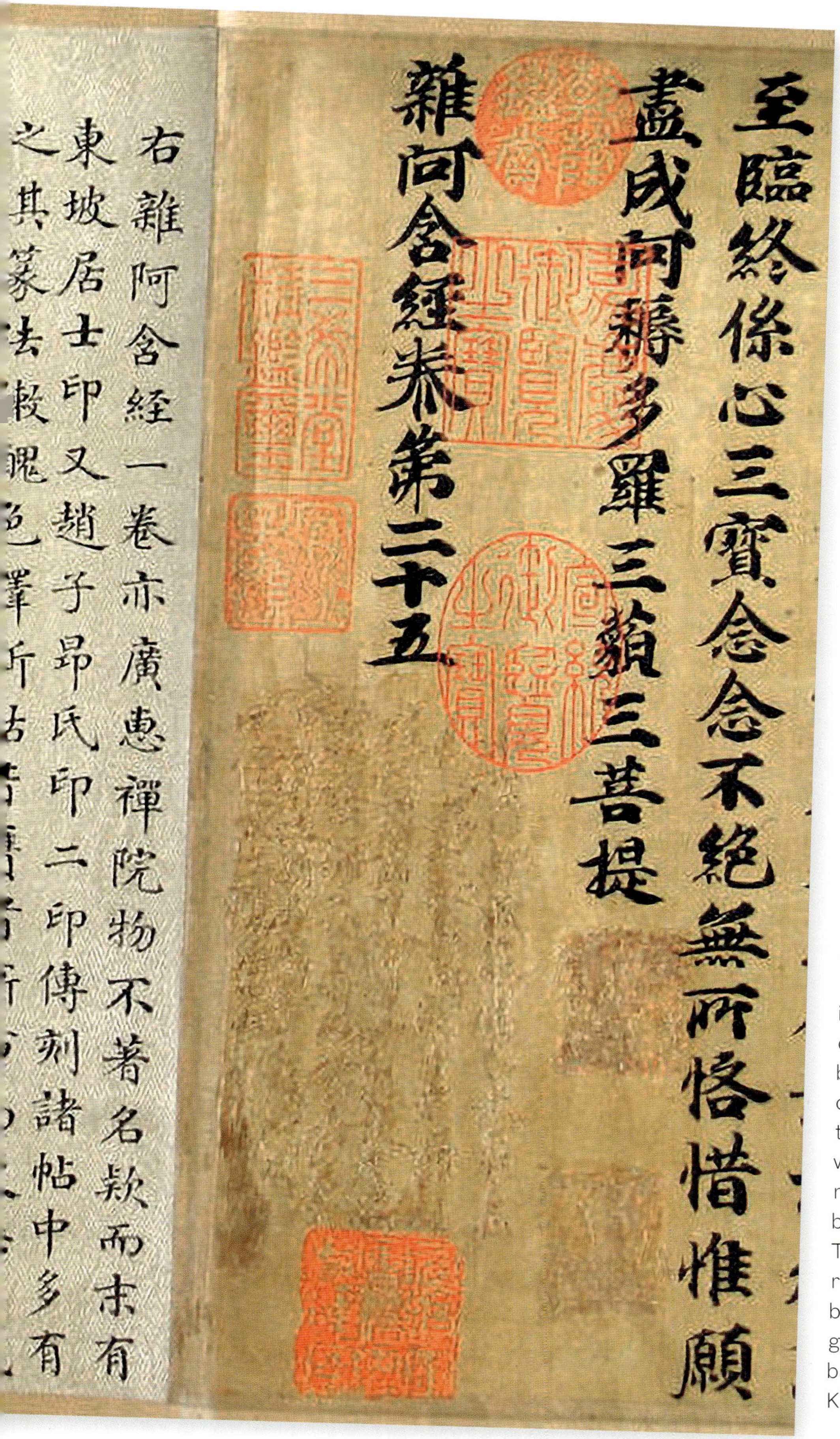

◂ An 11th-century handscroll of *Samyutagama Sutra* from the *Jinsushan Tripitaka*, a collection of Buddhist scriptures.

10th century CE as captions for picture scrolls, meant to cheer up an unhappy princess. The scrolls have been lost, but the caption stories survive. It narrates the tale from Valmiki's *Ramayana* in which Dasharatha tells his queen Kaushalya that his separation from Rama was the consequence of his own actions—because he had at one point accidentally killed Shravana, a young and dutiful man who was serving his old parents. In *Sambo-ekotoba*, that dutiful son is named Semu, and the story has a happy ending—Semu is revived by the king of gods, Indra, after being moved by the distressed cries of his grieving parents.

Another Japanese text based on the *Ramayana* is the *Hobutsushu* (Jewel Collection), in which a king, Tathagata Sakyamuni, withdraws into the mountains after a famine sweeps through his kingdom. His queen retires with him, and is abducted by a dragon king disguised as an ascetic. A giant bird tries to save her, but is struck down. An army of monkeys serves the king in his quest to rescue his wife—building a bridge, fetching medicinal herbs, and fighting a battle against the dragon king. The story ends with Sakyamuni returning to his hermitage, and becoming king again—without getting to the parts about Sita's banishment or the birth of Kusha and Lava.

MYANMAR AND THAILAND

CHRONICLE OF CULTURAL REINVENTION

Through innovations in format and characterization, communities in Myanmar and Thailand have adopted the *Ramayana* as their own since ancient times—infusing it with their unique cultural sensibilities.

The oral tradition of the *Ramayana* in Burma, what is now Myanmar, dates back to the 11th century, with the movement of Indian traders into the region. Lithic inscriptions, stone sculptures, terracotta plaques, and frescoes offer proof of Rama being recognized as an incarnation of Vishnu in Hindu stories, as well as a Bodhisattva in Jataka stories.

Between the 13th and 16th centuries, Burmese *Ramayana* stories were being transmitted orally as the *Rama Zatdaw*, and between the 16th and 18th centuries, they were documented as written text. The first known written Burmese adaptation of the *Ramayana* with an ascribed date is the *Rama Thagyin*, compiled by 1775. It narrates the story from Ravana's birth to his defeat at the hands of Rama but does not mention most events of the last chapter in Valmiki's *Ramayana*. An undated prose version of the story, *Rama Vatthu*, may have been composed earlier than *Rama Thagyin*, in the 17th century, by possibly the same balladeer. *Rama Vatthu* draws on Valmiki's plot but differs significantly in its narrative order and motifs. Today, the *Rama Zatdaw* tradition remains alive in Myanmar through theater and marionette shows, featuring dialogue, poetry, music, song, and dance —art forms that flourished from the 18th century onward with royal patronage.

Around the 13th century, when Myanmar's *Ramayana* started being transmitted orally, Rama's story was introduced to neighboring Thailand, possibly from the Khmer kingdom (present-day Cambodia). There was a strong belief that the events of the *Ramayana* occurred on Thai soil, leading to the association of many places with the legend. For instance, King U-Thong founded a new city in 1350 CE named Ayutthaya, after Ayodhya. The town of Lopburi, north of Ayuthhaya, is linked to Rama's son Lava. The first complete Thai version of the story, *Ramakien* (*Glory of Rama*), was composed by King Rama I in the 18th century. Subsequent rulers, Rama II, III, IV, V, and VI rewrote the story in prose, dialogue, and song.

The *Ramakien* versions have become an inexhaustible source of material for creative artists, inspiring expressions in literature, mural paintings, sculpture, wood carving, puppetry, shadow plays, and masked theater in Thailand. Thai shadow play, known as Nang, exclusively features *Ramakien* episodes, and classical Thai drama, such as the Khon, also draws solely from the *Ramakien*. In Khon, performers, except those portraying divine and human roles, wear masks and enact the story with musical accompaniment and recitations based on classical poetry by ancient poets.

Today, visitors to Thailand can also explore the legend at the Grand Palace in Bangkok, built during the reign of Rama I. The Wat Phra Kaew temple within its grounds features walls adorned with lavish paintings of *Ramakien* episodes.

▼ Pages from an 1870 *parabaik* (folding-book manuscript) with painted scenes from the Myanmarese *Ramayana*.

Khon is a dance-drama genre from Thailand. Here, we see Kumbhakarna, Ravana's brother, awake and in action.

INDONESIA AND MALAYSIA

CONFLUENCE OF TRADITIONS

The *Ramayana*'s themes permeated Indonesian literature, flourishing under Hindu-Buddhist rulers. With Islam's arrival in the 16th century, the narrative was adapted to reflect the cultural shifts in the Indonesian-Malay archipelago.

That the *Ramayana* was a familiar story in Java, Indonesia, by the end of the 9th century CE is evident from the stunning series of reliefs carved into the walls of the grand Prambanan Temple around 900 CE. The Javanese courts had strong connections with those in Bengal, and the island was home to merchants and monks from regions as far away as present-day Gujarat and Sri Lanka. This provided an easy route for the epic's journey. The first literary version in Old Javanese, the *Kakawin Ramayana*, appeared a century later.

It was not based directly on Valmiki's story but on a later Indian poetic work called *Bhattikavya*, composed in the 7th century. While the composer followed *Bhattikavya* for a part of the narrative, they developed certain aspects to ground it in Javanese cultural ideas. For instance, unlike Valmiki's *Ramayana*, in which Rama has little to say to Vibhishana when he crowns him the new king of Lanka, the *Kakawin Ramayana* features Rama's discourse on the virtues of a ruler.

▼ Interior of the Ramayana Cave at the Batu Caves complex in Kuala Lumpur, Malaysia.

Islamic influence

With the spread of Islam across Java from the 15th century onward, the heavily Indian-influenced Old Javanese culture migrated to Bali. Nearly all Old Javanese literary works survived primarily in Bali, although the shadow puppet theater tradition of Java continued to depict the stories. That tradition, Wayang Kulit, has existed in Java for at least 1,000 years. A significant medium for *Ramayana* tales, it contributed to the subject's popularity in illustrated palm-leaf manuscripts until the 20th century.

The spread of Islam in the region influenced the creation of the *Ramayana* canon in neighboring Malaysia as well. By the 16th century, rulers in Sumatra, the Malay Peninsula, and Java had embraced Islam. The state chronicles, known as *Hikayat* and *Sejarah*, started incorporating Islamic legends and titles. In the Malay Muslim courts, literary traditions retained their Hindu and Buddhist influences while using the Arabic script. Between the 13th and 15th centuries, a prose narrative of the story of the *Ramayana* was written down as the *Hikayat Seri Rama*. It begins with Ravana's origin story and his exile to an island after troubling his playmates. During this time, a prophet visits him and prays that he is granted powers. In some versions, Dasharatha is described as the Prophet Adam's descendant, integrating Rama's story into Malaysia's broader tradition.

Beyond textual adaptations, the *Ramayana* is alive in Malaysia today through various folk traditions, such as the Wayang Kulit shadow puppet play and the Penglipur lara storytelling tradition. The most popular form of Malay shadow play, Wayang Kulit Siam, centers on the Rama story but includes unique motifs such as Ravana having seven or 12 heads, Rama shooting through palm trees on a serpent's back during the contest for Sita's hand, and more. The play is frequently performed in cultural centers and theaters in Kelantan and Kuala Lumpur. The Penglipur lara tradition, meanwhile, involves oral narrative performances often accompanied by music. It is practiced during cultural festivals and in rural communities, particularly in the northern regions of peninsular Malaysia.

▲ Artwork from the *Serat Rama Keling* manuscript—a modern Javanese version of the *Ramayana*—published in 1814.

Bali

More than 83 percent of its population identifies as Hindu, and it is the heart of Hinduism in Indonesia. The *Ramayana* tradition here exists as part of two unique performing art forms. The stylized Sendratari, a ballet form, combines dance and drama, and is performed by a large troupe. The Kecak dance, meanwhile, has roots in rituals, such as those meant to ward off evil spirits. The *Ramayana* story was incorporated into this dance form in the 1930s by Balinese dancer Wayan Limbak and German artist Walter Spies. Today, the Kecak dance is performed widely across Bali.

▲ The *Reamker* frescoes in the gallery surrounding the Silver Pagoda in the Royal Palace compound in Phnom Penh, Cambodia.

CAMBODIA AND LAOS

LONG ORAL TRADITIONS

While it may have taken time for the *Ramayana* to become a written text in Cambodia and Laos, its influence permeated the local oral traditions and cultural practices from much earlier.

Like the Thai *Ramayana*, the Cambodian *Ramayana* is an old text which is closer to Valmiki's version than most other retellings in southeast Asia. Unlike the Thai version, however, it took centuries for the stories to be written down as a body of text. The earliest evidence that the stories of the *Ramayana* were known in what is now Cambodia dates back to the 5th century. Funan, the ancient state of Cambodia, was the first important one in southeast Asia to be Hinduized—Sanskrit literature was popular in Khmer regions during this period. Stone inscriptions from the 5th century show that the *Ramayana* tale was known in these parts. The oldest known text of these stories in Cambodia, however, can only be traced back to the 16th century.

This literary version, *Reamker*, is written in the Khmer language and inspired dance-dramas. It tells the story in Valmiki's *Ramayana* but changes the order—the story begins with the origin of Ravana and the monkey army. Another change is in the circumstances that lead up to Sita's banishment. Unlike the public gossip that leads to Rama's decision to send Sita away in Valmiki's *Ramayana*, the decision in some versions of the *Reamker* comes after Rama discovers a portrait of Ravana that Sita had drawn.

Performance arts

In contemporary times, the *Reamker* serves as an inspiration for various performance genres in Cambodia, including classical dance-drama, all-male masked dance-drama, and shadow puppetry. The popular masked dance drama, Ikhon khol, draws from specific *Reamker* episodes, integrating Rama's role as a former incarnation of the Buddha, a theme beautifully preserved in Cambodia's Royal Ballet repertoire to this day.

The story of the *Ramayana* in neighboring Laos is called *Phra Lak Phra Ram* or *Phra Lak Phra Lam* (in modern Lao, "r" is often replaced with "l"), but the date of its composition appears difficult to ascertain. Lao legends attribute the composition to the first king of the ancient kingdom of Lane Xang, what is now Laos, in the 14th century. Meanwhile, historical evidence of the origins of the story in oral traditions suggests that it was composed some time in the 19th century and compiled as a written text much later.

Vietnam

The ancient kingdom of Champa existed between the 2nd and 17th centuries CE. Its 7th-century ruler Prakashdharma built a temple dedicated to Valmiki. A stone inscription at the temple narrates a part of Valmiki's story and refers to Vishnu's incarnations. A localized version of the story incorporated the geography of the kingdom into the narrative—Champa as the kingdom of Ravana, Annam (a town to the north) the kingdom of Dasharatha.

This adaptation appears to have come into Laos in a process of gathering influences from neighboring countries like Thailand and Cambodia over time. The story has some significant variations. Thao Ravana (Ravana) is portrayed with only one head. He is handsome and rebellious. The story unfolds along the Mekong River, following the adventures of Lam (Rama) and Lak (Lakshmana) from the northern city-kingdom of Vientiane. They embark on a quest, riding flying horses, to rescue their older sister Canda, abducted by their cousin Ravana. Despite pleas from his mother, Ravana refuses to return Canda until the brothers intervene, retrieving her from Indraprastha. Ravana later agrees to Rama's terms, marries Canda, and pledges loyalty to Rama in Vientiane.

Phra Lak Phra Ram is not merely a tale but also a cultural touchstone for Laos. It has been depicted in mural paintings and wood relief carvings on temple structures, and historically, it was a central theme in the repertoire of the Lao Royal Ballet. Today, performances of *Phra Lak Phra Ram* are staged every alternate night at the Royal Palace Museum theater, the most popular tourist destination, in Luang Prabang, Laos.

▸ A mid-1100s altarpiece from Cambodia with Buddha enthroned.

THE RAMAYANA TRAILS IN INDIA

These trails lead you to sites where history and legend converge. Stand in the serene Chitrakoot, where Rama endured his exile, visit temples that echo with Hanuman's devotion, and feel the haunting whispers of Sita's abduction in the ancient Sita Gufa. From the soul-stirring aartis in Varanasi to the breathtaking Thanjavur paintings, each path immerses you in a living tapestry of India's divine mythology.

Across the spiritual north

Day 1 Begin your adventure in **Delhi**. Take a short drive to Bisrakh, a quaint village in Uttar Pradesh, where you can visit the Ravana Temple. Head back to Delhi to unwind and spend the night in the capital. If you are in Delhi a month or two before Dussehra, visit Titarpur, located in the western part of the city. As the largest effigy market in Asia, this bustling market is where hundreds of artisans prepare the iconic Ravana effigies for the upcoming Ramlila celebrations.

Day 2 Take a train to **Ayodhya**, one of India's holiest cities. Upon arrival, take a leisurely stroll through the town, and in the evening, experience the tranquility of the aarti at the ghats—an ideal way to start your spiritual journey in Ayodhya.

Day 3 Start your day by visiting Hanuman Garhi. Afterward, take a short walk to Kanak Bhawan and visit Dashrath Mahal. In the evening, witness the aarti at the Ram Janmabhoomi Temple—an emotional and powerful experience.

Day 4 Set out early to drive to Shringverpur, a small village located a few hours south of Ayodhya. Here, visit the temple believed to be the meeting point of Rama and the tribal king Guha. If you are planning this trip around Dussehra, drive to **Varanasi**, or drive for just under an hour to **Prayagraj**.

▼ Effigies of Ravana displayed for sale ahead of the Dussehra Festival in Titarpur.

▲ Ancient bas-relief at the renowned temple in Khajuraho.

Day 5 In Varanasi, take a ferry to Ramnagar Fort across the river and immerse yourself in the grand month-long Ramlila performance—a vibrant spectacle not to be missed.

Day 6 Drive to Prayagraj, where you will begin your exploration with a visit to the Bharadvaja Ashram, followed by a visit to the Sangam Ghat, the confluence of the Ganga, Yamuna, and the mythical Sarasvati Rivers. If the weather is pleasant, you can opt for a peaceful boat ride. A short walk from the ghat is the hidden underground Hanuman Temple, a sacred site believed to be where Hanuman took a break after setting Lanka on fire. Finish the day by visiting the picturesque Khusro Bagh, a Mughal-era garden, just before sunset.

Day 7 Take a day trip to Sita Samahit Sthal in Bhadohi. Here, marvel at the magnificent statue of Hanuman and explore the serene lake, said to possess healing properties. In the evening, return to Prayagraj for a sunset boat ride at the Triveni Sangam, where the three rivers meet.

Day 8 Drive to **Chitrakoot**, a tranquil town. Once settled, make your way to Sphatik Shila, a peaceful spot by the Mandakini River. Spend a calm evening here before returning to the town for an overnight stay.

Day 9 Begin your day with a hike up Kamadgiri Hill, where you can visit Lakshman Pahari and Bharat Milap on the way. In the afternoon, explore the hidden Gupt Godavari caves, then visit Ram Ghat to experience the evening aarti.

Day 10 Drive to Piprawan, an hour's journey from Chitrakoot, to visit the serene Sarbhanga Ashram. Take a short 10-minute drive to Selaha and visit the Sutikshna Ashram. Return to Chitrakoot for the night.

Day 11 Drive to **Khajuraho** to explore the most magnificent temples in India. These temples, built between the 9th and 10th centuries, are renowned for their intricate carvings and sculptures, which blend artistry with divine expression. Visit the Lakshmana Temple, dedicated to Hindu god Vishnu, and explore other temples that stand as a testament to the cultural zenith of the Chandela era. As you wander through the temple complex, take a moment to reflect on the sheer scale and beauty of the structures, their details, and the stories they whisper. Spend the night in Khajuraho or make your way home.

Devotees gathered at Dashashvamedh Ghat in Varanasi, India, to offer prayers to the sacred Ganga as the evening sky is illuminated by the glow of oil lamps and the air is filled with the chants of devotion.

▲ Kailasha Temple in the Ellora caves complex in Maharashtra.

Westward pilgrimage

Day 1 Begin your journey in **Mumbai**, India's bustling metropolis. Take a ferry from the Gateway of India to Elephanta Island and explore the Elephanta Caves, a UNESCO World Heritage Site known for its spectacular rock-cut architecture. It is a scenic hour-long walk from the ferry dock to the caves, where you will have 3–4 hours to marvel at the ancient sculptures and intricate carvings. Return to Mumbai for the night to rest after your cultural immersion.

Day 2 From Mumbai, take a scenic drive to **Nashik**, one of the four Kumbh Mela hosts. Visit the Sita Gufa, where it is believed that Ravana abducted Sita. Spend the day in Panchavati, the riverside neighborhood known for its sacred sites. Wander through the temples and take in the peaceful atmosphere along the Ram Kund ghat in the evening. Be sure to visit the revered Kalaram Temple before winding down for the night.

Day 3 Embark on a picturesque drive to Deolali Cantonment and visit the Khandoba Temple, dedicated to Shiva, a striking 500-year-old shrine. Continue your journey to the Pandav Leni Caves atop Trirashmi Hill, an impressive complex with serene idols of Buddha and Jain Tirthankaras, as well as ancient rock-cut water tanks. Afterward, return to Nashik, where you can relax and even indulge in some wine tasting, as Nashik is known for its thriving vineyards.

Day 4 Start your day with a trek up Anjaneri Mountain, believed to be the birthplace of Hanuman. Next, venture to Kavnai Fort in the village of Igatpuri. The fort offers a relatively less-explored ascent through the Sahyadri ranges and rewards trekkers with breathtaking panoramic views. Return to Nashik for a well-deserved rest after your adventure-filled day.

Day 5 Start early for a 2–3-hour drive to Ellora Caves, a monumental rock-cut cave complex near **Aurangabad**. Spend the day exploring the magnificent sculptures and exquisite art dating back to the 5th to 10th centuries. The area surrounding the caves is closed to vehicles, so be prepared for a walk to reach the site. After soaking in the history and beauty, drive to Aurangabad for an overnight stay.

Day 6 From Aurangabad, drive toward **Nagpur** and continue on to Ramtek (about 1.5 hours). Here, visit the Ramtek Gad Mandir, a beautiful temple atop Ramgiri Hill dedicated to Lord Rama. Spend some time soaking in the peaceful surroundings before returning to Nagpur for your overnight stay.

Day 7 From Nagpur, take a bus to **Tamia Hill Station**, a serene retreat perched above the mystical Patalkot Valley, believed to be the gateway to the netherworld, Meghanada's realm. Set up camp amid the stunning natural beauty of this area, where ancient rock formations, dense mangroves, and waterfalls paint a picturesque landscape. Spend the day soaking in the tranquility of the region, lost in its timeless charm. The next day, return to **Nagpur** to catch your flight.

Southward bound

Day 1 Start your journey in **Kochi** in Kerala and then embark on a scenic 2-hour drive to Thrissur. Visit the Payammal Shatrughna Temple, a quiet but deeply spiritual place. Return to Kochi for the night.

Day 2 Drive to **Madurai**, a city that will captivate you with its labyrinthine streets and vibrant energy. Visit the Meenakshi Temple, renowned for its riotous colors and bustling atmosphere.

Day 3 Drive for a short excursion to the Sanjeevi Hills, a region rich in trekking trails and dotted with ancient temples dedicated to Hanuman. These hills also hold great mythological significance, making them an enriching destination for both nature lovers and spiritual seekers. Return to Madurai for the night.

Day 4 Drive to **Rameswaram** from Madurai. The journey to Rameswaram will captivate you as you approach this breathtaking coastal city. Don't forget to pack your camera, as the views along the way are unforgettable. In Rameswaram, start at the Kothandaramaswamy Temple, marking the spot where Ravana's brother, Vibhishana, sought refuge with Rama. Next, visit the mysterious ruins of Dhanushkodi, once a thriving town before it was destroyed by a cyclone. Afterward, explore the Panchamukhi Hanuman Temple on Pamban Island.

Day 5 Early morning, drive to **Thanjavur** and marvel at the 12th-century Airavatesvara Temple, adorned with detailed carvings and inscriptions. If you have time, witness the creation

▲ Pamban railway bridge that connects the town of Rameswaram to mainland India.

of Thanjavur paintings and purchase authentic works directly from the artisans.

Day 6 Set out on a drive to **Mahabalipuram**. While the journey is long, it offers stunning, picturesque views that make the ride truly memorable. Explore the stunning Shore Temple, one of India's most iconic coastal temples. Take a stroll through this ancient port town, which was once a flourishing center of culture and trade. Stay the night in Mahabalipuram and immerse yourself in its tranquil beauty.

Day 7 Drive for two hours to **Kanchipuram**, an ancient city that was once the capital of powerful 6th-century rulers in southern India. Visit the Muktesvara Temple, known for its exquisite Ravananugraha frieze, and make sure to stop by the Kailasanatha Temple, renowned for its intricate architecture and sacred significance. Spend the night in Kanchipuram, or drive to **Chennai** to catch a flight.

From the Deccan to the eastern shores

Day 1 Start your journey in **Tirupati**, in Andhra Pradesh, home to the famous Sri Venkateswara Temple, which rests on Tirumala Hill. Explore the Anjanadri Hill, believed to be the birthplace of Hanuman. Later, visit Srikalahasti to witness the intricate art of Kalamkari weaving, where artisans create stunning tapestries depicting stories from the *Ramayana*.

Day 2 Drive to the village of **Lepakshi**. Marvel at the massive statue of the vulture king, Jatayu. Explore the Veerabhadra Temple and make your way to the ornate sculpture of the sacred bull, Nandi. Spend the night here in Lepakshi.

Day 3 Drive to **Bengaluru**, India's tech capital. From there, take a 2-hour drive to the tranquil hamlet of Avani, home to the Ramalingeshwara Temple. This temple, showcasing stunning Dravidian architecture, is believed to be the birthplace of Lava and Kusha. The rugged surroundings also offer a perfect setting for a trekking adventure. After your visit, head back to Bengaluru and unwind in the vibrant Indiranagar neighborhood, where you can enjoy the buzzing nightlife in pubs and karaoke bars. Take an overnight bus to **Gokarna**, a sacred city steeped in legend. It is believed that Ravana placed a Shivalinga here, containing the essence of Shiva.

Day 4 In Gokarna, visit the Mahabaleshwar Temple, dedicated to this deity. Spend the evening relaxing at Gokarna

▲ Kailasanatha Temple in Kanchipuram, Tamil Nadu, is one of the oldest temples in the region, built by Pallava king Rajasimha in the 8th century, dedicated to Shiva.

▲ Ancient bas-relief at the renowned temple in Khajuraho.

Beach, soaking in the serene atmosphere.

Day 5 Drive to **Bagalkot.** After some rest, continue to drive to Badami, where you will find the magnificent 7th-century Mahakuteswara Temple. This complex is home to a large group of temples, each offering unique insights into ancient architecture and spirituality. After your exploration, drive to Bagalkot for an overnight stay.

Day 6 Depart early in the morning for Pattadakal, known for its exceptional Virupaksha Temple, which houses one of the most detailed Ravananugraha sculptures. With over 150 temples in the area, focus on the 10 most prominent ones to make the most of your visit. After a day of exploration, return to Bagalkot for the night.

Day 7 Drive to **Hampi**, which may take 5–6 hours. Once you check into your resort, spend a relaxing evening in this ancient UNESCO World Heritage Site.

Day 8 Put on comfortable shoes and clothes for a full day of exploring Hampi's awe-inspiring ruins. Start with the Virupaksha Temple, an architectural marvel that dates back to the 7th century. Visit Sugriva's Cave, Anjaneya Hill, and the peaceful Pampa Sarovar, each steeped in rich history and spiritual significance. End your day by witnessing a stunning sunset from Hemakuta Hill, where the landscape comes alive as the sun dips below the horizon, casting a magical glow over the ruins.

Day 9 Hampi is famous for its bouldering, so rise early to try your hand at climbing the giant rocks before the heat of the day sets in. After your climb, unwind along the banks of the Tungabhadra River, enjoying the tranquility and scenic beauty.

Day 10 Fly from Hampi to **Visakhapatnam** and then take a 4-hour drive to **Kakinada**. Here, visit the Ravana Temple, where Ravana is believed to have installed the Shivalinga. Afterward, relax at Kakinada Beach or take a ferry to Hope Island, a peaceful getaway in the Bay of Bengal. Stay overnight in Kakinada.

Day 11 Drive back to **Visakhapatnam** and catch a flight or spend the day at one of the city's many beaches.

(Although these itineraries are thoughtfully crafted to inspire your journey, use them as a starting point. Adjust them based on your own time, budget, and interests. After all, the beauty of travel lies in the freedom to create your own path.)

Kalaram Temple in Nashik, Maharashtra

Hanuman Garhi Temple in Ayodhya

A satellite view of **Adam's Bridge**, a chain of limestone shoals that connect Sri Lanka to India

THE RAMAYANA TRAILS IN SRI LANKA

Winding through the epic landscape of the *Ramayana,* these trails in Sri Lanka draw you into a world of timeless power and mystery. From the sacred Ram Setu, the very span built by Rama to rescue his beloved Sita, to the majestic palace of Mandodari, and the mystical Rumassala, forever tied to Hanuman's heroic voyage to get Sanjeevani—each step on this path takes you closer to the pulse of an ancient, divine story.

A sacred journey through hills and coast

Day 1 Start your journey in **Kandy**, a UNESCO World Heritage Site and home to temples, breathtaking gardens, and sites steeped in history. Make sure to visit Sri Dalada Maligawa, also known as the Temple of the Tooth. This Buddhist temple is where the left upper canine of the Buddha has been preserved since 1590. After paying homage to the Buddha, visit the *devalas*, or shrines, of the four guardian deities—Natha, Vishnu, Kataragama, and Pattini. These shrines are integral to the grandeur of the Kandy Esala Perahera, one of Sri Lanka's most sacred festivals. In the evening, immerse yourself in the vibrant traditional Kandyan dance performance.

Day 2 Start your day with a visit to Sita Kottuwa, located in the mist-laden Dumbara Valley, where the palace of Mandodari, Ravana's queen, is said to have stood. The peaceful atmosphere is perfect for reflection and meditation at the ancient Buddhist *padhanagara* (house of meditation). After a peaceful morning, return to Kandy for lunch. In the afternoon, visit the Bhakthi Hanuman Temple in Ramboda. If your visit coincides with a full-moon day, you will be treated to special rituals during which the statue is adorned with flowers and silk. In the evening, make your way to the picturesque hill station of **Nuwara Eliya** for an overnight stay.

▼ Kandyan dancers on the streets of Kandy during the Day Perahera, the grand finale of the Esala Perahera in Sri Lanka.

▲ Unawatuna Beach in Galle, known for its golden sands and crystal-clear waters.

Day 3 Begin with a visit to the Frofot Estate, known for its Chariot Path and Sita Tear Pond. Alternatively, explore the Labokelle Tea Estate for a tranquil experience in the scenic tea gardens. After lunch in Nuwara Eliya, continue your spiritual journey with a visit to the Gayathri Peedum Temple in the afternoon.

Day 4 Explore the Sita Amman Temple, a revered site connected to the *Ramayana*. Take a leisurely walk through Hakgala Gardens (Ashok Vatika), where Sita is believed to have spent time in captivity. Continue your journey with a visit to Divirumpola Temple. After lunch in **Ella**, spend your afternoon visiting the stunning Ravana Falls and the nearby Ravana Cave. Overnight in Ella, enjoy being surrounded by the serene beauty of the landscape.

Day 5 Drive toward the charming coastal city of **Galle**, where you will visit Rumassala, a location steeped in mythology and believed to be the site where the Sanjeevani herb was dropped. You can either choose to stay overnight in Galle, soaking in the coastal ambiance, or just enjoy a delightful lunch on your way out of the city. Stop by the Kelaniya Temple en route, to marvel at its intricate carvings and rich cultural heritage.

Day 6 If you spent the night in Galle, begin your final day with a visit to the Kelaniya Temple. Next, make your way to the Munneswaran Temple in **Chilaw**. Enjoy a leisurely lunch in Chilaw before leaving the city and marking the end of your spiritual journey.

From temples to mythical highlands

Day 1 Start your journey with a visit to the sacred Munneswaran Temple and Manawari Temple. After a day of spiritual exploration, spend the night in the peaceful town of **Chilaw**.

Day 2 Drive toward **Mannar**, where you will visit the legendary Ram Setu (Adam's Bridge) and the ancient Thiruketheeswaram Temple. After your visit, continue your journey to **Habarana** for an overnight stay.

Day 3 Start your day with a visit to the Sigiriya Rock Fortress, and then explore the Cobra Hooded Cave. After lunch in Sigiriya, head to the Ritigala Monastery, believed to be the site of the mythical Sanjeevani Drop. Return to Habarana for the night.

Day 4 Drive to the coastal city of **Trincomalee**, where you will visit the Koneswaran Temple, a significant Hindu temple perched atop a cliff offering breathtaking views of the surrounding ocean. Spend the night in Trincomalee.

Day 5 Travel to **Kurunegala** and visit Dolukanda, another key site connected to the legend of Sanjeevani. From here, you can either head to **Kandy** to join the first itinerary or continue your journey to **Colombo** for the night.

▲ The interior of Kelaniya Temple, with its vibrant murals.

Nine Arch Bridge, nestled between Ella and Demodara in Sri Lanka, is a stunning feat of colonial-era engineering surrounded by lush greenery.

▲ Sigiriya, the Lion's Rock Fortress, in the heart of Sri Lanka's lush forest.

Day 6 Toward the end of your journey, visit the Kelaniya Temple, a sacred Buddhist temple believed to be the site of Buddha's visit during his third and final journey to Sri Lanka. It is renowned for its stunning murals and intricate carvings, depicting scenes from the Buddha's life and Sri Lankan history. It is believed that Vibhishana was crowned the king of Lanka here, after Ravana's defeat in battle.

From ancient ruins to coastal legends

Day 1 Begin your journey in **Jaffna** with a visit to the legendary Adam's Bridge or Ram Setu and the ancient Thiruketheeswaram Temple. After immersing yourself in these sacred sites, enjoy a restful overnight stay in the port city of Jaffna.

Day 2 Drive from Jaffna to the coastal city of **Trincomalee**, where you will visit the revered Koneswaran Temple, perched high atop a cliff and offering panoramic views of the surrounding ocean. Spend the night in Trincomalee, soaking in the coastal beauty and tranquility.

Day 3 Head to the ancient Ritigala Monastery, believed to be connected to the Sanjeevani story. Afterward, make your way to Sigiriya for an overnight stay, preparing for the next day's adventure.

Day 4 Climb the majestic **Sigiriya Rock**, a UNESCO World Heritage Site famous for its ancient frescoes, stunning views, and rich history. Afterward, you have the option to either join the first itinerary or return to **Colombo**. Alternatively, you can drive from Kurunegala to **Chilaw**. Visit the sacred sites of Munneswaran Temple and Manawari Temple before ending your day with an overnight stay in **Negombo**.

Day 5 You could also choose to spend another day. Start with a visit to the Kelaniya Temple, an important Buddhist site known for its intricate murals. After your visit, you can return to **Colombo** for your departure, marking the end of your memorable journey.

(Although these itineraries are thoughtfully crafted to inspire your journey, use them as a starting point. Adjust them based on your own time, budget, and interests. After all, the beauty of travel lies in the freedom to create your own path.)

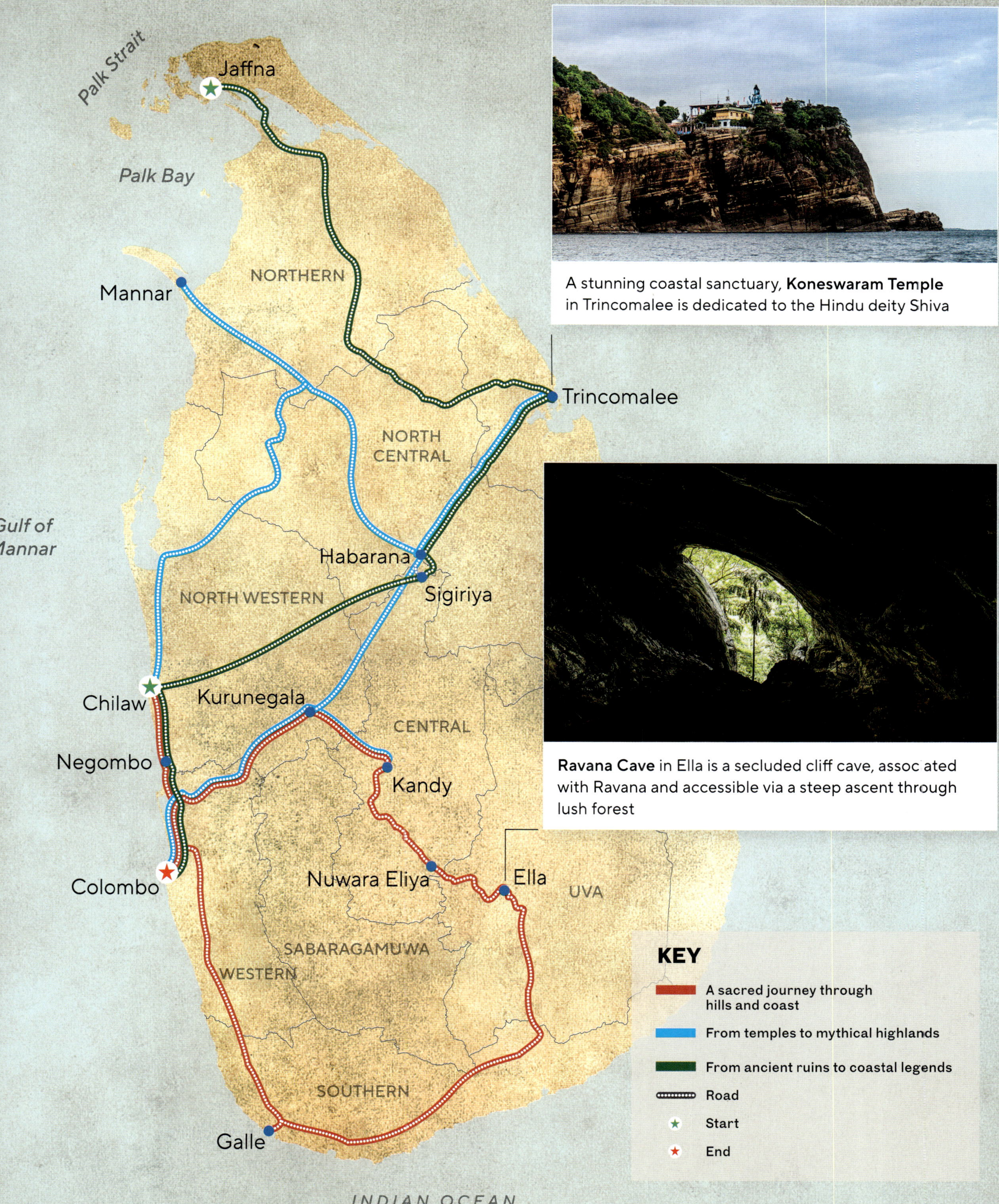

A stunning coastal sanctuary, **Koneswaram Temple** in Trincomalee is dedicated to the Hindu deity Shiva

Ravana Cave in Ella is a secluded cliff cave, assoc ated with Ravana and accessible via a steep ascent through lush forest

GLOSSARY

Aarti A ritual of worship where light, typically from a lamp with wicks soaked in ghee or camphor, is offered to deities.

Adharma A concept referring to actions or behaviors that go against the cosmic law of righteousness and justice, or dharma. Adharma leads to chaos and imbalance in the universe and is viewed as the antithesis of dharma.

Agni pariksha A trial by fire, traditionally symbolizing a test of purity or virtue. The practice is deeply symbolic of divine intervention and moral testing.

Apsara In Hindu and Buddhist mythology, apsaras are celestial nymphs or female spirits known for their supernatural beauty, grace, and dance.

Ashram A spiritual retreat or hermitage where individuals live and practice meditation, often under the guidance of a guru.

Asura A class of powerful beings often portrayed as the adversaries of the gods, or the devas. Asuras are typically linked to chaos and destruction, embodying the forces of darkness and disorder in the cosmos.

Avatar An avatar refers to the divine incarnation of a deity, particularly when the deity takes a physical form to restore cosmic order.

Bas-relief A sculptural technique in which figures project only slightly from a flat background.

Bhajan A devotional song or hymn sung in praise of a deity.

Bodhi tree The sacred fig tree under which Siddhartha Gautama, the Buddha, attained enlightenment.

Bodhisattva A being who has attained enlightenment but has chosen to remain in the cycle of birth, death, and rebirth to assist all sentient beings in achieving enlightenment.

Brahman A member of the highest of the four traditional social classes in Hindu society.

Caste system A traditional social hierarchy in India that divides people into four main categories—Brahmins (priests and scholars), Kshatriyas (warriors and rulers), Vaishyas (merchants and landowners), and Shudras (laborers and service providers).

Chaitya In Buddhist architecture, a chaitya is a prayer hall or shrine, often housing a stupa or relic. These spaces are designed for meditation and worship, emphasizing the sacredness of the Buddha's teachings and the journey toward enlightenment.

Charbagh layout A formal, Persian-inspired garden layout characterized by four quadrants, divided by water channels or pathways. It symbolizes paradise, and is commonly used in Mughal architecture, notably in the gardens surrounding tombs.

Curse A solemn invocation or prayer meant to bring about harm, misfortune, or divine retribution. In Indian traditions, curses are powerful spiritual acts that can alter the course of one's destiny, often associated with deities or powerful sages.

Dagoba A stupa or a dome-shaped structure that serves as a shrine or reliquary for sacred relics, typically of the Buddha or important Buddhist monks. The term is mainly used in Sri Lanka, whereas in other Buddhist regions, similar structures are called stupas (India and Nepal), chedis (Thailand), chortens (Tibet), or pagodas (China and Japan).

Danava Demons in Hindu mythology, descended from Sage Kashyapa and Danu.

Deva Deities or celestial beings who symbolize order and righteousness. They are often portrayed as the adversaries of the asuras and live in swarga (heaven).

Dham A sacred or religious site in Hinduism, particularly pilgrimage destinations.

Dharma The ethical, moral, and cosmic laws that govern the universe, guiding individuals in their duties and responsibilities.

Dholak A traditional two-headed drum used in Indian folk music and religious ceremonies.

Doha A couplet or verse in Hindi or Sanskrit poetry, often conveying moral or philosophical teachings.

Doha Dhani A style of folk music from Rajasthan, where bards recite dohas, or poetic couplets, while performing intricate classical music compositions in the rag dhani framework. This unique blend of poetry and music reflects a deep spiritual and cultural expression.

Dravidian architecture A South Indian temple architectural style that developed around the 7th century CE, characterized by grandiose gopurams, or pyramidal entrance towers, and intricately carved stone pillars. The layout often includes concentric enclosures surrounding the garbhagriha, or sanctum sanctorum, symbolizing spiritual ascent.

Dwarapala Guardian deities or statues placed at the entrances of temples, as protectors of the sacred space. They are often depicted as fierce, warriorlike figures, symbolizing the safeguarding of divine realms.

Ella A Sinhala term for a waterfall or stream, commonly used to describe cascading waters that hold spiritual and cultural significance in various local traditions.

Gandharva In Hindu and Buddhist traditions, gandharvas are celestial musicians and singers, often depicted as divine beings who entertain the gods through music and dance.

Gopuram A monumental, pyramidal entrance tower found in South Indian temples, particularly in Dravidian style.

Hindu calendar A traditional system of timekeeping in Hinduism, consisting of lunar and solar months, along with various religious festivals. It is used to determine the dates of significant events in the Hindu religious year and to guide spiritual practices.

Janapada Political entities, kingdoms, or regions of ancient India, especially in the Vedic period. These were the early societal formations before the rise of larger empires, with a strong emphasis on community and regional governance.

Jyotirlinga Sacred shrines dedicated to the god Shiva, where his divine presence is represented by a radiant column of light. There are twelve Jyotirlingas scattered across India, each associated with various legends that highlight Shiva's power and protection.

Khamaicha A traditional stringed instrument from Rajasthan, it is a type of lute that is played with a plectrum or the fingers.

Kotuwa In Sri Lankan architecture, kotuwa refers to a fortified structure or bastion, typically used as a defensive mechanism in ancient cities or forts.

Linga A symbolic representation of god Shiva, often a cylindrical stone or pillar. Typically, it is accompanied by a yoni, symbolizing the goddess Shakti, representing the union of masculine and feminine principles in the universe.

Mahajanapada Sixteen large and powerful kingdoms or republics in ancient India that existed from around 600 to 300 BCE.

Mantra A sacred utterance, syllable, or phrase used in Hinduism and Buddhism, often repeated during meditation or prayer. Mantras are believed to hold spiritual power and are used to focus the mind or invoke divine energies.

Maya It is a concept of illusion or deceptive nature of the material world. It suggests that the world as perceived by the senses is not the ultimate reality, but rather an illusion that veils the true nature of existence.

Moksha Liberation from the cycle of birth, death, and rebirth, which is understood to be the ultimate spiritual goal in Hinduism, Buddhism, and Jainism.

Naga-linga A sacred flower and tree associated with the god Shiva and revered for its resemblance to the hood of the serpent.

Nagara architecture A style of temple architecture predominant in North India, characterized by curvilinear spires or shikharas that rise above the main sanctum of the temple.

Patal Underworld or netherworld, a realm below the Earth where certain deities, demons, and other supernatural beings reside.

Padhanagara A city or settlement designed specifically to support the lives of monks and facilitate meditation and study.

Pamsukulika A type of ascetic or renunciant.

Parikrama A ritual practice in which devotees circumambulate a sacred object, temple, or site as an act of devotion.

Poya A Buddhist observance day in Sri Lanka and other countries following the lunar calendar and marking significant events in the life of the Buddha, including his birth, enlightenment, and passing away.

Qawwali A form of Sufi devotional music that originated in the Indian subcontinent and is characterized by powerful, rhythmic singing and the use of traditional instruments like the tabla, harmonium, and flute.

Raga A fundamental concept in Indian classical music, it is a melodic framework used for improvisation and composition. Each raga is associated with specific emotions, times of day, or seasons, and consists of a set of notes and rules for their arrangement and performance, designed to evoke particular moods or states of consciousness.

Rakshasa Supernatural beings who have the power to change their appearance by will, often depicted as demons or ogres. Brahma created them to protect the waters.

Ramkatha The narrative or retelling of the *Ramayana.*

Riksha Powerful bearlike warriors, led by their king, Jambavan.

Satra Monasteries and temples founded by Srimanta Sankardeva in Assam, serving as centers of Vaishnavism.

Sheshanaga The king of all serpents who is depicted as a massive multi-headed serpent, upon whose coils the god Vishnu rests.

Simhastha bathing festival A significant pilgrimage that occurs once every twelve years in Ujjain, marking an auspicious occasion for spiritual purification.

Stupa A dome-shaped structure used as a Buddhist shrine, typically housing relics of the Buddha or other revered figures

Sudarshan chakra A divine, spinning, discus-like weapon wielded by god Vishnu.

Tapasya Intense self-discipline or austerity undertaken as a means of spiritual purification or to gain divine favor.

Tirtha A sacred place or pilgrimage site, where devotees go to perform rituals, bathe, or meditate.

Tirthankara A spiritual teacher in Jainism who has attained complete enlightenment and helps others achieve liberation from the cycle of birth, death, and rebirth. There are 24 Tirthankaras, with Mahavira being the most recent and revered.

Vanara Monkeylike divine beings.

Vihara A Buddhist monastery or dwelling place for monks.

INDEX

BIBLIOGRAPHY

A

Agarwal, B. D. *Rajasthan District Gazetteers: Jodhpur*. Jaipur: Government of Rajasthan, 1960. http://archive.org/details/in.ernet.dli.2015.120399.

Alter, Stephen. *Sacred Waters: A Pilgrimage up the Ganges River to the Source of Hindu Culture*. New York: Harcourt, 2001. http://archive.org/details/sacredwaterspilg0000alte.

Anantharaman, Ambujam. *Temples of South India*. 2nd ed. Chennai: EastWest Books, 2006. http://archive.org/details/templesofsouthin0000anan.

Andhra Pradesh Tourism. 'Lepakshi.' https://aptourism.gov.in/destinations/21/lepakshi.

Archaeological Survey of India, Bhopal Circle. 'Lakshman Temple,' n.d. https://web.archive.org/web/20210924025543/https://asibhopal.nic.in/monument/chhatarpur_khajuraho_lakshmantemple.html#.

Archaeological Survey of India, Jaipur Circle. 'Mandor Fort,' n.d. https://asijaipurcircle.nic.in/Mandor%20Fort.html.

Arya, Samarendra Narayañ. 'Historicity of Ayodhya.' *Proceedings of the Indian History Congress* 51 (1990): 44–48.

Asia Society. 'Reamker: The Cambodian Version of the Ramayana.' https://asiasociety.org/education/reamker.

Awasthi, Tarinee. *The Illustrated Ramayana: The Timeless Epic of Duty, Love, and Redemption*. DK, 2021.

B

Balasubramanian, D. 'In Search of the Sanjeevani Plant of Ramayana.' *The Hindu*, 10 September 2009, sec. Science. https://www.thehindu.com/sci-tech/science/In-search-of-the-Sanjeevani-plant-of-Ramayana/article16880681.ece.

Barik, Bibhuti. 'Nature, Myth Converge at Mahendragiri.' *The Telegraph*, 11 October 2010. https://www.telegraphindia.com/odisha/nature-myth-converge-at-mahendragiri/cid/478112.

Batukbhai, Siddhapura Mayurkumar. 'Planning for Ecotourism in Sahyadri Hills Region: A Case Study Chinchli and Mahardar, Dand District, Gujarat.' Veer Narmad South Gujarat University, 2021. https://vnsgu.ac.in/iqac/naac/c1/c13/c134/files/1DtQ86QNthsZLeK1nRDvBOdCJZQqsMLjn.pdf.

Behl, Riya. 'The Many Masks of Majuli.' People's Archive of Rural India, 19 June 2023. https://ruralindiaonline.org/en/articles/the-many-masks-of-majuli/.

Bhattacharya, Abhik. 'Mandodari, The Lost Queen Of Ramayana.' Outlook India, 22 October 2023. https://www.outlookindia.com/national/mandodari-the-lost-queen-of-ramayana-magazine-325480.

Biswas, Jaya. 'Lepakshi Temple: Time Travel to the Royal Past, Where Every Stone Tells a Story.' *The Telegraph*, 3 August 2023.

Bora, Tanuja, and Dhrubajyoti Nath. 'The Figure of Rama in India and Thailand: A Comparative Study.' *IOSR Journal of Humanities and Social Science* 19, no. 4 (April 2014): 38–43.

Boyle, Richard. 'The Paars of Mannar.' *Himal Southasian*, 29 January 2011. https://www.himalmag.com/comment/the-paars-of-mannar.

Brohier, R. L. *Seeing Ceylon: In Vistas of Scenery, History, Legend and Folklore*.

C

Colombo: Lake House Investments Limited, 1965. http://archive.org/details/seeingceyloninvi0000rlbr.

Chatterjee, Arup. 'Do You Believe in Ram Setu? Adam's Bridge, Epistemic Plurality and Colonial Legacy.' *Island Studies Journal*, 2022. https://doi.org/10.24043/isj.405.

Clarke, Arthur C. 'Ceylon and the Underwater Archaeologist,' May 1964. https://www.penn.museum/sites/expedition/ceylon-and-the-underwater-archaeologist/.

Cleveland Museum of Art. 'The Great Miracle at Shravasti.' https://www.clevelandart.org/art/1975.102.

Crosby, Josiah. 'Buddhism in Ceylon.' *Journal of the Royal Asiatic Society of Great Britain and Ireland*, no. 1 (April 1947): 41–52.

D

Dallapiccola, Anna L. *Kalamkari Temple Hangings*. Mapin Publishing and V&A Publishing, 2015.

Dastkari Haat Samiti. 'Madhubani Art in Public Spaces.' Google Arts & Culture. https://artsandculture.google.com/story/madhubani-art-in-public-spaces/ewWxNHUUmZ3cKA.

Debroy, Bibek, trans. *The Valmiki Ramayana*. Penguin, 2017.

Desai, Santosh N. 'Ramayana—An Instrument of Historical Contact and Cultural Transmission between India and Asia.' *The Journal of Asian Studies* 30, no. 1 (1970): 5–20. https://doi.org/10.2307/2942721.

Devi, Sita. *Painting*. ca 1973. Painted in ink and colored paint on paper, 1983 dimensions are from the accession register. Victoria & Albert Museum South & South East Asia Collection. https://collections.vam.ac.uk/item/O82400/painting-devi-sita/.

Dhanaseeli, J. Delphine Prema. 'Pamban Rail Bridge—A Historical Perspective.' *Specialty Journal of Humanities and Cultural Science* 4, no. 4 (2019): 18–23.

Doniger, Wendy. *Splitting the Difference: Gender and Myth in Ancient Greece and India*. University of Chicago Press, 1999.

Doniger, Wendy. 'Sita and Helen, Ahalya and Alcmena: A Comparative Study.' *History of Religions* 37, no. 1 (1997): 21–49.

E & F

Eck, Diana L. *India: A Sacred Geography*. Harmony Books, 2012.

Embassy of Sri Lanka in Stockholm, Sweden. 'Horton Plains.' https://www.stockholm.embassy.gov.lk/en/sri_lanka/horton-plains/.

Forbes, Jonathan. *Eleven Years in Ceylon: Comprising Sketches of the Field Sports and Natural History of That Colony, and an Account of Its History and Antiquities*. 2 vols. London: Richard Bentley, 1840. http://archive.org/details/elevenyearsince01turngoog.

G

Gallop, Annabel Teh. 'The Ramayana in Southeast Asia: Indonesia and Malaysia.' Asian and African studies blog, British Library. https://blogs.bl.uk/asian-and-african/2014/05/the-ramayana-in-southeast-asia-4-indonesia-and-malaysia.html.

Gaur, Abhishek. 'Devotees Worship Ravana in Mandore.' *Deccan Herald*, 7 March 2019.

Gazetteer of the Bombay Presidency: Kanara. Vol. 15, Part 2. Bombay: Government Central Press, 1883. http://archive.org/details/dli.ministry.08150.

Gazetteer Of The Bombay Presidency: Nasik. Vol. 16. Bombay: Government Central Press, 1883. http://archive.org/details/in.ernet.dli.2015.537304.

Gazetteer of the Karnal District. Lahore: Mufid-i-Am Press, 1892.

Godakumbura, Bandula. 'Seetha Kotuwa Site Can Throw Light on King Rawana's Reign.' *Daily Mirror*, 20 April 2012. https://www.pressreader.com/sri-lanka/daily-mirror-sri-lanka/20120420/282054799025876.

Godakumbura, C. E. 'Rāmāyana in Śrī Lankā and Lankā of the Rāmāyana.' *Journal of the Royal Asiatic Society of Sri Lanka* 59, no. 2 (2014): 55–83.

Goldman, R., and J. Masson. 'Who Knows Rāvana ?—A Narrative Difficulty in the Vālmīki Rāmāyana.' *Annals of the Bhandarkar Oriental Research Institute* 50, no. 1/4 (1969): 95–100.

Goldman, Robert P. and Sally J. Sutherland Goldman, eds. *The Rāmāyana of Vālmīki: The Complete English Translation*. Princeton and Oxford: Princeton University Press, 2022.

Goldman, Robert P. 'Historicising the Ramakatha: Valmiki's Ramayana and Its Medieval Commentators.' *India International Centre Quarterly* 31, no. 4 (2005): 83–97.

Google Arts & Culture. 'Masks, Other Worlds,' n.d. https://artsandculture.google.com/story/masks-other-worlds/eAXh-66YoqD6KA.

Goss, Frederick. 'Literature in Transmigration: The Rama Story in Southeast Asia.' *Asian Review* 30, no. 1 (2017): 87–107.

H

Ha, Do Thu. 'Localizing India's Values of Ramayana in Southeast Asia—The Case of Hikayat Seri Rama.' *International Journal of Religion* 5, no. 11 (2024): 910–20. https://doi.org/10.61707/4vqpgs68.

Hartmann, John. Review of *The Rama Jataka in Laos: A Study in the Phra Lak Phra Lam. Vol. I, Vol. II*, by Sachchidanand Sahai. *Crossroads: An Interdisciplinary Journal of Southeast Asian Studies* 13, no. 1 (1999): 150–53.

Hazra, Sneh. 'Vaidehi—Sita Beyond the Body.' *The Statesman*, October 23 2022.

Henry, Justin W., and Sree Padma. 'Lankapura: The Legacy of the *Ramayana* in Sri Lanka.' *South Asia: Journal of South Asian Studies* 42, no. 4 (August 2019): 726–31. https://doi.org/10.1080/00856401.2019.1626127.

Henry, Justin W. *Ravana's Kingdom: The Ramayana and Sri Lankan History from Below.* Oxford University Press, 2022.

Henry, Justin W. 'Explorations in the Transmission of the Ramayana in Sri Lanka.' *South Asia: Journal of South Asian Studies* 42, no. 4 (4 July 2019): 732–46. https://doi.org/10.1080/00856401.2019.1631739.

Hess, Linda. 'Rejecting Sita: Indian Responses to the Ideal Man's Cruel Treatment of His Ideal Wife.' *Journal of the American Academy of Religion* 67, no. 1 (1999): 1–32.

I

Igunma, Jana. 'The Ramayana in Southeast Asia: Cambodia.' Asian and African studies blog, British Library. https://blogs.bl.uk/asian-and-african/2014/04/the-ramayana-in-southeast-asia-1-cambodia-.html.

Igunma, Jana. 'The Ramayana in Southeast Asia: Thailand and Laos.' Asian and African studies blog, British Library. https://blogs.bl.uk/asian-and-african/2014/04/the-ramayana-in-southeast-asia-2-thailand-and-laos.html.

Ilias, M.H. 'Mappila Muslims and the Cultural Content of Trading Arab Diaspora on the Malabar Coast.' *Asian Journal of Social Science* 35, no. 4/5 (2007): 434–56.

Iyengar, Kodaganallur R. Srinivasa. *Asian Variations in Ramayana*. Sahitya Akademi, 2005.

J

Jaiswal, Suvira. 'Historical Evolution of the Ram Legend.' *Social Scientist* 21, no. 3/4 (1993): 89–97. https://doi.org/10.2307/3517633.

Jayasingha, Pathmakumara, Robert Armstrong Lee Osborne, and Ross E. Pogson. 'Sthreepura Cave at Kiriwanagama, South Central Sri Lanka: A Network Cave in Saprolite and Proterozoic Quartzite.' *Acta Carsologica* 47/2-3 (n.d.).

Jose, Alaina. 'Payammal Sree Shathrugna Swamy Temple.' University of Calicut, 2021. https://web.archive.org/web/20240613145313/https://dspace.christcollegeijk.edu.in:8080/jspui/bitstream/123456789/1422/2/CCASADER14.pdf.

Joshi, Esha Basanti. *Gazetteer of India, Uttar Pradesh: Mathura District.* Lucknow: Government of Uttar Pradesh, 1968. http://archive.org/details/dli.csl.3090.

Joshi, Esha Basanti. *Uttar Pradesh District Gazetteers: Faizabad.* Allahabad: Government of Uttar Pradesh, 1960. http://archive.org/details/dli.csl.2988.

K

Kariyawasam, Tissa. 'The Rāmāyana and Folk Rituals of Sri Lanka.' *Journal of the Royal Asiatic Society of Sri Lanka* 59, no. 2 (2014): 91–102.

Katupotha, Jinadasa. 'Pearl Fishery Industry in Sri Lanka.' *WildLanka* Vol. 7, no. 1 (2019): pp. 033–049.

Kaung, U. Thaw. 'Ramayana in Myanmar Literature and Performing Arts.' *Myanmar Historical Research Journal*, no. 9 (June 2002): 73–99.

Kinsley, David. *Hindu Goddesses: Vision of the Divine Feminine in the Hindu Religious Tradition.* Delhi: Motilal Banarsidass, 1987.

Kochhar, Rishi. 'Journeying through the Lands of Ramayana.' *Deccan Herald*, 27 June 2021. https://www.deccanherald.com/features/journeying-through-the-lands-of-ramayana-1001425.html.

Kolaba District Gazetteer. 'Elephanta,' n.d. https://web.archive.org/web/20091125210514/http://www.maharashtra.gov.in/english/gazetteer/KOLABA/places_Elephanta.html.

Koning, Deborah de. 'The Many Faces of Ravana, Ravanisation: The Revitalisation of Ravana among Sinhalese Buddhists in Post-War Sri Lanka.' Tilburg University, 2021. https://pure.uvt.nl/ws/portalfiles/portal/59020919/De_Koning_The_Many_15_12_2021_incl_kaft.pdf.

Kumar, Mukesh. 'The Art of Resistance: The Bards and Minstrels' Response to Anti-Syncretism/Anti-Liminality in North India.' *Journal of the Royal Asiatic Society* 29, no. 2 (April 2019): 219–47. https://doi.org/10.1017/S1356186318000597.

Kumar, N. *Bihar District Gazetteers: Ranchi.* Patna: Government of Bihar, 1970. http://archive.org/details/dli.csl.2983.

L

Law, Bimala Churn. *Historical Geography of Ancient India*. Paris: Société Asiatique de Paris, 1954. http://archive.org/details/dli.pahar.3008.

Law, Bimala Churn. *Memoirs of the Archaeological Survey of India: Sravasti in Indian Literature.* 50, 1935. http://archive.org/details/in.ernet.dli.2015.106958.

Longhurst, A. H. *Hampi Ruins: Described and Illustrated.* Madras: Government Press, 1917. http://archive.org/details/HampiRuins.

Lothspeich, Pamela. 'Introduction: The Field of Ramlila.' *Asian Theatre Journal* 37, no. 1 (2020): 3–33.

Lutgendorf, Philip. *Hanuman's Tale: The Messages of a Divine Monkey.* New York: Oxford University Press, 2007. https://doi.org/10.1093/acprof:oso/9780195309225.001.0001.

Lutgendorf, Philip. 'My Hanuman Is Bigger Than Yours.' *History of Religions* 33, no. 3 (1994): 211–45.

Lutgendorf, Philip. 'Words Made Flesh: The Banaras Rāmlīlā as Epic Commentary.' In *Boundaries of the Text: Epic Performances in South and Southeast Asia*, 83–104. University of Michigan Press, 1991. https://www.jstor.org/stable/10.3998/mpub.19503.10.

M & N

Madhya Pradesh Tourism. 'Mandsaur & Vidisha: Towns in MP Is Worshipped,' 29 July 2020. https://www.mptourism.com/towns-in-mp-where-ravana-is-worshipped.html.

Madhya Pradesh Tourism. 'Meeting The Bharia Tribes In Patalkot Valley,' April 28 2022. https://www.mptourism.com/bharia-tribes-patalkot-valley-madhya-pradesh.html.

Maharashtra State Gazetteers: Nasik District. Bombay: Government of Maharashtra, 1975.

MAP Academy. 'Bhaona Masks,' n.d. https://mapacademy.io/article/bhaona-masks/.

MAP Academy. 'Bhaona.' https://mapacademy.io/article/bhaona/.

MAP Academy. 'Gomera Masks.' https://mapacademy.io/article/gomera-masks/.

MAP Academy. 'Kalamkari.' https://mapacademy.io/article/kalamkari/.

MAP Academy. 'Madhubani Painting.' https://mapacademy.io/article/madhubani-painting/.

MAP Academy. 'Murals at Virabhadra Temple, Lepakshi.' https://mapacademy.io/article/murals-at-virabhadra-temple-lepakshi/.

MAP Academy. 'Ravana Chhaya.' https://mapacademy.io/article/ravana-chhaya/.

MAP Academy. 'Ravananugrahamurti.' https://mapacademy.io/article/ravananugrahamurti/.

MAP Academy. 'Tanjore Painting.' https://mapacademy.io/article/tanjore-painting/.

MAP Academy. 'Tholpavakoothu.' https://mapacademy.io/article/tholpavakoothu/.

'Mask Making Tradition of Assam,' November 11 2021. https://blog.mygov.in/mask-making-tradition-of-assam/.

May, San San. 'The Ramayana in Southeast Asia: Burma.' Asian and African studies blog, British Library. https://blogs.bl.uk/asian-and-african/2014/05/the-ramayana-in-southeast-asia-3-burma.html.

Mazumdar, B. P. 'Rāma Cult in Early Medieval India.' *Proceedings of the Indian History Congress* 19 (1956): 140–44.

Media Studies. 'Vladimir Propp's Narrative Functions,' 2024. https://media-studies.com/narrative-functions/.

NASA Jet Propulsion Laboratory (JPL). 'Adam's Bridge, India-Sri Lanka, n.d. https://www.jpl.nasa.gov/images/pia24949-adams-bridge-india-sri-lanka.

'Nirala,' Narendra Narayan Sinha. 'Madhubani: A Contemporary History (1971-2011).' *Proceedings of the Indian History Congress* 71 (2010): 1243–50.

P

Padma, Sree. 'Borders Crossed: Vibhishana in the *Ramayana* and Beyond.' *South Asia: Journal of South Asian Studies* 42, no. 4 (4 July 2019): 747–67. https://doi.org/10.1080/00856401.2019.1631738.

Pande, Vikrant, and Neelesh Kulkarni. *In The Footsteps Of Rama: Travels with the Ramayana*. Harper Collins, 2021.

Pankaj, Bhavana. 'Who Was Mandodari? Each Version of the Ramayana Gives Ravana's Wife a Different Role and Story.' Scroll.in, December 8 2019. https://scroll.in/article/946091/who-was-mandodari-each-version-of-the-ramayana-gives-ravanas-wife-a-different-role-and-story.

Pargiter, F. E. 'The Geography of Ráma's Exile.' *Journal of the Royal Asiatic Society of Great Britain and Ireland*, 1894, 231–64.

Parmar, Shyam. *Folklore of Madhya Pradesh.* New Delhi: National Book Trust, India, 1972. http://archive.org/details/in.ernet.dli.2015.219846.

Patnaik, Sunil Kumar, and Sarita Nayak. 'The Mountain Mahendragiri—An Eco-Heritage Tourist Destination.' *Odisha Review*, November 2020.

Patra, Benudhar. 'Kalinga and Champa: A Study in Ancient Maritime Relations.' *Odisha Review*, November 2017.

Paul, Meenakshi F. 'Ram as Folk Hero in the "Ramains" of Himachal Pradesh.' *Indian Literature* 51, no. 4 (240) (2007): 178–87.

Percival, Robert. *An Account of the Island of Ceylon: Containing Its History, Geography, Natural History, with the Manners and Customs of Its Various Inhabitants.* 2nd ed. London: C. and R. Baldwin, 1805. http://archive.org/details/dli.ministry.00030.

Pillai, N. Vanamamalai. *The Setu and Rameswaram.* Rameswaram: V Narayanan & Bror., 1929. http://archive.org/details/in.gov.ignca.9894.

Pou, Saveros. 'Indigenization of Rāmāyana in Cambodia.' *Asian Folklore Studies* 51, no. 1 (1992): 89–102. https://doi.org/10.2307/1178423.

R

Raghavan, V., ed. *The Ramayana Tradition In Asia.* Sahitya Akademi Publications, 1998.

Ramachandran, T. N. 'Find of Tempera Painting in Sītābhiñji, District Keoñjhār, Orissa.' *Artibus Asiae* 14, no. 1/2 (1951): 4–25. https://doi.org/10.2307/3248685.

Ramnath, Kalyani. 'Transit.' *Invisible Histories.* https://histecon.fas.harvard.edu/invisible-histories/captions/transit/index.html.

Ravi, S. 'Meet Hem Chandra Goswami, a Master Mask-Maker from Majuli.' *The Hindu*, 22 August 2019, sec. Art. https://www.thehindu.com/entertainment/art/the-magician-of-majuli-hem-chandra-goswami/article29221124.ece.

Richman, Paula, ed. *Many Ramayanas: The Diversity of a Narrative Tradition in South Asia.* University of California Press, 1991. http://ark.cdlib.org/ark:/13030/ft3j49n8h7/

Richman, Paula, ed. *Questioning Ramayanas: A South Asian Tradition.* University of California Press, 2001.

Richman, Paula, ed. *Ramayana Stories in Modern South India: An Anthology.* Bloomington: Indiana University Press, 2008.

S

Saran, Malini. 'The Ramayana in Indonesia: Alternate Tellings. *India International Centre Quarterly* 31, no. 4 (2005): 66–82.

Sax, William S. 'The Ramnagar Ramlila: Text, Performance, Pilgrimage.' *History of Religions* 30, no. 2 (1990): 129–53.

Schechner, Richard, and Linda Hess. 'The Ramlila of Ramnagar [India].' *The Drama Review: TDR* 21, no. 3 (1977): 51–82. https://doi.org/10.2307/1145152.

Seneviratne, Maureen. *Selected Essays.* Colombo: Wimal Enterprises, 2001. http://archive.org/details/selectedessays0000sene.

Shankar, Kartikeya. 'Hidden Wonders: Nuwara Eliya, The "Little England" Of Sri Lanka.' Outlook Traveller, 2 March 2024. https://www.outlooktraveller.com/destinations/international/did-you-know-about-nuwara-eliya-sri-lankas-little-england.

Silk Roads Programme. 'Great Basses Wreck.' https://en.unesco.org/silkroad/silk-road-themes/underwater-heritage/great-basses-wreck.

Singaravelu, S. 'The Rāma Story in the Malay Tradition.' *Journal of the Malaysian Branch of the Royal Asiatic Society* 54, no. 2 (240) (1981): 131–47.

Singh, Avadhesh Kumar. *Vālmiki Rāmāyana: Voices and Visions.* New Delhi: D. K. Printworld, 2017.

Siriwardana, Thilanka M., Nadeera H. Dissanayake, and Canan Çakırlar. 'Pearl Fisheries in South Asia: Archaeological Evidence from Pre-Colonial and Colonial Shell Middens around the Gulf of Mannar in Sri Lanka.' *International Journal of Historical Archaeology*, 16 May 2024. https://doi.org/10.1007/s10761-024-00739-5.

Sophearith, Siyonn. 'The Life of the Ramayana in Ancient Cambodia: A Study of the Political, Religious and Ethical Roles of an Epic Tale in Real Time.' University of California, Berkeley, 2003. https://cdn.angkordatabase.asia/libs/docs/publications/the-life-of-the-ramayana-in-ancient-cambodia-a-study-of-the-political-religious-and-ethical-roles-of-an-epic-tale-in-real-time/Siyonn-Sophearith_UDAYA06-07-2006-r.pdf.

Sri Lanka: Eyewitness Travel. DK Publishing, 2016.

Sri Lanka Biodiversity. 'Yala National Park.' https://lk.chm-cbd.net/protected-areas/yala-national-park.

Srivastava, Vartika. 'Mithilanchal: The Land of Madhubani Art.' *Outlook Traveller*, 18 November 2022.

Sundaram, P. S., trans. *Kamba Ramayana.* Penguin, 2002.

Sutherland, Sally J. 'Sita and Draupadi: Aggressive Behavior and Female Role-Models in the Sanskrit Epics.' *Journal of the American Oriental Society* 109, no. 1 (March 1989): 63–79.

Szanton, David L. 'The Politics of Mithila Painting,' n.d. https://orias.berkeley.edu/sites/default/files/the_politics_of_mithila_painting_2-2017.pdf.

T

Tennent, James Emerson. *Ceylon: A General Description of the Island, Historical, Physical, Statistical.* London: Longman, Green, Longman, and Roberts, 1860. http://archive.org/details/b29352770_0001.

Tharuvana, Azeez. *Living Ramayanas: Exploring the Plurality of the Epic in Wayanad and the World.* Westland Publications Private Limited, 2021.

The Mahavamsa. 'The Coming of Vijaya,' October 8 2011. https://mahavamsa.org/mahavamsa/original-version/06-coming-vijaya/.

'The Story of Ram in Ramlila.' *Asian Theatre Journal* 37, no. 1 (2020): 34–37. https://doi.org/10.1353/atj.2020.0024.

Thomas, Gavin. *The Rough Guide to Sri Lanka.* London : Rough Guides, 2012. http://archive.org/details/roughguidetosril0000thom_q5f3.

'Tirumala: Tirumala Tirupati Devasthanams.' Tirupati Central Excise, n.d. https://tirupaticentralexcise.gov.in/docs/tirumala.pdf.

Toru, Ohno. *A Study of Burmese Rama Story.* 24. Osaka University of Foreign Studies, 1999.

U & V

UNESCO. 'Elephanta Caves.' https://whc.unesco.org/en/list/244/.

UNESCO. 'Ellora Caves.' https://whc.unesco.org/en/list/243/.

UNESCO. 'Group of Monuments at Hampi.' https://whc.unesco.org/en/list/241/.

UNESCO. 'Group of Monuments at Mahabalipuram,' n.d. https://whc.unesco.org/en/list/249/.

UNESCO. 'Group of Monuments at Pattadakal.' https://whc.unesco.org/en/list/239/.

UNESCO. 'Khajuraho Group of Monuments,' n.d. https://whc.unesco.org/en/list/240/.

UNESCO. 'Ramlila, the Traditional Performance of the Ramayana,' n.d. https://ich.unesco.org/en/RL/ramlila-the-traditional-performance-of-the-ramayana-00110.

UNESCO. 'Sacred City of Anuradhapura.' https://whc.unesco.org/en/list/200/.

UNESCO. 'Sri Veerabhadra Temple and Monolithic Bull (Nandi), Lepakshi (The Vijayanagara Sculpture and Painting Art Tradition),' n.d. https://whc.unesco.org/en/tentativelists/6607/.

UNESCO. 'Temples of Kanchipuram,' n.d. https://whc.unesco.org/en/tentativelists/6528/.

Urban Development Authority, *Sri Lanka. Ella: Tourism Development Master Plan 2020-2030.* August 2020. https://www.sltda.gov.lk/storage/common_media/ELLA_VOLUME_1_Part_A_compressed679831860.pdf

Usha, B.N. 'In Conversation with Du Saraswathi.' *The Third Eye* (blog), 2 December 2022. https://thethirdeyeportal.in/body/in-conversation-with-du-saraswathi/.

Varadachary, V. *Tirumala: The Panorama of Seven Hills.* Tirupati: Tirumala Tirupati Devasthanama, 1999.

Vijay, Sandy N. 'Kishkindha Konnect.' *Deccan Herald*, January 7 2020.

W & Y

Wannaudorn, Smai, and Pathom Hongsuwan. '*Phra Lak Phra Lam*: The Representation of Cultural Ecology in Lao Society.' *The Journal of Lao Studies* 5, no. 1 (n.d.): 94–107.

Weerasooriya, Sahan. 'Charged by an Elephant at Wasgamuwa.' *The Island* 15 April 2022. http://island.lk/charged-by-an-elephant-at-wasgamuwa/.

Young, Jonathan, and Philip Friedrich. 'Mapping Lanka's Moral Boundaries: Representations of Socio-Political Difference in the *Ravana Rajavaliya.*' *South Asia: Journal of South Asian Studies* 42, no. 4 (4 July 2019): 768–80. https://doi.org/10.1080/00856401.2019.1633114.

ACKNOWLEDGMENTS

The publisher would like to thank the following people for their support, suggestions, and contributions during the planning and creation of the book:

Jennifer Moragoda for her continued support, ideas, and feedback throughout the bookmaking process
Roshni Fernando for crafting the Sri Lanka itinerary with care and attention to detail
Teesta Verma for her review and improvements to the India itinerary
Dr. Tarinee Awasthi for all the translations from Valmiki's *Ramayana*
Sachin Pradhan for cartography
Ankita Gupta for editorial support
Ira Sharma, **Devina Pagay**, **Rajoshi Chakraborty**, **Shipra Jain**, and **Devika Awasthi** for their design support
Manpreet Kaur for picture research administration support

Every effort has been made to acknowledge those individuals, organizations, and corporations that have helped with this book and to trace copyright holders. DK apologizes in advance if any omission has occurred. If an omission does come to light, DK will be pleased to insert the appropriate acknowledgment in subsequent editions of the book.

The publisher would like to thank the following for their kind permission to reproduce their photographs:

(Key: a-above; b-below/bottom; c-center; f-far; l-left; r-right; t-top)

All pages Dreamstime.com: Kadzenha (background texture) **1 The Cleveland Museum Of Art:** Severance and Greta Millikin Purchase Fund. **2-3 Alamy Stock Photo:** Planet Observer / UIG. **4 Brooklyn Museum:** Purchased with funds given by Dr. Bertram H. Schaffner. **6-7 Dreamstime.com:** Praveen Indramohan (b). **8-9 Dreamstime.com:** Saiko3p. **10 Alamy Stock Photo:** Dinodia Photos. **11 Los Angeles County Museum of Art:** Gift of Paul F. Walter. **12 © The Trustees of the British Museum. All rights reserved. 13 Wellcome Collection:** Ravana slaughtering Jatayu the vulture, while an abducted Sita looks away in horror. Chromolithograph by R. Varma. **14-15 The Metropolitan Museum of Art:** Purchase, Friends of Asian Art Gifts, 2008 (b). **16 Valmiki's Ramayana:** (cla). **Wellcome Collection:** Illustrated Sinhalese covers (inside) showing the events (cl). **16-17 National Museum of Asian Art, Smithsonian:** Freer Gallery of Art Collection (c). **17 Getty Images:** Sunil Ghosh / Hindustan Times (cr). **Ramavatarcharit:** (tc). **Ramayana Bahara:** (tr). **18 Alamy Stock Photo:** The History Collection. **19 Getty Images:** Universal History Archive / Universal Images Group. **20-21 Los Angeles County Museum of Art**: Gift of Paul F. Walter. **22 Los Angeles County Museum of Art:** Indian Art Special Purpose Fund. **23 Getty Images:** Pierce Archive LLC / Buyenlarge. **24-25 The Metropolitan Museum of Art:** Seymour and Rogers Funds, 1976. **26 Alamy Stock Photo:** The Picture Art Collection. **26-27 Los Angeles County Museum of Art:** Gift of Mr. and Mrs. Julian Ganz, Jr. **28 © The Trustees of the British Museum. All rights reserved. 29 Alamy Stock Photo:** Bambam Kumar Jha. **30 Alamy Stock Photo:** The Picture Art Collection. **32-33 Shutterstock.com:** AbhishekMittal. **34-35 The Cleveland Museum Of Art:** Edward L. Whittemore Fund. **36-37 Alamy Stock Photo:** Anil Dave (b). **36 Press Information Bureau:** (t). **38 Wellcome Collection:** Ahalya leaning on tree. Chromolithograph by R. Varma. **39 Dreamstime.com:** EPhotocorp. **40-41 Bridgeman Images:** © Lowe Art Museum / Gift of Mr. George P. Bickford (c). **41 Alamy Stock Photo:** Luis Dafos (tr). **42-43 University of California, Los Angeles (UCLA):** AIIS Center for Art & Archaeology Negatives & Slides. **44 Shutterstock.com:** Hari Mahidhar. **45 Alamy Stock Photo:** ephotocorp / Rajesh Avhad. **46-47 Getty Images:** Niharika Kulkarni / AFP. **48-49 Dreamstime.com:** Tanusree Mitra (t). **48 Shutterstock.com:** Itiprithul (br). **49 Dreamstime.com:** Tanusree Mitra (bl, cr). **Getty Images:** Avishek Das / SOPA Images / LightRocket (tr, br). **50-51 Alamy Stock Photo:** CPA Media Pte Ltd / Pictures From History. **52 Getty Images:** Arun Sankar / AFP. **53 Shutterstock.com:** CRS PHOTO. **54 Alamy Stock Photo:** Gainew Gallery (bl). **Getty Images:** Timothy Norris (t). **54-55 Alamy Stock Photo:** Prabhat Kumar Verma / ZUMA Wire (b). **55 Shutterstock.com:** reddees (tl). **56-57 Dreamstime.com:** Praveen Indramohan. **58 Dreamstime.com:** Michael Smith. **59 Dreamstime.com:** Evgeniy Fesenko. **60-61 Getty Images:** Historical Picture Archive / Corbis. **62 Getty Images:** The Image Bank Unreleased / Christophe Boisvieux (tl). **Shutterstock.com:** AjayTvm (b). **62-63 Shutterstock.com:** AjayTvm (t). **63 Shutterstock.com:** AjayTvm (bl); Anand Ganapathy (cl). **64-65 Alamy Stock Photo:** The Picture Art Collection. **66 Dreamstime.com:** Milosk50. **67 Alamy Stock Photo:** Penta Springs Limited / Artokoloro. **68 Getty Images:** Soltan Frédéric / Sygma (tl, tr). **Shutterstock.com:** bodom (b). **69 Getty Images:** Soltan Frédéric / Sygma (tl, bl). **70-71 Getty Images:** Moment / Evgenii Zotov. **72 Alamy Stock Photo:** Penta Springs Limited / Artokoloro. **73 Dreamstime.com:** Fortton. **74 National Museum of Asian Art, Smithsonian:** Gift of Charles Lang Freer. **76-77 Minneapolis Institute of Art:** The Helen Jones Fund for Asian Art. **78 Alamy Stock Photo:** GRANGER Historical Picture Archive. **80-81 Dreamstime.com:** Saiko3p. **82-83 Alamy Stock Photo**: The Picture Art Collection. **84-85 Getty Images:** Moment Open / Dhammika Heenpella / Images of Sri Lanka. **87 Depositphotos Inc:** mcmorabad. **88 Dreamstime.com:** Prabhakaran M. **89 Dreamstime.com:** Saiko3p. **90-91 Dreamstime.com:** Shafik Khan. **92 Getty Images:** Pierce Archive LLC / Buyenlarge. **93 Dreamstime.com:** Anil Dave. **94 Dreamstime.com:** Dmitry Rukhlenko (tr). **94-95 Shutterstock.com:** YAMOMOY (b). **95 Dreamstime.com:** Subhrajyoti Parida (br). **Getty Images:** Ajay Aggarwal / Hindustan Times (tr); Moment / Evgenii Zotov (tl). **Wellcome Collection:** Ravana, the ten headed demon god. Gouache painting by an Indian artist (cr). **96-97 © The Trustees of the British Museum. All rights reserved. 97 Dreamstime.com:** Wirestock (tr). **98-99 Getty Images / iStock:** ePhotocorp. **100 Alamy Stock Photo:** Ariadne Van Zandbergen (bl). **100-101 ESA:** Processed by EarthWatching (ESRIN) (t). **102-103 © The Trustees of the British Museum. All rights reserved. 104 Dreamstime.com:** Ajith Kumara. **105 Bridgeman Images:** From the British Library archive. **106-107 Dreamstime.com:** Anupong Intawong. **108 Alamy Stock Photo:** Alexander Mitrofanov. **109 Dreamstime.com:** Christian Offenberg. **110-111 Getty Images / iStock:** DigitalVision Vectors / duncan1890. **112 Shutterstock.com:** Emjay Smith (bl). **112-113 Shutterstock.com:** Chathura

Prasanga (b). **114 Getty Images:** Sanchit Khanna / Hindustan Times (tr); Moment / Anoop Negi (cr). **Shutterstock.com:** PradeepGaurs (br). **115 Alamy Stock Photo:** India Today / ZUMA Wir (tl). **Getty Images:** Sanchit Khanna / Hindustan Times (bl). **Shutterstock.com:** PradeepGaurs (tr). **Unsplash:** Anirudh (br). **116-117 Alamy Stock Photo:** Angelo Hornak. **118 Depositphotos Inc:** Klodien. **120-121 Alamy Stock Photo:** imageBROKER / Muthuraman V. **122 Bridgeman Images:** © Look and Learn. **123 Bridgeman Images:** From the British Library archive. **124-125 Depositphotos Inc:** shyamala (b). **125 Shutterstock.com:** Tenacity_1987 (tr). **126 Alamy Stock Photo:** Dinodia Photos RM (tl). **Shruti Subramani:** www.reflectionsbyshruti.com / @shrutisubramani (tc, b). **127 Dreamstime.com:** EPhotocorp (tl); Samrat35 (bl). **Shutterstock.com:** Harish Tyagi / EPA-EFE (cl). **128-129 Getty Images:** Arun Sankar / AFP. **130 Alamy Stock Photo:** Zoom Historical. **131 Award winning travel blogger, Arti Shah Agarwal blogging at:** www.myyatradiary.com. **132 The Cleveland Museum Of Art:** Gift in honor of Madeline Neves Clapp; Gift of Mrs. Henry White Cannon by exchange; Bequest of Louise T. Cooper; Leonard C. Hanna Jr. Fund; From the Catherine and Ralph Benkaim Collection. **133 Dreamstime.com:** Kavkirat Kaur. **134-135 Dreamstime.com:** Dmitry Rukhlenko. **136-137 Wellcome Collection. 137 Lanka Excursions Holidays:** Ando Sundermann (br). **138-139 Los Angeles County Museum of Art:** Purchased with funds provided by Christian Humann (t). **139 Dreamstime.com:** Saiko3p (b). **140 Lanka Excursions Holidays:** Ando Sundermann (bl). **140-141 Alamy Stock Photo:** CPA Media Pte Ltd / Pictures From History (t). **142-143 © The Trustees of the British Museum. All rights reserved. 144-145 Alamy Stock Photo:** imageBROKER / Muthuraman V. **145 Goshan Colombathantrige:** (tr). **146 Alamy Stock Photo:** Dinodia Photos RM (tr, b). **Dreamstime.com:** Venkatajalandar A S (tl). **147 Alamy Stock Photo:** mauritius images GmbH / Rene Mattes (tl); The Picture Art Collection (bl). **148 Trisha Ghosh:** (bl). **148-149 Los Angeles County Museum of Art:** Gift of Jane Greenough Green in memory of Edward Pelton Green. **150 Shutterstock.com:** Srinivasa S. **151 Alamy Stock Photo:** Art Collection 2. **152-153 Los Angeles County Museum of Art:** Gift of Paul F. Walter. **154 Alamy Stock Photo:** Ivan Vdovin. **155 Los Angeles County Museum of Art:** Gift of Jane Greenough Green in memory of Edward Pelton Green. **156-157 Alamy Stock Photo:** Margarete Lovison. **158-159 Bridgeman Images:** From the British Library archive. **160 Alamy Stock Photo:** Tim Gainey. **161 The Metropolitan Museum of Art:** Gift of Steven Kossak, The Kronos Collections, in celebration of the Museum's 150th Anniversary, 2020. **162 Dreamstime.com:** EPhotocorp (tr). **Getty Images / iStock:** IVANVIEITO (tl, b). **163 Dreamstime.com:** Satish Parashar (bl); Radiokafka (tl). **164 Getty Images / iStock:** Chaitra Kukanur. **165 Bridgeman Images:** © Look and Learn. **166-167 National Museum of Asian Art, Smithsonian:** Gift of Charles Lang Freer. **168 Getty Images:** Moment / CR Shelare. **169 Shutterstock.com:** CRS PHOTO. **170-171 Philadelphia Museum of Art:** Purchased with the Director's Discretionary Fund, 1970. **172 Dreamstime.com:** Esignn. **173 Getty Images:** 500px / Ranya Al Ghazi. **174-175 Getty Images:** Sanjay Kanojia / NurPhoto. **176 Brooklyn Museum:** Gift of Mr. and Mrs. Robert L. Poster. **177 Dreamstime.com:** Byheaven87 (cra); Mihir Joshi (tr). **178 Getty Images / iStock:** Chandan Patra (bl). **178-179 Alamy Stock Photo:** Lebrecht Music & Arts (t). **180 Getty Images:** Moment Open / Dhammika Heenpella / Images of Sri Lanka. **181 National Museum of Asian Art, Smithsonian:** Gift of Charles Lang Freer. **182 Depositphotos Inc:** richie0703. **183 Alamy Stock Photo:** Art Collection 2. **184-185 The Metropolitan Museum of Art:** Gift of Cynthia Hazen Polsky, 1987. **185 Alamy Stock Photo:** Dinodia Photos RM (tr). **186-187 Minneapolis Institute of Art:** The Jane and James Emison Endowment for South Asian and Indian Art and the Helen Jones Fund for Asian Art (c). **187 Getty Images:** Moment Open / Dhammika Heenpella / Images of Sri Lanka (br). **188 Alamy Stock Photo:** Diganta Talukdar (bl); travelib asia (r). **Shutterstock.com:** Talukdar David (tl); Abhilekh Saikia (cl). **189 Getty Images:** David Talukdar / NurPhoto (bl). **Shutterstock.com:** Talukdar David (tl); Sankar Ghose (cl). **190 Shutterstock.com:** chetansoni (bl). **190-191 Alamy Stock Photo:** The History Collection. **Unsplash:** Annie Spratt (background). **193 The Cleveland Museum Of Art:** Severance and Greta Millikin Purchase Fund. **194 Alamy Stock Photo:** Dinodia Photos / Indian Pictures RF. **195 Getty Images / iStock:** Andrey Danilovich. **196-197 Shutterstock.com:** Flying Islander. **198 Dreamstime.com:** Dudlajzov (bl). **198-199 Alamy Stock Photo:** Historic Collection. **200 Dreamstime.com:** Nila Newsom. **201 Dreamstime.com:** Hilda Weges (br). **202 Image is sourced from Temples of India:** https://templesofindia.org (cr). **Los Angeles County Museum of Art:** Gift of Anna Bing Arnold (br). **National Museum of Asian Art, Smithsonian:** Freer Gallery of Art Collection (tr). **203 Alamy Stock Photo:** Danvis Collection. **204 Alamy Stock Photo:** Leonid Plotkin. **205 National Museum of Asian Art, Smithsonian:** Gift of Charles Lang Freer. **206 Alamy Stock Photo:** Dinodia Photos RM (b); IndiaPicture / V. Muthuraman (t). **207 Alamy Stock Photo:** Dinodia Photos RM (cl, bl). **Getty Images:** V. Muthuraman / IndiaPictures / Universal Images Group (tl). **208-209 The Metropolitan Museum of Art:** Purchase, Friends of Asian Art Gifts, 2021. **210-211 Acadèmy Antiques:** Anthony Dixon. **212-213 Dreamstime.com:** Cowardlion. **214 Dreamstime.com:** Jackmalipan. **215 Getty Images:** Marc Dozier. **216-217 Dreamstime.com:** Aliaksandr Mazurkevich. **218 Alamy Stock Photo:** Shim Harno (tr). **Shutterstock.com:** Abrahamleander (cl). **218-219 Shutterstock.com:** Sigit Adhi Wibowo (c). **219 Alamy Stock Photo:** Nina Adams (cr). **Getty Images / iStock:** E+ / brytta (tr). **Leiden University Libraries:** (tl). **220-221 The Metropolitan Museum of Art:** Bequest of John M. Crawford Jr., 1988. **222-223 Library of Congress, Washington, D.C.:** Ramayana. [Place of Publication Not Identified: Publisher Not Identified, 1870] Pdf. https://www.loc.gov/item/2021668039/. (x3). **224-225 Dreamstime.com:** Sutiponmm. **226-227 Dreamstime.com:** Leonid Andronov (b). **227 Getty Images:** Pictures From History / Universal Images Group (tr). **228 Getty Images / iStock:** nimu1956. **229 The Cleveland Museum Of Art:** Purchase from the J. H. Wade Fund. **230 Getty Images:** Sanchit Khanna / Hindustan Times. **231 Shutterstock.com:** Storm Is Me. **232-233 Shutterstock.com:** Onkar Abhyankar. **234 Dreamstime.com:** Aliaksandr Mazurkevich. **235 Dreamstime.com:** Lalam Mandavkar. **236 Shutterstock.com:** lego 19861111. **238 Shutterstock.com:** CRS PHOTO (tl). **239 Alamy Stock Photo:** Planet Observer / UIG (br). **Dreamstime.com:** Denisvostrikov (tr). **240 Dreamstime.com:** Thomas Wyness. **241 Getty Images:** The Image Bank / Tuul & Bruno Morandi (t); The Image Bank / John Elk III (b). **242-243 Getty Images:** Thilina Kaluthotage / NurPhoto. **244 Shutterstock.com:** Radchuk O.S. **245 Dreamstime.com** Matyas Rehak (tr). **Getty Images / iStock:** Matthew Starling (cr)

Cover images: *Front:* **Los Angeles County Museum of Art:** Indian Art Special Purpose Fund; *Back:* **Alamy Stock Photo:** Dinodia Photos RM tl, Planet Observer / UIG cla; **Dreamstime.com:** Dudlajzov bl; **Getty Images:** Moment / Evgenii Zotov clb

Project Editor Chandrima Banerjee
Senior Editors Vatsal Verma, Suefa Lee
US Editor Sharon Lucas
US Executive Editor Lori Hand
Senior Art Editor Bhavika Mathur
Senior Cover Designer Suhita Dharamjit
Senior Cover DTP Designer Harish Aggarwal
Assistant Picture Researcher Nunhoih Guite
Team Lead, Picture Research Sumedha Chopra
Preproduction Designer Anurag Trivedi
Preproduction Image Editor Vijay Kandwal
Preproduction Coordinator Tarun Sharma
Deputy Manager, Picture Research Virien Chopra
Preproduction Manager Balwant Singh
Preproduction Image Manager Pankaj Sharma
Managing Editors Chitra Subramanyam, Gareth Jones
Managing Art Editor Neha Ahuja Chowdhry
Senior Managing Editor Rohan Sinha
Consulting Publisher Aparna Sharma
Publishing Director Georgina Dee

Writers MadhuMadhavi Singh, Arushi Mathur
Proofreaders Ankita Gupta, Sushmita Choudhury
Indexer Tarun Khanna

First American Edition, 2025
Published in the United States by DK Publishing,
a division of Penguin Random House LLC
1745 Broadway, 20th Floor, New York, NY 10019

25 26 27 28 29 10 9 8 7 6 5 4 3 2 1
001– 355870–Nov/2025

Published in India and Great Britain by Dorling Kindersley Limited

ISBN: 979-8-2171-3532-5

Printed and bound in India

www.dk.com

This book was made with Forest Stewardship Council™ certified paper—one small step in DK's commitment to a sustainable future.
Learn more at www.dk.com/uk/information/sustainability